HILLSIDE HOMES

208 SLOPING-LOT
— & —
MULTI-LEVEL DESIGNS

1,000 to Over 5,500 square feet

HOME PLANNERS, LLC
Wholly owned by Hanley-Wood, LLC

Published by Home Planners, LLC
Wholly owned by Hanley-Wood, LLC

Editorial and Corporate Offices:
3275 West Ina Road, Suite 110
Tucson, Arizona 85741

Distribution Center:
29333 Lorie Lane
Wixom, Michigan 48393

Patricia Joseph/President
Stephen Williams/Director of Sales & Marketing
Jan Prideaux/Executive Editor
Paulette Mulvin/Project Editor
Sara Lisa/Manufacturing Coordinator
Paul Fitzgerald/Senior Graphic Designer
Chester E. Hawkins/Graphic Designer

Photo Credits

Front Cover: Bob Greenspan

Back Cover: Bob Greenspan

First Printing: September 1999

10 9 8 7 6 5 4 3 2

Printed in the United States of America

Library of Congress Catalog Card Number: 99-73033

ISBN: 1-881955-62-1

On the front cover: Accommodating a hillside lot with perfect aplomb, our Design 7402 is both elegant and practical. For more information and to see floor plans, turn to page 28. Cover photo of the home is shown in reverse of the actual floor plans.

On the back cover: Contemporary by style, hillside by nature, Design 3311 offers a walkout basement that opens to the rear for convenience. For more information and to see floor plans, turn to page 58.

TABLE OF CONTENTS

Design P345
see page 6

Homes for Front- or Side-Sloping Lots...4

Traditional Homes with Walkout Basements.................................47

Contemporary Homes with Walkout Basements.........................95

Bi-Level, Split-Level and Split-Foyer Designs..............................111

Homes with Livable Basements...159

Homes with Raised Foundations...203

How to Order Blueprints for the Homes......................................212

DESIGN P240

Square Footage: 1,124

The combination of stucco and stone, arched and square windows gives this home a very attractive exterior. A perfect size for retirement, it offers three bedrooms, but one could easily be used as a study or hobby room. The living area is essentially one big open space, with the front door opening directly into the great room, which is separated from the breakfast room by an arch topped with a plant shelf.

A fireplace warms the entire area, just as light from the bayed breakfast area will brighten it. The master suite is sumptuous, with a tray ceiling, huge walk-in closet and a vaulted bath with a separate tub and shower and a double-bowl vanity. A laundry alcove sits in the central hallway to the bedrooms. Please specify basement or crawlspace foundation when ordering.

Design By
© FRANK BETZ
ASSOCIATES, INC.

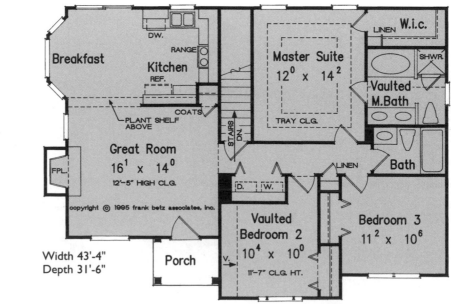

DESIGN 7508

Main Level: 2,124 square feet
Lower Level: 112 square feet
Total: 2,236 square feet

Horizontal siding, cedar shingles and stone accents adorn this modified Craftsman-style home. It is designed for a home that slopes to the side and holds a two-car garage, plus storage space and a stairwell on the lower level. The main level has excellent livability and open spaces. The formal dining room is defined by columns and has a box-bay window. Just beyond is the great room, with fireplace and pass-through to the kitchen. Connecting the great room and the kitchen is a sunny nook overlooking the deck. A cozy den and three bedrooms dominate the right side of the plan. The master suite is graced by a tray ceiling and a bath with a spa tub, a walk-in closet and double sinks. Family bedrooms share the use of a full bath. The laundry is nearby.

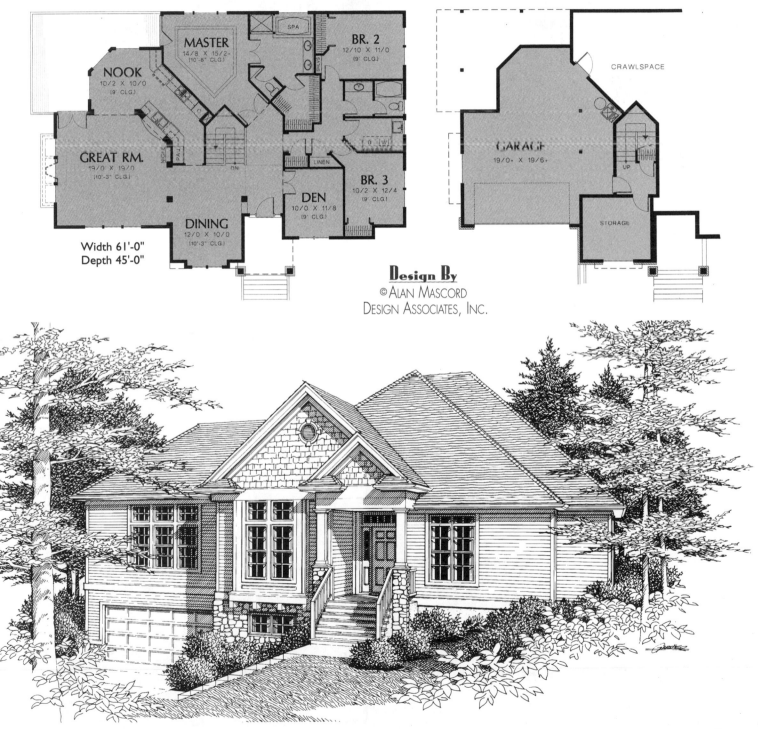

Width 61'-0"
Depth 45'-0"

Design By
© ALAN MASCORD
DESIGN ASSOCIATES, INC.

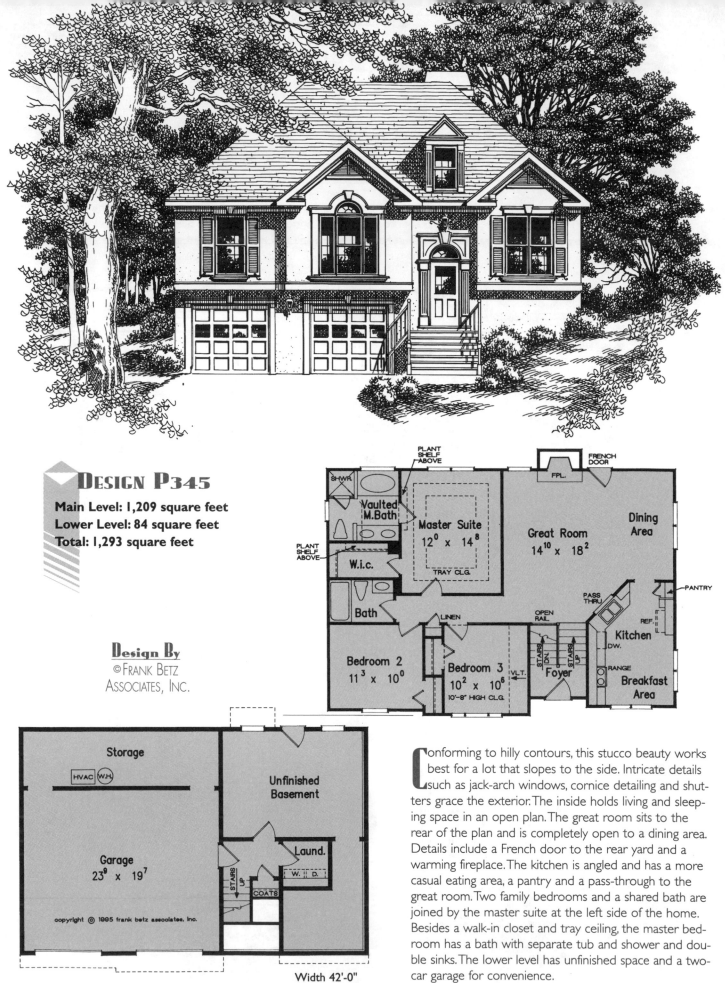

Design P345

Main Level: 1,209 square feet
Lower Level: 84 square feet
Total: 1,293 square feet

Design By
© Frank Betz
Associates, Inc.

PLANT SHELF ABOVE

SHWR.

Vaulted M.Bath

PLANT SHELF ABOVE

W.i.c.

Bath

LINEN

Master Suite
12⁰ x 14⁸

TRAY CLG.

FRENCH DOOR

FPL.

Great Room
14¹⁰ x 18²

Dining Area

PASS THRU.

PANTRY

REF.

Bedroom 2
11³ x 10⁰

Bedroom 3
10² x 10⁶

10'-8" HIGH CLG.

OPEN RAIL

VLT.

STAIRS DN.

STAIRS UP

Foyer

Kitchen

DW.

RANGE

Breakfast Area

Storage

HVAC   W.H.

Unfinished Basement

Garage
23⁹ x 19⁷

STAIRS UP

COATS

Laund.

W.   D.

copyright © 1995 frank betz associates, inc.

Width 42'-0"
Depth 31'-0"

Conforming to hilly contours, this stucco beauty works best for a lot that slopes to the side. Intricate details such as jack-arch windows, cornice detailing and shutters grace the exterior. The inside holds living and sleeping space in an open plan. The great room sits to the rear of the plan and is completely open to a dining area. Details include a French door to the rear yard and a warming fireplace. The kitchen is angled and has a more casual eating area, a pantry and a pass-through to the great room. Two family bedrooms and a shared bath are joined by the master suite at the left side of the home. Besides a walk-in closet and tray ceiling, the master bedroom has a bath with separate tub and shower and double sinks. The lower level has unfinished space and a two-car garage for convenience.

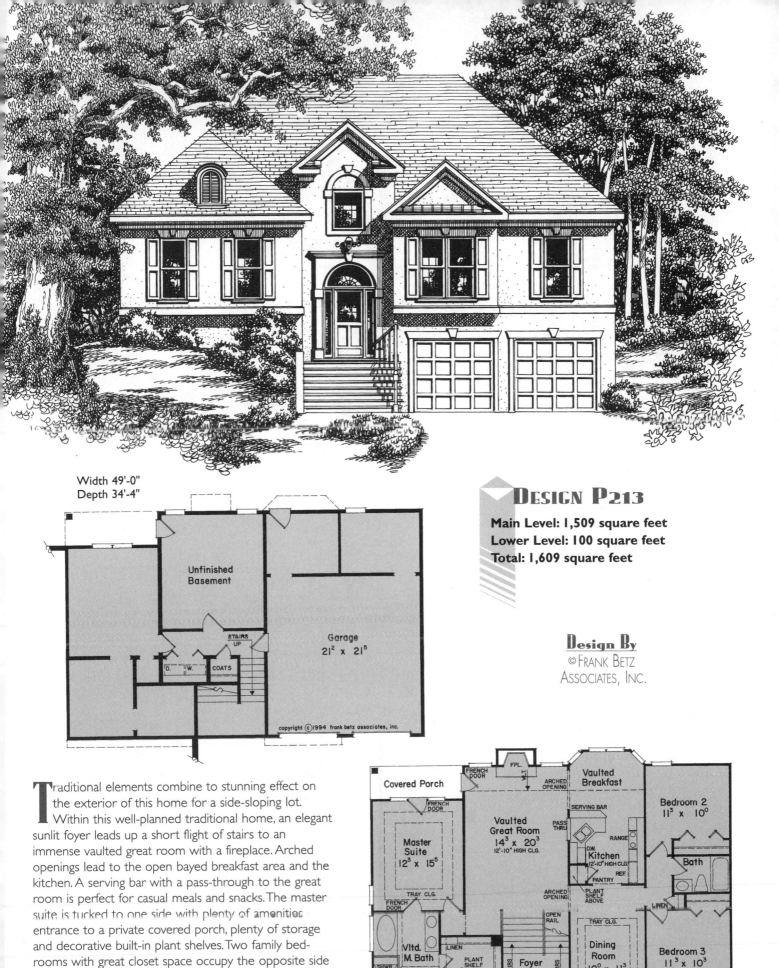

Width 49'-0"
Depth 34'-4"

Unfinished
Basement

STAIRS
UP

D. W. COATS

Garage
21² x 21⁵

copyright © 1994 frank betz associates, inc.

DESIGN P213

Main Level: 1,509 square feet
Lower Level: 100 square feet
Total: 1,609 square feet

Design By
© FRANK BETZ
ASSOCIATES, INC.

Traditional elements combine to stunning effect on the exterior of this home for a side-sloping lot. Within this well-planned traditional home, an elegant sunlit foyer leads up a short flight of stairs to an immense vaulted great room with a fireplace. Arched openings lead to the open bayed breakfast area and the kitchen. A serving bar with a pass-through to the great room is perfect for casual meals and snacks. The master suite is tucked to one side with plenty of amenities entrance to a private covered porch, plenty of storage and decorative built-in plant shelves. Two family bedrooms with great closet space occupy the opposite side of the home and share a full bath. An unfinished basement provides for future lifestyle needs.

Covered Porch

FRENCH DOOR

FPL.

ARCHED OPENING

Vaulted Breakfast

SERVING BAR

Bedroom 2
11³ x 10⁰

FRENCH DOOR

Master Suite
12³ x 15⁵

Vaulted Great Room
14³ x 20³
12'-10" HIGH CLG.

PASS THRU

RANGE

D.W. Kitchen
12'-10" HIGH CLG.

REF

Bath

TRAY CLG.

FRENCH DOOR

PANTRY

ARCHED OPENING

PLANT SHELF ABOVE

LINEN

Vltd. M. Bath

SHWR

LINEN

PLANT SHELF ABOVE

OPEN RAIL

STAIRS UP

Foyer

STAIRS DN

Dining Room
10⁰ x 11³

TRAY CLG.

Bedroom 3
11³ x 10³

W.i.c.

7

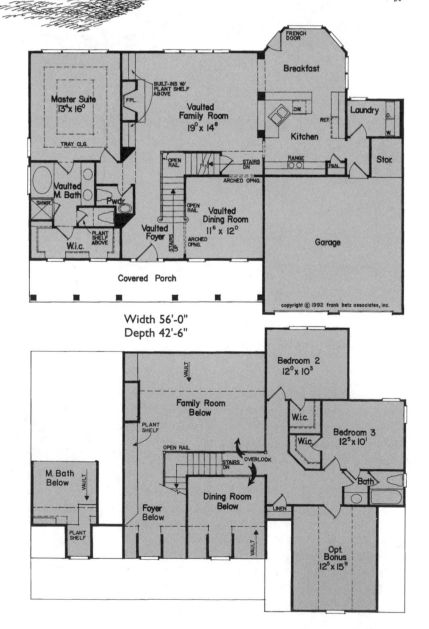

DESIGN P140

First Floor: 1,414 square feet

Second Floor: 502 square feet

Total: 1,916 square feet

Bonus Room: 208 square feet

For lots that slope slightly to the side, this quaint home opens with a full-width covered porch. The sunny breakfast room of this country home is the perfect place to start your day. The breakfast room and adjacent kitchen lead to a vaulted family room with scenic views and a fireplace flanked by built-in cabinets and plant shelves. The dining room is conveniently close to the kitchen but with enough separation to cut down on disruptive cooking and clean-up noises. A luxurious master suite, with a vaulted bath and huge walk-in closet, is on the first floor. Two family bedroom share a full bath upstairs. An optional bonus room can be developed as another bedroom, an office, a study or a game room. Please specify basement or crawlspace foundation when ordering.

Design By
© FRANK BETZ
ASSOCIATES, INC.

Width 56'-0"
Depth 42'-6"

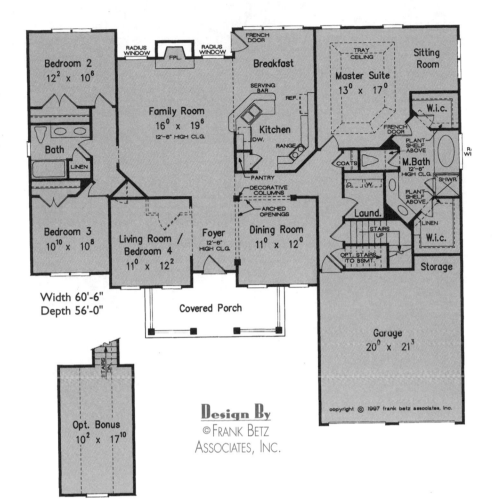

Bedroom 2
12² x 10⁶

RADIUS WINDOW
FPL.
RADIUS WINDOW

Bath
LINEN

Bedroom 3
10¹⁰ x 10⁸

Family Room
16⁰ x 19⁶
12'-6" HIGH CLG.

SERVING BAR

Kitchen
DW.
RANGE
REF.

PANTRY

DECORATIVE COLUMNS
ARCHED OPENINGS

Living Room /
Bedroom 4
11⁰ x 12²

Foyer
12'-6" HIGH CLG.

Dining Room
11⁰ x 12⁰

Breakfast
FRENCH DOOR

TRAY CEILING

Master Suite
13⁰ x 17⁰

Sitting Room

FRENCH DOOR

W.i.c.

PLANT SHELF ABOVE

M.Bath
12'-6" HIGH CLG.

PLANT SHELF ABOVE

SHWR.

COATS

D. W.

Laund.

LINEN

W.i.c.

STAIRS UP

OPT. STAIRS TO BSMT.

Storage

Width 60'-6"
Depth 56'-0"

Covered Porch

Garage
20⁰ x 21³

STAIRS DN.

Opt. Bonus
10² x 17¹⁰

Design By
©FRANK BETZ
ASSOCIATES, INC.

copyright © 1997 frank betz associates, inc.

DESIGN P366

Square Footage: 2,056
Bonus Room: 208 square feet

For a lot with a slight side slope, this design works well. The entry begins with a covered, columned porch and opens through a glass door to a foyer with a twelve-foot ceiling. On the left is the living room (or make it Bedroom 4 with the addition of a closet); on the right is the formal dining room. Decorative columns separate the dining room from the foyer and hallway. A gigantic family room sits at the center of the home. It also has a twelve-foot ceiling and is warmed by a hearth flanked with two radius windows. Bedrooms 2 and 3 are on the left. The master suite is on the right, behind the two-car garage. Special details in the master suite deserve attention: tray ceiling, sitting room, two walk-in closets, plant shelves and a separate tub and shower. A bonus room over the garage could become a home office or an additional bedroom. Please specify basement or crawlspace foundation when ordering.

Design 7280

Square Footage: 1,429

With fine traditional details, this home for a side-sloping lot is handsome as well as practical. The elegant entry leads to a great room with a vaulted ceiling. A fireplace in the great room acts as a focal point. A formal dining room resides to the front and is easily served by the kitchen. L-shaped counters and a boxed window add character and convenience to the kitchen. The breakfast area expands views with a bay window. The master suite, on the right side of the plan, opens to a walk-in closet and a private bath. Secondary bedrooms feature boxed windows and share a centrally located hall bath. The basement level leads to the two-car garage and holds a laundry area and space for expansion.

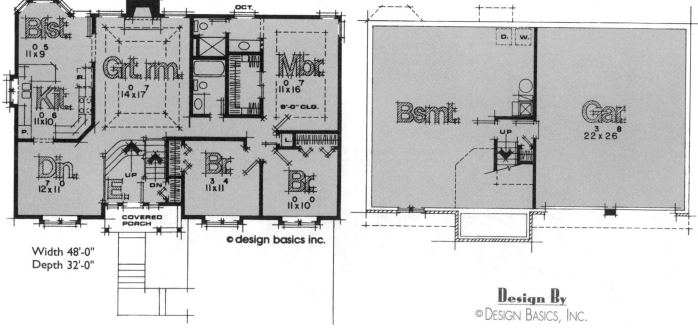

Width 48'-0"
Depth 32'-0"

© design basics inc.

Design By
© Design Basics, Inc.

10

DESIGN 7517

Main Level: 2,124 square feet
Lower Level: 112 square feet
Total: 2,236 square feet

Design By
© ALAN MASCORD
DESIGN ASSOCIATES, INC.

MASTER
14/8 X 15/2+
(10'-8" CLG.)

SPA TUB

BR. 2
12/10 X 11/0
(9' CLG.)

NOOK
10/2 X 10/0
(9' CLG.)

GREAT RM.
19/0 X 19/0
(10'-3" CLG.)

MEDIA BELOW

SHELVES BELOW

REF.

PAN

NICHE

DN

LINEN

D W

BR. 3
10/2 X 12/4
(9' CLG.)

DEN
10/0 X 11/8
(9' CLG.)

DINING
12/0 X 10/0
(10'-3" CLG.)

CRAWLSPACE

GARAGE
19/0+ X 19/6+

UP

STORAGE / FUTURE BONUS SPACE

Width 61'-0"
Depth 45'-0"

Don't let a sloped lot deter you from getting the plan you want. This grand home accommodates a side slope without losing any livability. The lower level has a two-car garage and a storage area or bonus space. On the main level, the great room and dining room are open and divided only by two decorative columns. A nearby nook and galley kitchen have access to a rear deck. For quieter times, the den sits to the right of the foyer. Three bedrooms include two family bedrooms with shared bath and a master suite. Look for a spa tub, walk-in closet and tray ceiling in the master suite.

Design P302

Main Level: 1,258 square feet
Lower Level: 60 square feet
Total: 1,318 square feet

Design By
© FRANK BETZ
ASSOCIATES, INC.

An impressive front entrance adds interest to the gable roofline of this livable design for side-sloping lots. Inside, high ceilings add a senses of spaciousness. Ascend from the front foyer to a vaulted dining room, family room and kitchen. Sliding glass doors lead out from the dining room to the rear yard. Note the fireplace in the family room. The sleeping wing is tucked away on the left side of the plan and includes two family bedrooms sharing a hall bath and a luxurious master suite with tray ceiling and vaulted master bath. An unfinished basement area offers room for future expansion. The two-car garage sits on the lower level and has a large storage room.

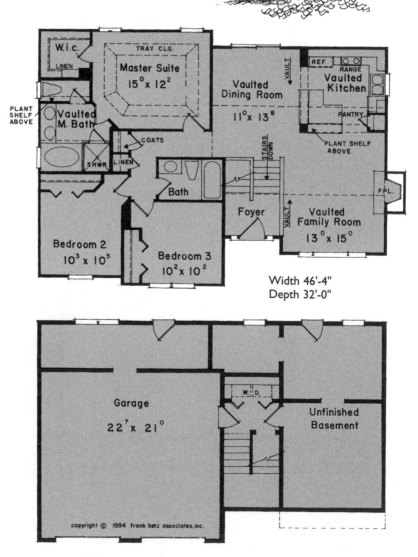

W.i.c.
LINEN
TRAY CLG.
Master Suite
15⁰ x 12²
Vaulted Dining Room
11⁰ x 13⁸
REF.
RANGE
Vaulted Kitchen
PANTRY
PLANT SHELF ABOVE
Vaulted M. Bath
COATS
SHWR
LINEN
Bath
STAIRS DOWN
PLANT SHELF ABOVE
FPL.
VAULT
Foyer
Vaulted Family Room
13⁰ x 15⁰
Bedroom 2
10³ x 10⁵
Bedroom 3
10² x 10²

Width 46'-4"
Depth 32'-0"

Garage
22⁷ x 21⁰
W.D.
Unfinished Basement

copyright © 1994 frank betz associates, inc.

DESIGN 7278

Square Footage: 1,125

This convenient, split-entry ranch design is perfect for a home that slopes to the side. The lower level features a two-car garage and additional space for a washer and dryer, plus bonus space to use as you wish. The large entry, with a coat closet, is dramatically designed: it has an angled staircase that leads to the great room. A cathedral ceiling in the great room expands its spaciousness. The dining room and kitchen are nearby, separated by a snack bar counter. The dining room has sliding glass doors to the rear yard. The kitchen sink has a box window above it. A long hallway leads to the three bedrooms. Double doors open to a large master bedroom with vaulted ceiling, master bath and walk-in closet. The secondary bedrooms share a convenient hall bath.

Design By
© DESIGN BASICS, INC.

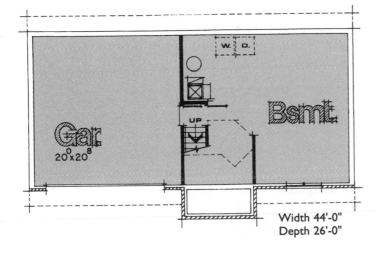

Width 44'-0"
Depth 26'-0"

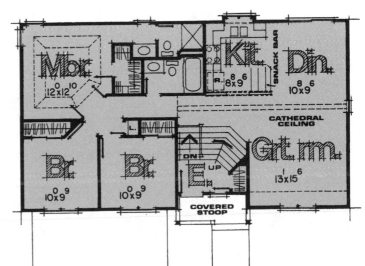

DESIGN 9410

First Floor: 1,484 square feet
Second Floor: 1,402 square feet
Total: 2,886 square feet
Bonus Room: 430 square feet

This impressive Tudor is designed for lots that slope up slightly from the street—the garage is five feet below the main floor. Just to the right of the entry, the den is arranged to work well as an office. Formal living areas include a living room with fireplace and an elegant dining room. The family room also has a fireplace and is close to the bumped-out nook—a great casual dining area. Double doors in the nook lead out to the rear yard. All the bedrooms are generously sized, especially the master suite, which features all the amenities, plus a huge walk-in closet. A large vaulted bonus room is provided with convenient access from both the family room and the upper hallway.

Width 63'-0"
Depth 51'-0"

Design By
© ALAN MASCORD
DESIGN ASSOCIATES, INC.

14

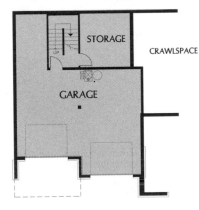

STORAGE

CRAWLSPACE

UP

GARAGE

Width 52'-0"
Depth 36'-0"

Design by
©ALAN MASCORD DESIGN
ASSOCIATES, INC.

BR. 2
10/0 X 12/6

DN

BR. 3
10/8 X 12/6

LINEN

LINEN

WINDOW
SEAT

VAULTED
MASTER
13/8 X 14/6

OPEN TO
LIVING RM
BELOW

DINING
10/10 X 13/6 +/-
(9' CLG)

KIT.
13/10 X 16/6 +/-

NOOK
10/0 X 10/0
(9' CLG)

UP   DN

REF.

DN

PAN.

VAULTED
FAMILY
13/4 X 14/8

WET
BAR

DN

DEN
13/6 X 12/2
(9' CLG)

VAULTED
LIVING RM
13/0 X 17/10

DECK

DESIGN
HPTHH20001

First Floor: 1,501 square feet
Second Floor: 921 square feet
Total: 2,509 square feet

Side-sloping lot? No problem for this plan. It was designed specifically to accommodate with a double garage underneath and living space above. The main level opens from a raised porch to a receiving hall with decorative columns and flanking living and family rooms. An airy island kitchen with attached breakfast nook is close to the formal dining room. A wet bar separates the dining room and living room. Tucked away on the left side of the plan are a den with private deck, the laundry area and a half-bath. Three bedrooms reside on the upper level. The owners suite has a private bath with separate tub and shower, a walk-in closet and double sinks. Note the large storage area in the lower level.

Design HPTHH20002

Main Level: 2,464 square feet
Lower Level: 1,887 square feet
Total: 4,351 square feet

From the front, this classy design appears to be a one-story plan. But if you're building on a site that slopes to the side, you'll appreciate the hillside nature of the plan that allows for a walkout basement. The entry admits access to columned living areas: a great room and a dining room, both with tray ceilings. A vaulted den is hidden away in a cozy corner and features a half-bath and built-ins. The island kitchen and nook lie just beyond the living area, with a large laundry connecting the kitchen to the garage. The owners bedroom is on the main floor and contains a bath with a huge, glass-enclosed shower and whirlpool spa. Family bedrooms—there are three—and a games room are on the lower level. There is also a wet bar and wine cellar on this level.

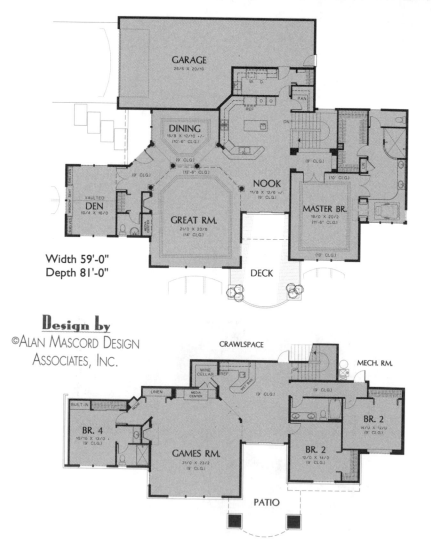

Width 59'-0"
Depth 81'-0"

Design by
©ALAN MASCORD DESIGN ASSOCIATES, INC.

Design 9573

First Floor: 1,502 square feet
Second Floor: 954 square feet
Total: 2,456 square feet

Come home to the spectacular views and livability supplied by this lovely hillside home. It tucks a garage into the lower level; two full stories accommodate family living patterns. A two-story living room shares a see-through fireplace with the formal dining room. Quiet time may be spent in the den, which opens through double doors to a deck. The sunken family room also enjoys a fireplace and isn't too far from the kitchen and breakfast nook. The kitchen features a cooktop island. On the second floor, a vaulted master suite enjoys privacy from the two secondary bedrooms. These two family bedrooms share a full bath that sits between them. The master bath has a spa-style tub, double sinks and a separate shower.

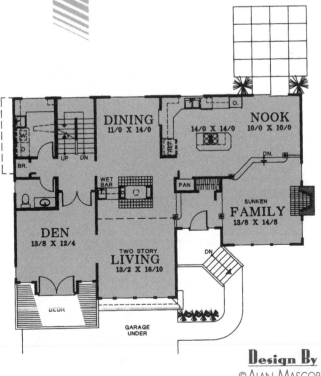

DINING
11/0 X 14/0

NOOK
10/0 X 10/0

BR.

WET BAR

PAN

DN.

SUNKEN
FAMILY
13/8 X 14/8

DEN
13/8 X 12/4

TWO STORY
LIVING
13/2 X 16/10

DN

GARAGE
UNDER

DECK

Design By
© Alan Mascord
Design Associates, Inc.

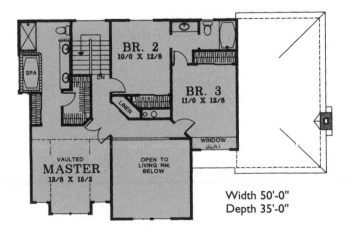

SPA

BR. 2
10/0 X 12/8

BR. 3
11/0 X 12/8

LINEN

DN

VAULTED
MASTER
13/8 X 15/2

OPEN TO
LIVING RM.
BELOW

WINDOW
SEAT

Width 50'-0"
Depth 35'-0"

17

HOLZHAUER INC.

Design 7510

First Floor: 813 square feet
Second Floor: 726 square feet
Total: 1,539 square feet

MASTER
15/0 X 13/0

BR. 3
10/2 X 11/10

LINEN

DN

BR. 2.
10/0 X 11/4

Design By
© Alan Mascord
Design Associates, Inc.

Vertical and horizontal wood siding combine with a covered front porch on this home for a side-sloping lot. The lower level holds the garage and lots of storage space, with stairs to the first floor. Living spaces are open and well-appointed with a dining room, living room and island kitchen. Note the built-ins and fireplace in the living room and the dining room access to the rear deck. A half-bath, storage closet and laundry alcove are just to the right of the entry foyer. Bedrooms are on the second level and include two family bedrooms with a shared bath and a master suite with its own bath.

LIVING
15/0 X 17/8 +/-
(10' CLG.)

DINING
13/4 X 15/4 +/-
(10' CLG.)

9/0 X 14/0

PAN
REF

UP

BUILT-IN

STORAGE

DN

D W

STORAGE
15/0 X 8/0

UNFINISHED
STORAGE
10/2 X 8/6
(7' CLG.)

GARAGE
24/0 X 19/0

UP

Width 36'-0"
Depth 34'-0"

18

DESIGN 7509

Main Level: 954 square feet
Upper Level: 348 square feet
Lower Level: 409 square feet
Total: 1,711 square feet

Perched on a sloping lot, this home combines fine design with open floor planning. On the lower level are a two-car garage and a bedroom with full bath and two closets. Stairs lead up to the main level, which can also be accessed from outside through an entry foyer with a few steps up. The living room, dining room and kitchen are open to one another. The kitchen features an island work surface, while the living room has a fireplace surrounded by built-ins. A door in the living room leads to a front-facing deck. The upper level holds an additional bedroom with full bath and two closets.

Width 30'-0"
Depth 40'-0"

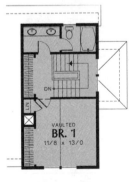

Design By
© ALAN MASCORD
DESIGN ASSOCIATES, INC.

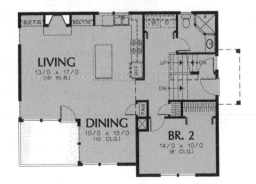

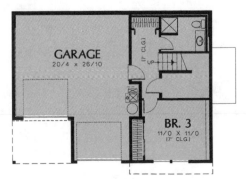

DESIGN 9509

First Floor: 1,022 square feet
Second Floor: 813 square feet
Total: 1,835 square feet

This house not only accommodates a narrow lot, but it also fits a sloping site. Notice how the two-car garage is tucked away under the first level of the house. The angled corner entry gives way to a two-story living room with a tiled hearth. The dining room shares an interesting angled space with this area and enjoys easy service from the efficient kitchen. A large pantry and an angled corner sink add character to this area. The family room offers double doors to a refreshing balcony. A powder room and a laundry room complete the main level. Upstairs, three bedrooms include a vaulted master suite with a private bath. Bedrooms 2 and 3 each take advantage of direct access to a full bath.

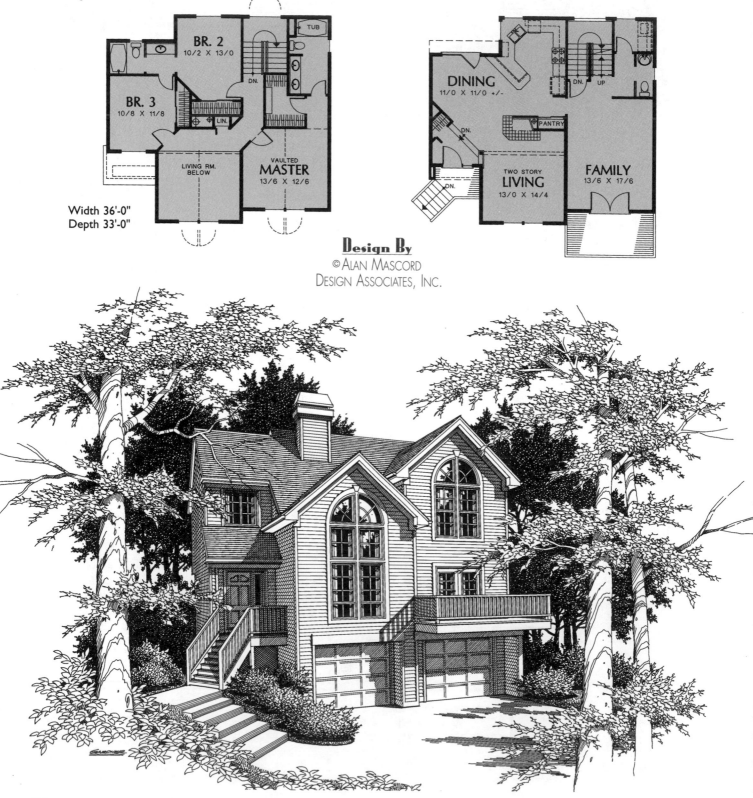

Width 36'-0"
Depth 33'-0"

Design By
© ALAN MASCORD
DESIGN ASSOCIATES, INC.

Design By
© ALAN MASCORD
DESIGN ASSOCIATES, INC.

DESIGN 7516

First Floor: 913 square feet
Second Floor: 811 square feet
Total: 1,724 square feet

DINING
14/6 × 10/2
[10' CLG.]

LIVING
17/0 × 16/0 +/-
[10' CLG.]

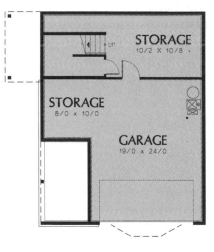

STORAGE
10/2 × 10/8 +

STORAGE
8/0 × 10/0

GARAGE
19/0 × 24/0

BR. 3
11/0 × 11/10

BR. 2
10/0 × 10/2

MASTER
13/8 × 13/8 +/-

Width 38'-0"
Depth 33'-6"

A difficult lot is no challenge for this fine design—it works best on a sloping lot. The garage level has space for two cars and has abundant storage and a stair to the first floor. Living areas on the first floor include a living room with bay window, fireplace and built-ins; a dining room; and a kitchen with island work area. A walk-in pantry, half bath and large laundry room are also on the first floor. The second floor features three bedrooms: two family bedrooms with shared bath and a master suite with private bath. The master bath is grand with double sinks, separate tub and shower and huge walk-in closet.

Design 7469

First Floor: 1,106 square feet
Second Floor: 872 square feet
Total: 1,978 square feet

Design By
© Alan Mascord
Design Associates, Inc.

BR. 3
11/0 X 10/8

BR. 2
11/0 X 10/0

LOFT

FOYER
BELOW

LIVING
BELOW

LIN

VAULTED
MASTER
15/2 X 12/0

OPT FR
DRS

DINING
10/6 X 12/0+

DW
15/0 X 9/0

NOOK
13/10 X 8/4

2 STORY
LIVING
13/0 X 14/0

FAMILY
13/10 X 20/8

DECK

Cedar shingles brighten the exterior of this Craftsman adaptation. The layout of the home makes it perfect for a sloping lot. The first floor can be accessed through a front entry or from the garage level where there is space for two cars. A two-story living room with pass-through fireplace to the family room is joined by a nook and U-shaped island kitchen on this level. Double doors in the family room open to a front-facing deck. Optional French doors in the dining room offer rear deck availability. A half-bath and laundry complete the floor. The second floor is graced by a vaulted master suite with full bath and two bedrooms with shared bath. Don't miss the large walk-in closet in the master suite.

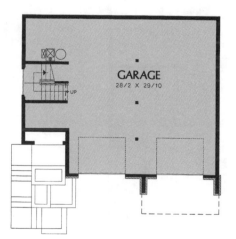

GARAGE
28/2 X 29/10

Width 38'-0"
Depth 35'-0"

16/8 X 9/6

PAN | REF

DINING
18/8 X 11/6
(10' CLG.)

STOR

DN

DN

UP

LIVING
17/0 X 17/2
(10' CLG.)

Width 34'-0"
Depth 38'-0"

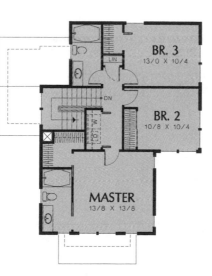

BR. 3
13/0 X 10/4

LIN

DN

BR. 2
10/8 X 10/4

W

MASTER
13/8 X 13/8

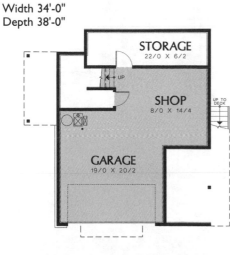

STORAGE
22/0 X 6/2

UP

SHOP
8/0 X 14/4

UP TO
DECK

GARAGE
19/0 X 20/2

DESIGN 7515

First Floor: 898 square feet
Second Floor: 777 square feet
Total: 1,675 square feet

Shingle siding covers this narrow-lot home, creating an exterior that weathers and improves with age. Inside, open planning begins with the living room, dining room and kitchen—separated only by an island countertop, making this area perfect for festive as well as casual gatherings. The upper level houses two family bedrooms and a master bedroom with a private bath. A large workshop at the garage level will be a haven for the handyman in the family.

Design By
© Alan Mascord
Design Associates, Inc.

DESIGN 7474

First Floor: 2,005 square feet
Second Floor: 689 square feet
Total: 2,694 square feet
Bonus Room: 356 square feet

Shingles and stone combine to present a highly attractive facade on this spacious three-bedroom home. The Craftsman-style influence is very evident and adds to the charm, also. The two-story foyer is flanked by a large, yet cozy, den on the right and on the left, beyond the staircase, is the formal dining room with built-ins. The vaulted great room also offers built-ins, as well as a fireplace. The U-shaped kitchen will surely please the gourmet of the family with its planning desk, corner sink, cooktop island and plenty of counter and cabinet space. The vaulted master suite is complete with a plant shelf, a walk-in closet and a lavish bath. Two secondary bedrooms make up the sleeping zone upstairs, each with a walk-in closet and having access to the full bath. A large bonus room is available for use as a guest suite.

Design By
© ALAN MASCORD
DESIGN ASSOCIATES, INC.

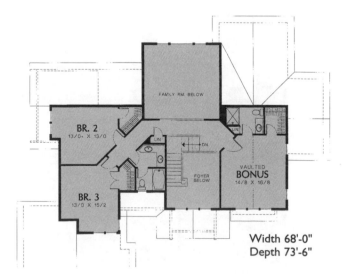

Width 68'-0"
Depth 73'-6"

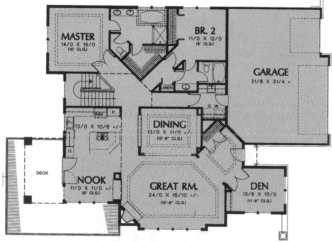

DESIGN 7441

Main Level: 2,057 square feet
Lower Level: 1,373 square feet
Total: 3,430 square feet

Multi-pane windows, a sloping lot and fine details are what make this home a true gem. Inside, a cozy den with double doors opens off the foyer. A spacious great room with a tray ceiling and a fireplace is near the formal dining room and the island kitchen. For dining alfresco, the casual dining nook offers direct access to the deck. A lavish master bedroom is located to the rear of the first floor and is enhanced by a walk-in closet and an amenity-filled bath. A secondary bedroom completes this level. Downstairs, two more family bedrooms share a full bath and a large games room with a fireplace.

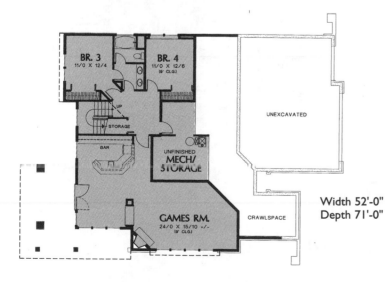

Width 52'-0"
Depth 71'-0"

Design By
© ALAN MASCORD
DESIGN ASSOCIATES, INC.

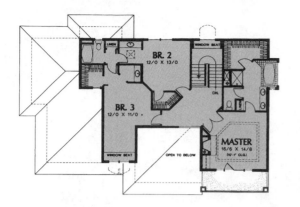

BR. 2
12/0 X 13/0

BR. 3
12/0 X 11/0

LINEN

WINDOW SEAT

DN.

MASTER
16/6 X 14/8
(10'-0" CLG.)

WINDOW SEAT

OPEN TO BELOW

NOOK
10/0 X 17/0

FAMILY
18/0 X 16/0

WINDOW SEAT

GALLERY

DINING
13/6 X 14/8

VAULTED
LIVING
15/0 X 15/0

DEN
15/0 X 12/8 +/-

10' CLG.

DESIGN 9554

Main Level: 1,989 square feet

Upper Level: 1,349 square feet

Lower Level: 105 square feet

Total: 3,443 square feet

Bonus Room: 487 square feet

Design By
© ALAN MASCORD
DESIGN ASSOCIATES, INC.

CRAWLSPACE

STORAGE

SHOP
10/10 X 16/4

BONUS RM.
19/6 X 20/6

STORAGE/GAMES

GARAGE
32/10 X 25/10

Width 63'-0"
Depth 48'-0"

Dramatic balconies and spectacular window treatment enhance this stunning luxury home. Inside, a through-fireplace warms the formal living room and a restful den. Both living spaces open onto a balcony that invites quiet reflection on starry nights. The banquet-sized dining room is easily served from the adjacent kitchen. Here, space is shared with an eating nook that provides access to the rear grounds and a family room with a corner fireplace perfect for casual gatherings. The upper level contains two family bedrooms and a luxurious master suite that enjoys its own private balcony. The lower level accommodates a shop and a bonus room for future development.

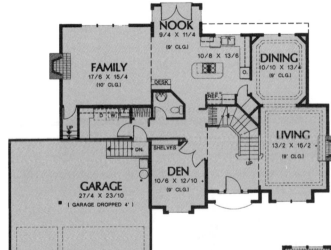

NOOK
9/4 X 11/4
(9' CLG.)

DINING
10/10 X 13/4
(9' CLG.)

FAMILY
17/6 X 15/4
(10' CLG.)

DESK

10/8 X 13/6

O.

REF.

LIVING
13/2 X 16/2
(9' CLG.)

SHELVES

UP

D. W.

UP

DN.

GARAGE
27/4 X 23/10
(GARAGE DROPPED 4')

DEN
10/6 X 12/10
(9' CLG.)

Design By
© ALAN MASCORD
DESIGN ASSOCIATES, INC.

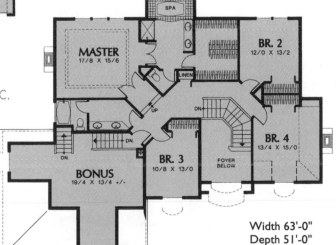

SPA

MASTER
17/8 X 15/6

BR. 2
12/0 X 13/2

LINEN

UP

DN.

DN.

BR. 4
13/4 X 15/0

DN.

BR. 3
10/8 X 13/0

FOYER
BELOW

BONUS
19/4 X 13/4 +/-

Width 63'-0"
Depth 51'-0"

DESIGN 9561

First Floor: 1,564 square feet
Second Floor: 1,422 square feet
Total: 2,986 square feet
Bonus Room: 430 square feet

Keystones, stucco and dramatic rooflines create a stately exterior for this traditional home. The formal living and dining rooms invite elegant occasions, while the clustered family room, breakfast nook and gourmet kitchen take care of casual gatherings. A quiet den with built-in shelves opens off the foyer—perfect for a library or home office. The second-floor master suite, a few steps up from the central hall, features a coffered ceiling and a divided walk-in closet. The master bedroom opens to the spa bath through French doors. Three family bedrooms share a full bath. Unfinished bonus space above the garage can be developed into a hobby or study room.

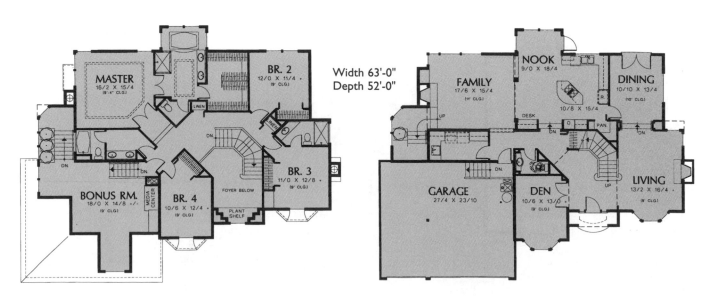

Design 7402

First Floor: 1,740 square feet
Second Floor: 1,477 square feet
Total: 3,217 square feet
Bonus Room: 382 square feet

Design By
© Alan Mascord
Design Associates, Inc.

If you have a lot that slopes slightly to the front, this design will accommodate with a garage that is sunken from the main house. Or you may grade your site to fit the design! The entry is opulent and inviting and opens to a den with bay window on the left and a formal living room with fireplace on the right. Down a few steps from the living room is the formal dining room, with French doors to the rear property. The kitchen and nook are also down a few steps. Note the convenient work areas in the kitchen. The family room connects directly to the kitchen and features another fireplace. Family bedrooms join the master suite on the second floor. Bedroom 3 has a private bath, while Bedrooms 2 and 4 share a hall bath. A bonus room can become a fifth bedroom or hobby space as needed.

Width 63'-0"
Depth 52'-0"

DESIGN 7503

First Floor: 1,747 square feet
Second Floor: 1,146 square feet
Total: 2,893 square feet

Design By
© ALAN MASCORD
DESIGN ASSOCIATES, INC.

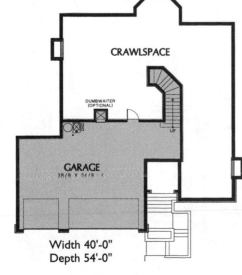

Width 40'-0"
Depth 54'-0"

Graceful form and wonderful function meet in this elegant design for a front-sloping lot. The lower level holds garage space for two cars and has a curved staircase to the first floor. Or enter the first floor from a dramatic entry with arched window. Formal rooms are on the right: a living room with fireplace and a dining room—both have tray ceilings. A media room (or fifth bedroom) and cozy den are on the left. Casual living areas are to the back of the plan and include a family room with fireplace and nook with double doors to the outside. The U-shaped kitchen has an island cooktop, large pantry and planning desk. Bedrooms are on the second floor. Three family bedrooms share a full bath with double sinks. The master suite has a tray ceiling and marvelous bath with garden spa tub, huge walk-in closet and vaulted ceiling.

DESIGN P365

First Floor: 1,972 square feet
Second Floor: 579 square feet
Total: 2,551 square feet
Bonus Room: 256 square feet

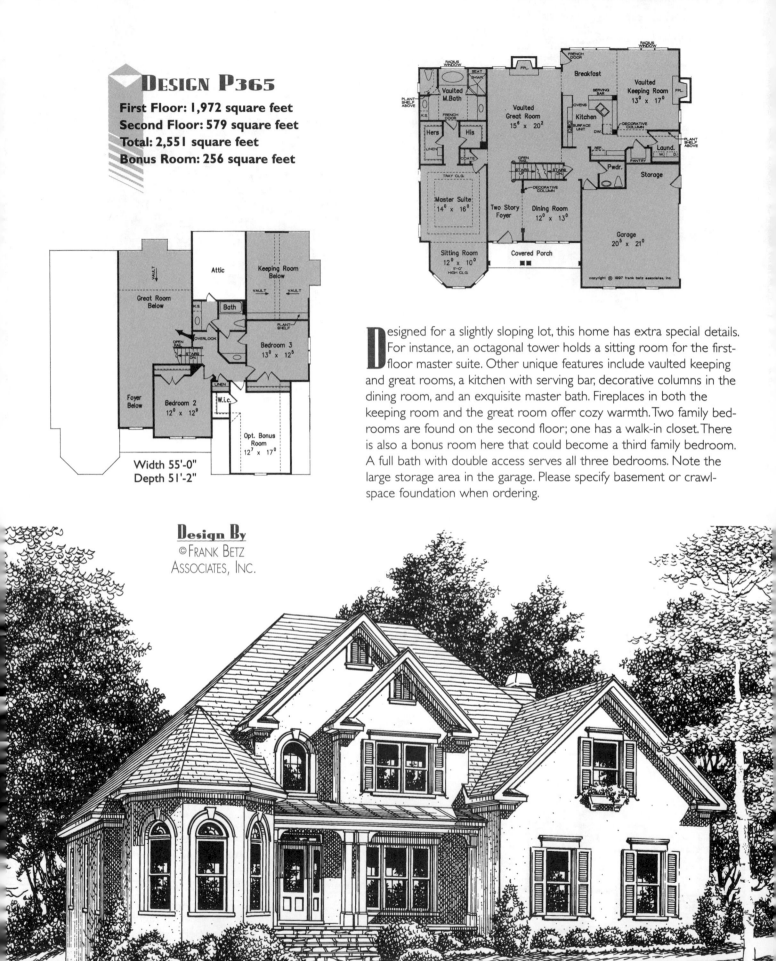

Width 55'-0"
Depth 51'-2"

Design By
© FRANK BETZ
ASSOCIATES, INC.

Designed for a slightly sloping lot, this home has extra special details. For instance, an octagonal tower holds a sitting room for the first-floor master suite. Other unique features include vaulted keeping and great rooms, a kitchen with serving bar, decorative columns in the dining room, and an exquisite master bath. Fireplaces in both the keeping room and the great room offer cozy warmth. Two family bedrooms are found on the second floor; one has a walk-in closet. There is also a bonus room here that could become a third family bedroom. A full bath with double access serves all three bedrooms. Note the large storage area in the garage. Please specify basement or crawl-space foundation when ordering.

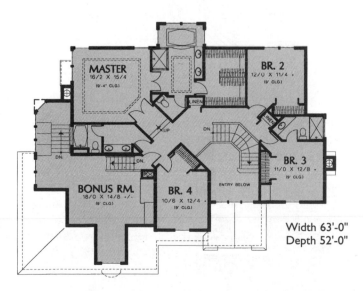

DESIGN 7442

First Floor: 1,728 square feet

Second Floor: 1,477 square feet

Total: 3,205 square feet

Bonus Room: 382 square feet

Design By
© ALAN MASCORD
DESIGN ASSOCIATES, INC.

Double French doors are a motif in this gracious home. From the foyer, the first set of French doors opens into a den. Through the living room, with its focal-point fireplace, the dining room has French doors that open to the rear yard. On the way to the family room through the kitchen, notice the cooktop island and walk-in pantry. A laundry room and powder room complete this floor. Upstairs, enter the master suite through French doors and from there through another set of French doors into the master bath. Three family bedrooms, two baths and a bonus room are also on this floor.

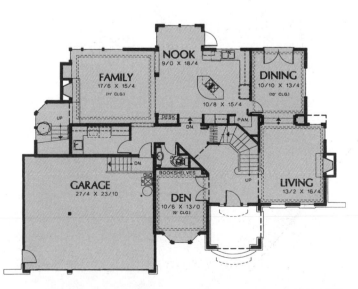

Width 63'-0"
Depth 52'-0"

Design 9538

First Floor: 1,538 square feet
Second Floor: 1,089 square feet
Total: 2,627 square feet

Design By
© Alan Mascord
Design Associates, Inc.

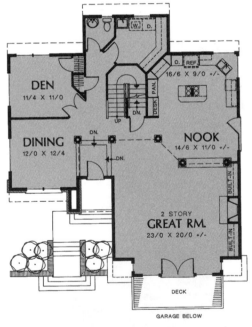

DEN
11/4 X 11/0

DINING
12/0 X 12/4

16/6 X 9/0 +/-

NOOK
14/6 X 11/0 +/-

2 STORY
GREAT RM.
23/0 X 20/0 +/-

DECK

GARAGE BELOW

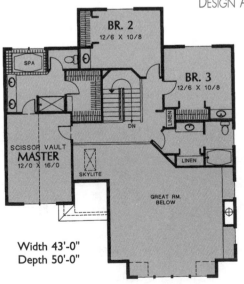

BR. 2
12/6 X 10/8

SPA

BR. 3
12/6 X 10/8

LINEN

LINEN

DN

SCISSOR VAULT
MASTER
12/0 X 16/0

SKYLITE

GREAT RM.
BELOW

Width 43'-0"
Depth 50'-0"

This attractive two-story home will fit a sloping lot and fulfill seaside views. The foyer opens to interior vistas through decorative columns, while the two-story great room boasts lovely French doors to a front deck. The gourmet kitchen features an island cooktop counter, a sunny corner sink and a nook with a pass-through to the great room. A formal dining room, a secluded den and a sizable laundry complete the first floor. The second-floor master suite employs a scissor-vault ceiling and a divided-light window for style, and a relaxing bath with a spa tub for comfort. Two family bedrooms, each with a private lavatory, share a full bath on this floor.

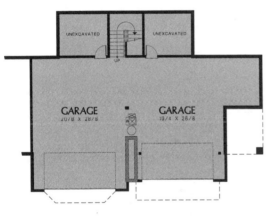

Design By
© ALAN MASCORD
DESIGN ASSOCIATES, INC.

DESIGN 7507

First Floor: 1,765 square feet
Second Floor: 907 square feet
Total: 2,672 square feet

In stucco and horizontal siding, this design is reminiscent of Prairie styling and works best on a sloping lot. The lower level contains double garages and leads up to the main level with a U-shaped stair. The first floor can also be reached through a front entry with two garden landings. Up a few steps from the entry foyer are a two-story great room with fireplace and a dining room with tray ceiling. The kitchen is nearby. To the rear is a laundry room and walk-in pantry. A casual breakfast nook accesses a front-facing terrace. Two family bedrooms and a shared bath are also on this level. The upper level is devoted to a master suite with private deck and luxurious bath with spa tub. A tucked-away den complements the master suite and holds a wet bar, fireplace and built-ins.

Width 65'-0"
Depth 42'-6"

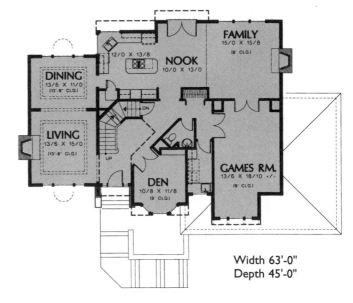

DESIGN 7432

Main Level: 1,793 square feet
Upper Level: 1,330 square feet
Lower Level: 163 square feet
Total: 3,286 square feet

Palladian windows, multiple rooflines and a three-car garage give this home plenty of curb appeal. Inside, an angled staircase leads up to the second floor, while a double-door den offers a bay window for comfort. The living and dining rooms both have tray ceilings, with the living room featuring a fireplace. The efficient kitchen is full of amenities, including a corner sink with a window, a cooktop work island and a walk-in pantry. The spacious family room presents a second fireplace and double doors into a huge games room. Upstairs, three family bedrooms share a full hall bath, while the master suite is lavish with its amenities.

Width 63'-0"
Depth 45'-0"

Design By

© ALAN MASCORD
DESIGN ASSOCIATES, INC.

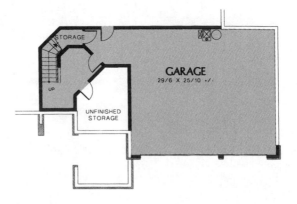

34

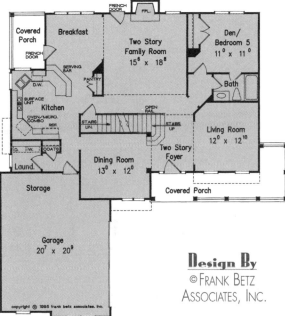

Design By
© FRANK BETZ ASSOCIATES, INC.

copyright © 1995 frank betz associates, inc.

DESIGN P155

First Floor: 1,409 square feet
Second Floor: 1,300 square feet
Total: 2,709 square feet

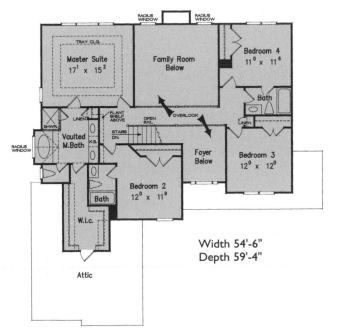

Width 54'-6"
Depth 59'-4"

Country elegance is highly evident in this two-story, five-bedroom home. The two-story foyer is flanked by the formal living and dining rooms. The gourmet kitchen—with a corner sink, a pantry and dining bar shared with the breakfast room—is sure to please. A two-story family room offers a fireplace and access to the rear yard. On the upper level, one family bedroom is graced with its own bath, while the other two bedrooms share a full bath. The deluxe master suite is enhanced by a tray ceiling, a huge walk-in closet, and a vaulted bath complete with a whirlpool tub, separate shower, twin vanities, and a toilet compartment. Please specify basement or crawlspace foundation when ordering.

Design Q263

Square Footage: 1,100
Unfinished Lower Level:
770 square feet

Room on the lower level for future expansion makes this split level as practical as it is appealing. Sharing this level with the two-car garage and laundry room is space for a recreation room, half bath and fourth bedroom. On the main level, living space includes a living room with fireplace and bayed dining room with deck overlook. A door in the kitchen accesses the rear deck. The master bedroom is tucked away in a windowed bay at the opposite end of the home. It shares a bath with two family bedrooms with box-bay windows.

Design By
© Select Home Designs

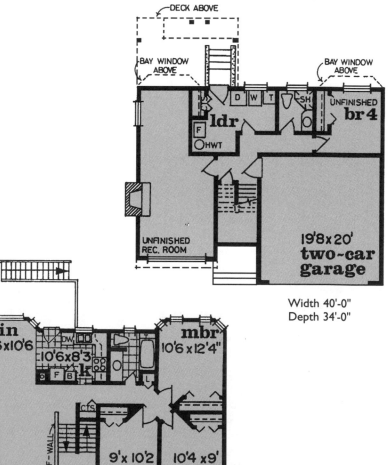

DECK ABOVE

BAY WINDOW ABOVE

BAY WINDOW ABOVE

ldr

UNFINISHED br 4

HWT

UNFINISHED REC. ROOM

19'8x20'
two-car garage

Width 40'-0"
Depth 34'-0"

din
9'6x10'6

10'6x8'3
k

mbr
10'6 x 12'4"

HALF-WALL

9'x 10'2
br3

10'4 x9'
br2

12'6 x 19'6
liv

GARAGE BELOW

DESIGN 7439

First Floor: 1,402 square feet
Second Floor: 848 square feet
Total: 2,250 square feet

Palladian windows and clapboard siding blend to create a modern look on this comfortable home. Inside, formal rooms are open to one another, defined by lovely columns and archways. The kitchen overlooks a bright morning nook with views to the outdoors. A vaulted family room enjoys a fireplace and built-in bookshelves. To the rear of the plan, Bedroom 4 easily converts to a den or guest room, with a nearby bath. Upstairs, the master suite has a vaulted ceiling and a deluxe bath with a garden tub and a walk-in closet. The width of the home is 40 feet with a two-car garage.

Design By
© ALAN MASCORD
DESIGN ASSOCIATES, INC.

Width 50'-0"
(40'-0" with 2-car garage)
Depth 50'-0"

VAULTED
MASTER
15/0 X 13/0 +/-

FAMILY RM.
BELOW

DN.

PLANT
SHELF

LINEN

FOYER
BELOW

BR. 2
10/2 X 11/0 +/-

VAULTED
BR. 3
12/0 X 10/2

DEN/ BR. 4
12/5 X 10/8

BUILT-IN

VAULTED
FAMILY
14/8 X 16/0 +/-

NOOK
11/0 X 9/0
(9' CLG.)

11/0 X 13/0

DN.

UP

DINING
13/0 X 11/0 +/-
(9' CLG.)

GARAGE
19/0 X 22/6

10/0 X 21/2

VAULTED
LIVING
13/0 X 12/10 +/-

DESIGN T112

Square Footage: 1,770
Lower-Level Storage:
526 square feet

Width 49'-6"
Depth 47'-0"

BREAKFAST
10'-10" X 9'-4"

MASTER BATH

FAMILY ROOM
14'-0" X 19'-0"

KITCHEN
10'-10" X 11'-0"

MASTER
BEDROOM
13'-0" X 15'-6"

W.I.C.

DN

DINING ROOM
13'-6" X 10'-6"

FOYER
7'-6" X 18'-0"

BATH

BEDROOM NO.2
12'-0" X 10'-6"

UP

STOOP

BEDROOM NO.1
12'-0" X 10'-0"

Design By
STEPHEN FULLER

This fine family home will delight for years to come. It utilizes the contours of your lot to the best advantage. A recessed front door opens to a columned dining room that shares space with the family room. A bayed breakfast nook enjoys expansive rear views and direct service from the kitchen. Up a short flight of stairs, three bedrooms include two family bedrooms and a master suite. Bedroom 2 gains access to the compartmented hall bath. Bedroom 1 has a raised ceiling. In the master suite, French doors lead to a private deck. An expansive, secluded bath offers dual lavatories, a corner garden tub and a walk-in closet. This home is designed with a basement foundation.

© American Home Gallery, Ltd.

DESIGN 7501

Main Level: 1,744 square feet
Upper Level: 470 square feet
Lower Level: 127 square feet
Total: 2,341 square feet

Two levels of living and a lower-level garage with a shop provide all the space your family will ever want. The exterior is a mixture of materials for a classic look: horizontal wood siding, stone and cedar shingles. The main entry is raised and recessed and opens to a foyer that leads to a den with built-in bookshelves on the right and the formal dining room on the left. The great room is a bit beyond the dining room and is graced by an optional fireplace with built-ins and double doors to the rear deck. The nook adjoins the kitchen— note the walk-in pantry and pass-through counter. A vaulted master bedroom is on the main level and has a grand bath. Two family bedrooms are on the upper level. They share a full bath with linen closet.

BR. 3
11/0 X 10/2

OPEN TO BELOW

OPEN TO BELOW

BR. 2
12/0 X 10/6

Design By
© ALAN MASCORD
DESIGN ASSOCIATES, INC.

NOOK
12/2 X 10/0
(8' CLG.)

VAULTED
MASTER
13/2 X 16/0

SPA

GREAT RM.
19/0 X 19/0
(12'-4' CLG.)

DINING
12/0 X 10/2
(9' CLG.)

DEN
12/0 X 10/2
(9' CLG.)

Width 53'-0"
Depth 38'-0"

SHOP

CRAWLSPACE

GARAGE
22/0 X 20/0

STOR.

STORAGE

Design 7422

First Floor: 1,476 square feet
Second Floor: 886 square feet
Total: 2,362 square feet

Gabled rooflines, arched-topped windows and a three-car garage combine to give this hillside home plenty of curb appeal. The two-story foyer has a cozy den opening directly to the left, with a formal dining room nearby. The angled kitchen offers a corner sink and a snack bar into a sunny nook. A two-story great room features a wall of windows and a corner fireplace. A bedroom, full bath and laundry room inhabit the main level. Upstairs, two family bedrooms share a full bath, while the master bedroom suite is complete with a walk-in closet, sumptuous bath and vaulted ceiling.

Design By
© Alan Mascord
Design Associates, Inc.

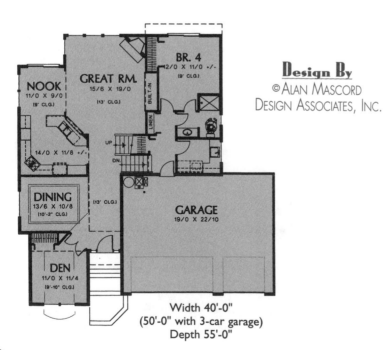

Width 40'-0"
(50'-0" with 3-car garage)
Depth 55'-0"

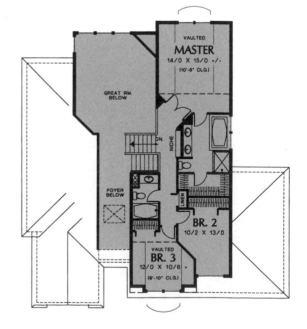

Width 30'-0"
Depth 44'-6"

CRAWLSPACE

GARAGE
19/0 X 23/2

DINING
11/0 X 12/6
(12' CLG.)

LIVING
13/6 X 12/0
(9' CLG.)

BUILT-INS
UP
DN.
REF
PAN
UP
BUILT-INS
BUILT-INS
W   D
DN.

STUDY
12/0 X 10/2+
(9' CLG.)

(VAULTED)
MASTER
13/6 X 12/0

BUILT-INS

DN

OPEN TO BELOW

(VAULTED)
BR. 2
12/0 X 10/2

Design
HPTHH20003

First Floor: 1,005 square feet
Second Floor: 620 square feet
Total: 1,625 square feet

Problem lot? No problem! This design makes a beautiful property out of a site that slopes to the front. Efficient use of space puts the garage on the lower level with living and sleeping areas above. The main level features formal living and dining rooms, plus a quiet study with built-ins. The L-shaped kitchen has an angled sink that overlooks the living/dining area. A handy laundry room and half-bath are just beyond the study. The owners suite and one family bedroom are on the upper level. The owners bedroom is vaulted and has built-ins.

Design by
©ALAN MASCORD DESIGN
ASSOCIATES, INC.

DESIGN 7434

Main Level: 1,883 square feet
Lower Level: 80 square feet
Total: 1,963 square feet

Symmetrical gables offset a columned entry on this traditional home, and a glass-paneled door introduces a stunning interior fit for family living. The casual living area resides to the rear of the plan and features an angled hearth and access to the rear property. The kitchen overlooks the family area and a morning nook, which has a door to a private porch. French doors open to a deluxe master suite with a walk-in closet, a com-partmented toilet, a double-bowl vanity and a garden tub. Three family bedrooms share a full bath as well as linen storage in the hall. The lower floor offers a service entrance from the garage and space for a laundry or utility area.

Design By
© ALAN MASCORD
DESIGN ASSOCIATES, INC.

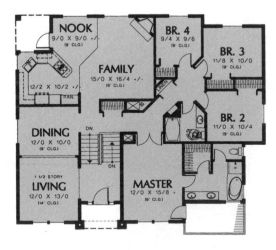

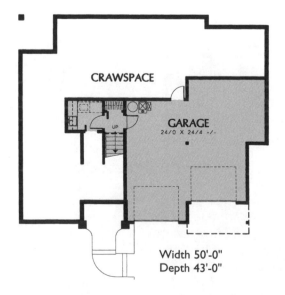

Width 50'-0"
Depth 43'-0"

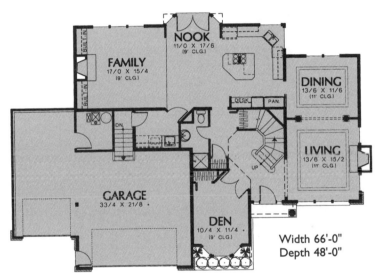

NOOK
11/0 X 17/6
(9' CLG.)

FAMILY
17/0 X 15/4
(9' CLG.)

DINING
13/6 X 11/6
(11' CLG.)

DESK   PAN.

LIVING
13/8 X 15/2
(11' CLG.)

DN.

UP

GARAGE
33/4 X 21/8

DEN
10/4 X 11/4
(9' CLG.)

Width 66'-0"
Depth 48'-0"

DESIGN 7548

First Floor: 1,572 square feet
Second Floor: 1,341 square feet
Total: 2,913 square feet

Design By
© ALAN MASCORD
DESIGN ASSOCIATES, INC.

Brick and horizontal siding work together to adorn the exterior of this fine traditional design. Combine this design with a sloping lot and you've got a home to last. The first floor sits a few steps up from the three-car garage and features formal living areas as well as casual spaces. Both the living room and dining room have tray ceilings. The den is isolated and graced by a bay window. The family room sits to the rear, near a breakfast nook and island kitchen, and has a fireplace flanked by built-ins. Bedrooms are on the second floor—three family bedrooms and a grand master suite. Note all the amenities of the master bath: a spa tub, separate shower, double sinks and a huge walk-in closet.

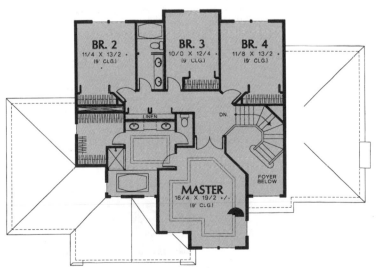

BR. 2
11/4 X 13/2
(9' CLG.)

BR. 3
10/0 X 12/4
(9' CLG.)

BR. 4
11/8 X 13/2
(9' CLG.)

LINEN

DN.

MASTER
16/4 X 19/2 +/-
(9' CLG.)

FOYER
BELOW

Design Q238

Square Footage: 1,276
Unfinished Lower Level:
967 square feet

If you'd like to start small and expand later as your family grows, this plan offers that option. The basement is unfinished but can be developed into a family room, bedroom and full bath in addition to the laundry room and two-car garage at this level. A large living/dining area is found on the main level. It is graced by a fireplace, buffet space and sliding glass doors to the rear deck. The L-shaped kitchen is efficiently designed and holds space for a breakfast table. Three bedrooms and two full baths include a master suite with walk-in closet.

Design By
© Select Home Designs

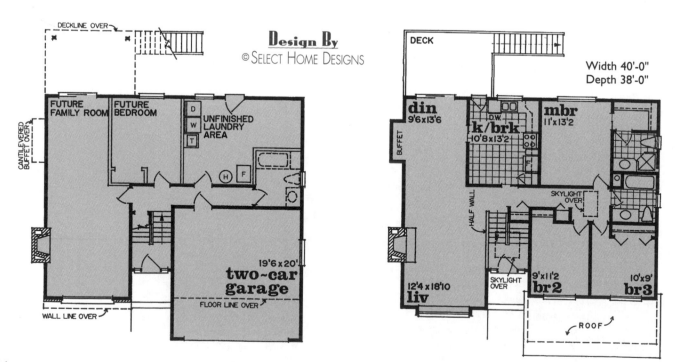

Width 40'-0"
Depth 38'-0"

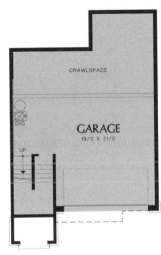

CRAWLSPACE

GARAGE
19/0 X 21/0

UP

PATIO

DINING
12/0 X 11/0
(9' CLG.)

(VAULTED)
LIVING
14/6 X 13/9

MEDIA

REF.

PAN.

UP

DN. UP

BUILT-IN

STUDY
12/0 X 11/6
(9' CLG.)

D. W.

DN.

Width 28'-0"
Depth 44'-0"

(VAULTED)
MASTER
13/6 X 12/0

OPEN TO
BELOW

LIN.

DN.

(VAULTED)
BR. 2
10/0 X 12/6

SH.

Design
HPTHH20004

First Floor: 993 square feet
Second Floor: 642 square feet
Total: 1,635 square feet

For the smaller family, this design, which slopes to the front, is accommodating without being overwrought. The garage is found on the lower level. The main level holds living and dining areas. Note the corner fireplace in the living room and the built-ins in the study. A patio opens off the living room for outdoor enjoyment. Two bedrooms inhabit the upper level: an owners suite and a family or guest bedroom. Each has its own bath and a vaulted ceiling. The owners bedroom has a giant walk-in closet in addition to a wall closet.

Design by
©ALAN MASCORD DESIGN
ASSOCIATES, INC.

Design P237

First Floor: 1,351 square feet

Second Floor: 1,257 square feet

Total: 2,608 square feet

Design By
© Frank Betz
Associates, Inc.

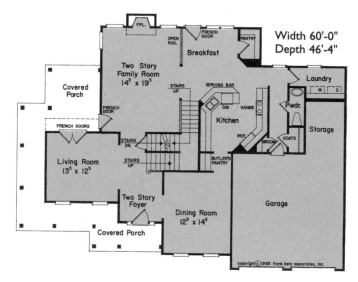

Width 60'-0"
Depth 46'-4"

Here's a new country home with a fresh face and a dash of Victoriana. Inside, the foyer leads to an elegant dining room and a spacious living room with French doors to the covered rear porch. The heart of the home is a two-story family room with a focal-point fireplace and its own French door to the rear property. A breakfast room offers a walk-in pantry and shares a snack bar with the kitchen, which leads to the formal dining room through a butler's pantry. The second-floor master suite features an impressive private bath with a vaulted ceiling and an optional sitting room. Please specify basement or crawlspace foundation when ordering.

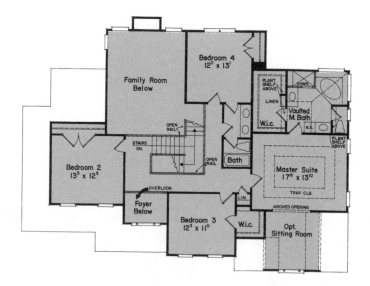

DESIGN T038

Square Footage: 1,800
Unfinished Lower Level:
981 square feet

This European-inspired cottage contains one of the most efficient floor plans available. From the formal dining room at the front of the plan to the commodious great room at the rear, it accommodates various lifestyles in less than 2,000 square feet. An opulent master suite with deck access and grand bath dominates the right wing of the house. Two family bedrooms and a full bath are found to the left. There's even a powder room for guests. The gourmet-style kitchen has an attached breakfast area with glassed bay for sunny brunches. Bonus space in the basement allows for future development. This home is designed with a walkout basement foundation.

Design By
STEPHEN FULLER

Width 54'-0"
Depth 52'-0"

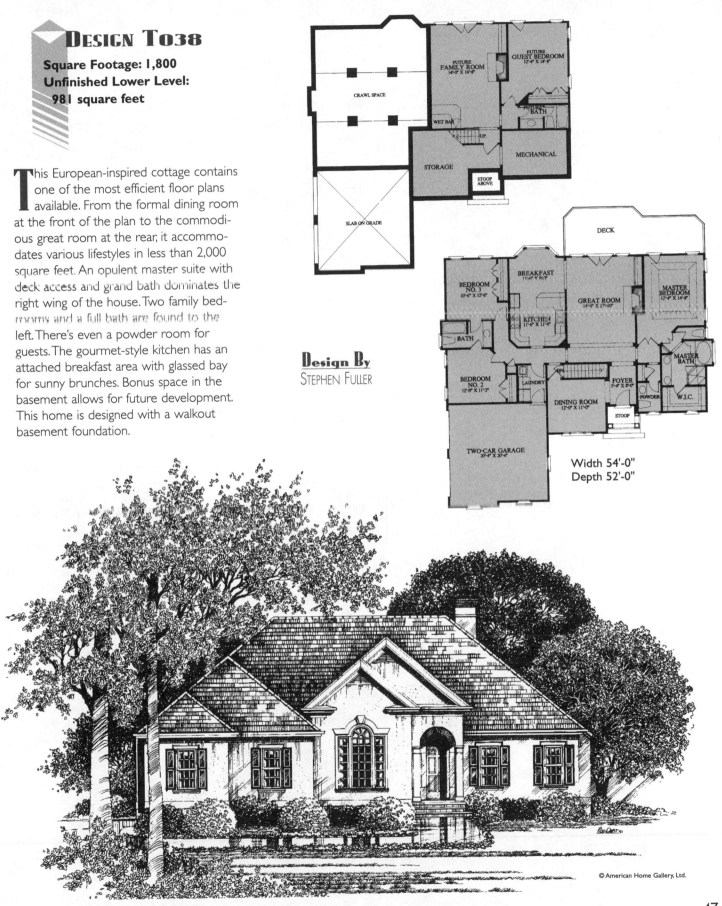

Design T021

First Floor: 2,070 square feet
Second Floor: 790 square feet
Total: 2,860 square feet
Unfinished Lower Level:
914 square feet

The striking combination of wood frame, shingles and glass creates the exterior of this classic cottage. The foyer opens to the main-level layout. To the left of the foyer is a study with a warming hearth and a vaulted ceiling. To the right is the formal dining room. A great room with an attached breakfast area is near the kitchen. A guest room is nestled in the rear of the plan for privacy. The master suite provides an expansive tray ceiling, a glass sitting area and easy passage to the outside deck. Upstairs, two bedrooms are accompanied by a sunken loft for a quiet getaway. This home is designed with a basement foundation.

Design By
Stephen Fuller

Rear View

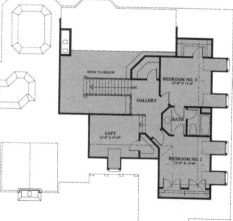

Width 58'-4"
Depth 54'-10"

Quote One®

Cost to build? See page 214
to order complete cost estimate
to build this house in your area!

DESIGN T191

First Floor: 2,502 square feet
Second Floor: 677 square feet
Total: 3,179 square feet
Unfinished Lower Level: 1,564 square feet
Bonus Room: 171 square feet

Rear View

Stone and stucco bring a chateau welcome to this Mediterranean-style home. The interior plan combines traditional formality with a relaxed contemporary spirit, with well-defined rooms and amenity-filled flowing spaces. A sensational sun room lights up the rear of the plan. Note the abundance of windows all across the rear of the home. A coffered ceiling and columned archways decorate the liv-ing area, which opens to the formal dining room. The first-floor sleeping wing offers a bayed master suite with rear deck access, a family or guest bedroom with private bath and a study that opens back into the foyer. Upstairs, two secondary bedrooms and a full bath enjoy privacy and easy kitchen access down a side stairway. There is plenty of future expansion in the walk-out basement foundation.

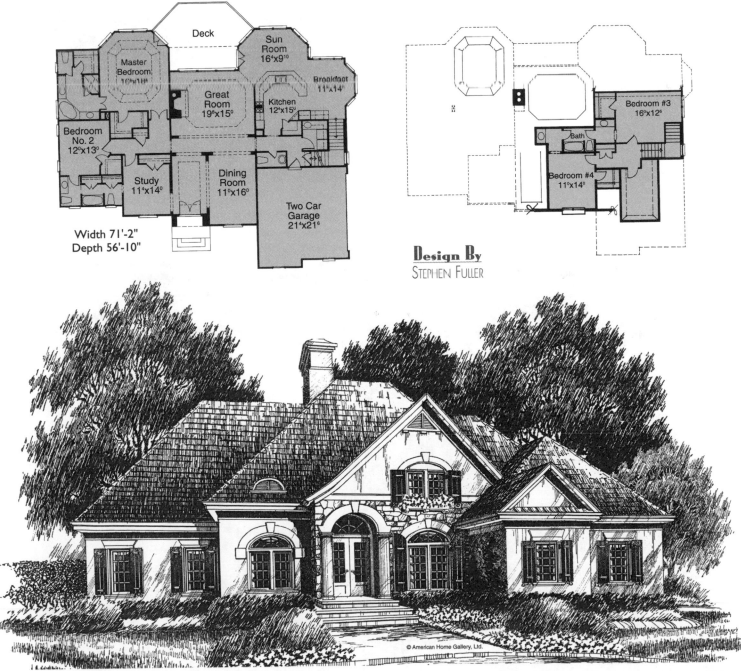

Deck

Sun Room 16⁴x9¹⁰

Master Bedroom 16⁰x18⁰

Great Room 19⁸x15⁰

Kitchen 12⁰x15⁰

Breakfast 11⁶x14⁰

Bedroom No. 2 12⁰x13⁰

Study 11⁴x14⁰

Dining Room 11⁰x16⁰

Two Car Garage 21⁴x21⁶

Width 71'-2"
Depth 56'-10"

Bedroom #3 16⁰x12⁶

Bath

Bedroom #4 11⁰x14⁰

Design By
Stephen Fuller

© American Home Gallery, Ltd.

DESIGN 7784

Main Level: 2,065 square feet
Lower Level: 1,216 square feet
Total: 3,281 square feet

For lots with rear views and a slope to the back, this traditional design has it all. The main level features a central great room with fireplace and rear-deck access, and is adjoined by a breakfast nook and convenient kitchen. More formal meals can occur in the front-facing dining room with tray ceiling. The master suite is on this level and holds a bath with His and Hers walk-in closets, separate tub and shower and double sinks. An additional bedroom may also become a study. The lower level has a huge media room with fireplace, wet bar and patio access. Two family bedrooms with baths flank the media room. The two-car garage has additional storage space.

Design By
DONALD A. GARDNER
ARCHITECTS, INC.

Width 82'-2"
Depth 43'-6"

PATIO

BED RM.
13-0 X 12-0

fireplace

MEDIA /
REC. RM.
22-6 X 16-0

shelves

BED RM.
13-0 X 12-0

bath

walk-in closet

wet bar

bath

walk-in closet

up

MECH RM.
14-0 X 6-4

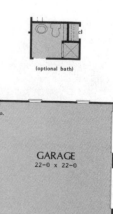

DECK

(optional bath)

MASTER
BED RM.
13-0 x 18-0

fireplace

GREAT RM.
24-6 x 16-0

(cathedral ceiling)

shelves

BRKFST.
13-0 x 10-0

KIT.
13-0 x 13-0

sto.

walk-in closet

walk-in closet

lin.
pd.
rm.

cl

down

pan.

GARAGE
22-0 x 22-0

FOYER
13-4 x 6-8

master bath

cl

BED RM./
STUDY
12-0 x 12-0

PORCH

DINING
12-0 x 14-0

d w

cl

storage

©1997 Donald A. Gardner Architects, Inc.

Rear View

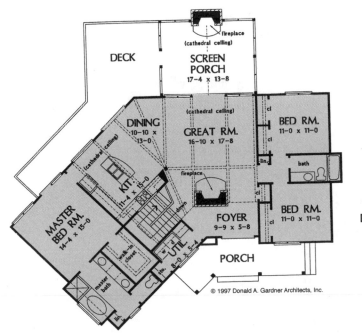

© 1997 Donald A. Gardner Architects, Inc.

DECK

SCREEN PORCH
17-4 x 13-8

fireplace
(cathedral ceiling)

DINING
10-10 x 13-0

(cathedral ceiling)

GREAT RM.
16-10 x 17-8

BED RM.
11-0 x 11-0

bath

KIT.
11-4 x 15-0

fireplace

BED RM.
11-0 x 11-0

MASTER BED RM.
14-4 x 15-0

walk-in closet

FOYER
9-9 x 5-8

UTIL.

master bath

PORCH

Width 62'-8"
Depth 59'-10"

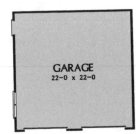

GARAGE
22-0 x 22-0

DESIGN 7632

Main Level: 1,680 square feet
Lower Level: 1,653 square feet
Total: 3,333 square feet

This rustic retreat is updated with contemporary angles and packs a lot of living into a small space. Indoor/outdoor relationships are well developed and help to create a comfortable home. Start off with the covered front porch, which leads to a welcoming foyer. The beam-ceilinged great room opens directly ahead and features a fireplace, a wall of windows, access to the screened porch (with its own fireplace!) and is adjacent to the angled dining area. A highly efficient island kitchen is sure to please with a cathedral ceiling, access to the rear deck and tons of counter and cabinet space. Two family bedrooms, sharing a full bath, are located on one end of the plan while the master suite is secluded for complete privacy at the other end. The master suite includes a walk-in closet and a pampering bath.

Design By
DONALD A. GARDNER
ARCHITECTS, INC.

Featuring great one-level livability, this design offers something additional—a walkout lower level to finish as you choose. The family room is at the heart of the home and offers a fireplace and corner built-ins. It opens through double doors to a breakfast room and adjoining sun room and then on to the U-shaped kitchen. A formal dining room connects to both the kitchen and the entry foyer for convenience. A wide side deck can be reached through a double door in the breakfast room or from a single door in the master bedroom. A craft room is just beyond the laundry at the service entrance. Note the tray ceiling in the master bedroom and the huge walk-in closet in its grand bath. Two family bedrooms are on the right side of the plan and share a full bath. One of these bedrooms would make a fine office. This home is designed with a basement foundation.

Design T243

Square Footage: 2,752
Unfinished Lower Level: 1,380 square feet

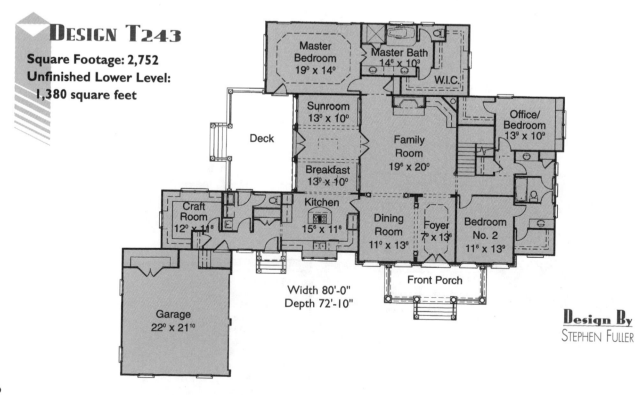

Width 80'-0"
Depth 72'-10"

Design By
STEPHEN FULLER

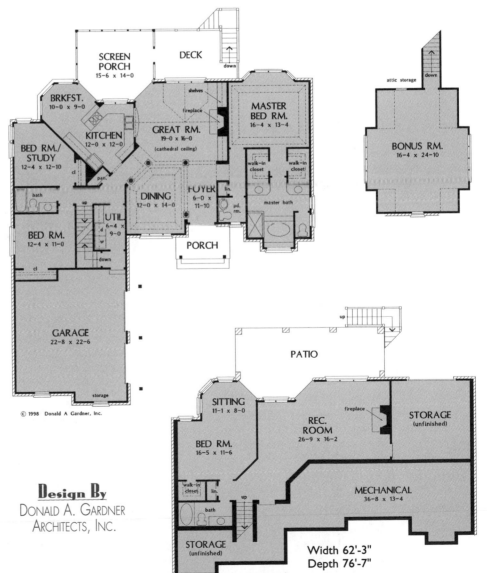

©1998 Donald A. Gardner, Inc.

Design 7797

Main Level: 2,094 square feet
Lower Level: 1,038 square feet
Total: 3,132 square feet
Bonus Room: 494 square feet

Looking and living like a custom home, this design has space on the basement level that adds to its appeal. The main level opens with an entry foyer with columns that separate it from the formal dining room and the great room. The great room has a fireplace, built-ins and access to a rear deck and screened porch. A kitchen nearby has an attached breakfast bay. The formal dining room is graced by a tray ceiling. Family bedrooms are on the left side of the plan and share a full bath. The master suite dominates the right side of the plan. Note the bay window in the bedroom and the double walk-in closets. The master bath features a spa tub and separate shower. An additional bedroom is found on the lower level, along with a recreation room and storage. Bonus space over the garage can be developed later. This home may also be built with a crawlspace foundation.

Design By
DONALD A. GARDNER
ARCHITECTS, INC.

SCREEN PORCH 15-6 x 14-0
DECK
BRKFST. 10-0 x 9-0
KITCHEN 12-0 x 12-0
GREAT RM. 19-0 x 16-0 (cathedral ceiling)
MASTER BED RM. 16-4 x 13-4
BED RM./STUDY 12-4 x 12-10
walk-in closet
walk-in closet
bath
DINING 12-0 x 14-0
FOYER 6-0 x 11-10
lin.
master bath
pd. rm.
BED RM. 12-4 x 11-0
UTIL. 6-4 x 9-0
up
down
PORCH
GARAGE 22-8 x 22-6
storage

© 1998 Donald A Gardner, Inc.

attic storage
down
BONUS RM. 16-4 x 24-10

up
PATIO
SITTING 11-1 x 8-0
REC. ROOM 26-9 x 16-2
fireplace
STORAGE (unfinished)
BED RM. 16-5 x 11-6
MECHANICAL 36-8 x 13-4
walk-in closet
lin.
up
bath
STORAGE (unfinished)

Width 62'-3"
Depth 76'-7"

53

© 1998 Donald A. Gardner, Inc.

DESIGN 7747

Main Level: 1,810 square feet
Lower Level: 1,146 square feet
Total: 2,956 square feet

Looking like a one-story plan, this home actually has a walk-out basement that adds dramatically to its floor space. The main level contains all you might ask for in a design: living room with fireplace and cathedral ceiling, dining room with porch access, U-shaped island kitchen, breakfast nook and two bedrooms with full baths. The master suite is of particular note, with a private porch, walk-in closet and bath with spa tub. The lower level adds a family room with fireplace and patio, and two family bedrooms with private patios. A huge storage area on the lower level is accessed from the outside. Note the walk-in closet in one of the lower-level bedrooms and the storage space in the garage. This home may be built with a crawlspace foundation.

Design By
DONALD A. GARDNER
ARCHITECTS, INC.

Width 68'-4"
Depth 60'-10"

DECK

KIT.
11-10 x 14-0

BRKFST.
10-0 x 14-0

fireplace

LIVING RM.
16-4 x 20-0

(cathedral ceiling)

MASTER
BED RM.
17-0 x 14-0

down

railing

BED RM.
12-0 x 13-0

UTIL.
7-4 x
9-0

DINING
13-0 x 14-4

FOYER
6-8 x
13-2

linen

master
bath

bath

walk-in
closet

bath

storage

BED RM./
STUDY
13-0 x 13-0

PORCH

© 1998 Donald A Gardner, Inc.

GARAGE
22-0 x 22-8

storage

Width 70'-10"
Depth 69'-10"

COVERED
PATIO

bath

fireplace

BED RM.
13-8 x 14-0

FAMILY RM.
16-4 x 20-0

BED RM.
14-8 x 12-4

pd.
rm.

storage

up

lin.

bath

© 1998 Donald A Gardner, Inc.

STORAGE
(unfinished)

DESIGN 7693

Main Level: 2,297 square feet
Lower Level: 1,212 square feet
Total: 3,509 square feet

A variety of exterior materials and interesting windows combine with an unusual floor plan to make this an exceptional home. It is designed for a sloping lot, with full living quarters on the main level, but with two extra bedrooms and a family room added to the basement level. A covered porch showcases a wonderful dining-room window and an attractive front door. The living room, enhanced by a fireplace, adjoins the dining room for easy entertaining. The island kitchen and a bayed breakfast room are to the left. Three bedrooms on this level include one that is well placed to serve as a study. There is also a master suite with dual vanities, a garden tub and a walk-in closet. A deck on this floor covers a patio off the lower-level family room, which has its own fireplace.

Design By
DONALD A. GARDNER
ARCHITECTS, INC.

B. NATHAN

© 1998 Donald A. Gardner, Inc.

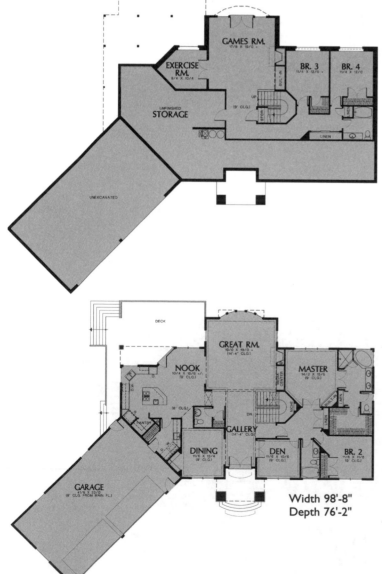

DESIGN 7550

Main Level: 2,437 square feet
Lower Level: 1,297 square feet
Total: 3,734 square feet

Design By
© ALAN MASCORD
DESIGN ASSOCIATES, INC.

Width 98'-8"
Depth 76'-2"

Complete on two levels, this home with walk-out basement is a fine example of hillside living. The main level allows for a great room with fireplace and curved bay-window wall, a formal dining room and a private den. A gallery leads to all three areas and holds the staircase to the lower level. The kitchen and breakfast nook sit just to the left of the great room and have access to a rear deck. Two bedrooms are on the right side of the main level: a family bedroom with full bath and the master suite with walk-in closet and elegant bath. The lower level is a complement to the main level. It features a games room with fireplace, exercise room and two additional bedrooms sharing a full bath. This home may also be built with a slab foundation.

Width 80'-0"
Depth 61'-0"

DESIGN 7551

Main Level: 2,157 square feet
Lower Level: 1,754 square feet
Total: 3,911 square feet

Design By
© ALAN MASCORD
DESIGN ASSOCIATES, INC.

Choose this gracious design for a hillside lot, and you'll always have the livability you're looking for. The main level is complete unto itself with an oversized great room with fireplace, a formal dining room and an island kitchen with nook. A wide deck wraps around the great room and the nook for outdoor access. The master suite is on this level and features a delightful bath. One additional bedroom could be used as a den. The lower level has a media room and a games room for the best in casual living. Two additional bedrooms on this level share a full bath. A wide patio stretches across the back of the lower level. This home may also be built with a slab foundation.

Design 3311

Main Level: 2,662 square feet
Lower Level: 1,548 square feet
Total: 4,210 square feet

L D

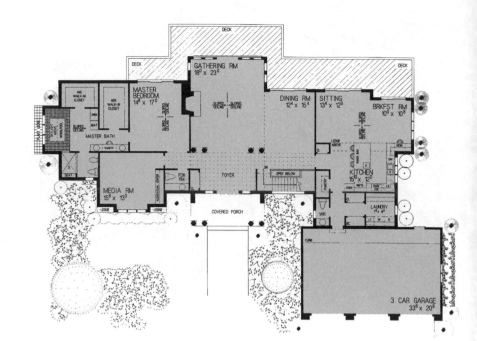

QUOTE ONE®

Cost to build? See page 214
to order complete cost estimate
to build this house in your area!

Width 98'-0"
Depth 64'-8"

Here's a hillside haven for family living with plenty of room to entertain in style. Enter the main level from a dramatic columned portico that leads to a large entry hall. The gathering room, graced by a fireplace and sliding glass doors to the rear deck, is straight back and adjoins a formal dining area. A true gourmet kitchen with plenty of room for casual eating and conversation is nearby. The abundantly appointed master suite on this level is complemented by a luxurious bath complete with His and Hers walk-in closets, a whirlpool tub in a bumped-out bay and a separate shower. Note the media room to the front of the house. On the lower level are two more bedrooms—each with access to the rear terrace, a full bath, a large activity area with fireplace and a convenient summer kitchen.

Design By
© HOME PLANNERS

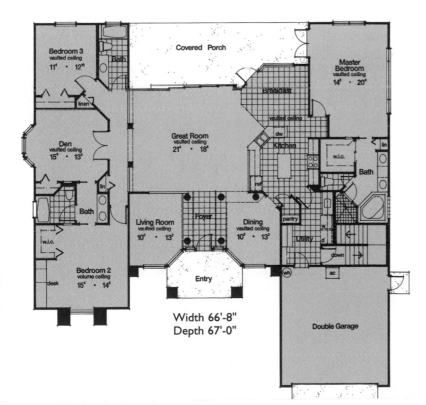

Width 66'-8"
Depth 67'-0"

DESIGN 8793

Square Footage: 2,742
Unfinished Lower Level:
2,667 square feet

Design By
© HOME DESIGN SERVICES, INC.

A walkout basement adds to the total living space of this one-of-a-kind hillside home. The entry is flanked by the formal living and dining rooms and then opens into a massive great room with a covered porch beyond. The kitchen and breakfast nook are open to the great room; the kitchen features an island work center. Two family bedrooms and a den are on the left side of the plan. Bedroom 3 has a private bath. The den is a focal point, seen through arches and double doors from the great room. The master suite is on the right side and has a walk-in closet, porch access and sumptuous bath. Space on the lower level can be developed later to accommodate additional bedrooms or a family room.

COPYRIGHT LARRY E. BELK

DESIGN 8153

Main Level: 2,773 square feet
Lower Level: 1,214 square feet
Total: 3,987 square feet

An understated stucco facade creates an elegant picture from the curb of this sloping-lot home. The grand foyer features a barrel-vaulted ceiling, which ties into the arched opening leading to the enormous great room and its fourteen-foot ceiling. Created for outdoor living, the ground floor provides views for the master suite, the great room, the kitchen and breakfast room. All of these areas provide access to the large deck that wraps the rear of the home. Downstairs, the basement includes two roomy bedrooms with private baths. The game room is a perfect location for a big-screen TV. Nine-foot ceilings in the basement give the rooms an open, spacious feeling. This home may also be built with a slab foundation.

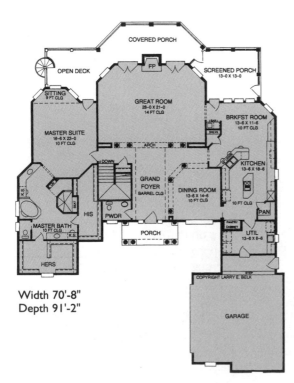

Width 70'-8"
Depth 91'-2"

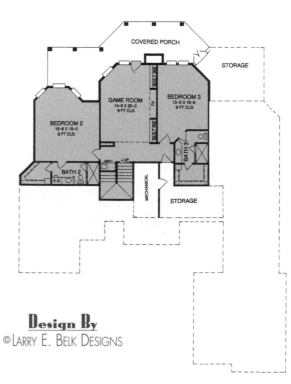

Design By
©Larry E. Belk Designs

Width 66'-0"
Depth 66'-0"

DESIGN 2846

Main Level: 2,341 square feet
Lower Level: 1,380 square feet
Total: 3,721 square feet

The street view of this contemporary Spanish-style home shows a beautifully designed one-story home, but now take a look at the rear elevation. This home has been designed to be built into a hill, so the lower level is open to the sun. With an abundance of casual living space on the lower level, including a games room, full bath, a lounge with a fireplace and even a summer kitchen with a full-sized snack bar; the formal living space can be reserved for the main floor. From the foyer, the formal living room and dining room take center stage. The large kitchen has an angled snack bar that is open to the family room. The master suite has a covered porch and split-vanity bath. Two family bedrooms share a full hall bath.

Design By
© HOME PLANNERS

Rear View

© 1998 Donald A. Gardner, Inc.

DESIGN 7665

Main Level: 1,472 square feet
Lower Level: 1,211 square feet
Total: 2,683 square feet

This charming European country home offers both traditional and casual space, and its comfortable heart is the great room, which has a fireplace and access to the rear porch. The U-shaped kitchen serves a formal dining room with a tray ceiling as well as a breakfast room, which leads outdoors. Two walk-in closets frame a dressing area in the master suite, which also has a garden tub. On the lower level, a media/recreation room shares a hall with two additional bedrooms and a full bath.

PORCH

DINING
12-0 x 12-2

MASTER BED RM.
15-0 x 13-4
(cathedral ceiling)

GREAT RM.
20-0 x 16-4
(cathedral ceiling)

fireplace

KITCHEN
17-4 x 11-4

walk-in closet

walk-in closet

railing

down

FOYER
6-8 x
7-4

pan.

pd. rm.

BRKFST.
11-2 x 9-2

lin.

master bath

PORCH

PORCH

covered walkway

© 1998 Donald A Gardner, Inc.

GARAGE
23-0 x 23-0

PATIO

COVERED PATIO

lin.

bath

BED RM.
11-6 x 13-0

walk-in closet

walk-in closet

BED RM.
12-0 x 13-0

MEDIA/ REC. RM.
16-6 x 31-10

STORAGE
(unfinished)

UTIL.
8-10 x
6-10

d w

up

Width 54'-0"
Depth 40'-8"

Design By
DONALD A. GARDNER
ARCHITECTS, INC.

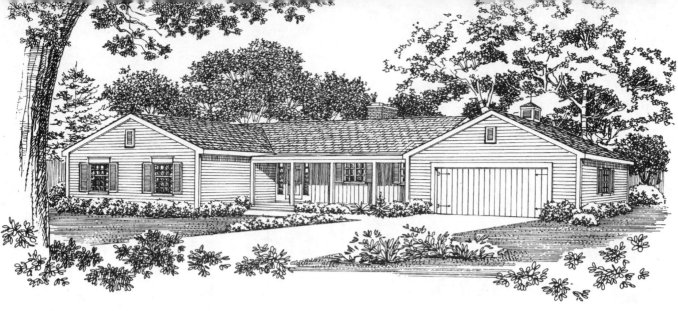

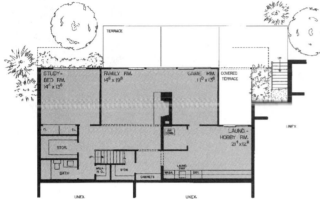

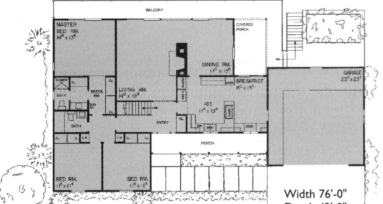

Width 76'-0"
Depth 42'-0"

DESIGN 1974

Main Level: 1,680 square feet
Lower Level: 1,344 square feet
Total: 3,024 square feet

You would never guess from looking at the front of this traditional design that it possessed such a strikingly different rear. From the front, it looks as though all the livability is on one floor. If you choose, you can build the home without finishing the lower level immediately, then adding it as your need for space increases. The main level includes grand livability on its own: a living and dining room, kitchen with breakfast room and three bedrooms with two full baths. The finished lower level would add a family room, a game room, a laundry and hobby room, a bedroom or study and another full bath.

Design By
© HOME PLANNERS

Rear View

Design HPTHH20005

Main Level: 1,230 square feet
Lower Level: 769 square feet
Total: 1,999 square feet

A quaint home with classic details, this design offers living on two levels: one at the main level and one on the lower level. A vaulted living and dining area dominates the main level and offers a fireplace and access to a rear deck. Just off the entry is a cozy den for quieter times. The kitchen lies between these two areas. The owners suite is also vaulted and contains a bath with spa tub, separate shower and double sinks. The lower level is devoted to a recreation room, two bedrooms and a full bath.

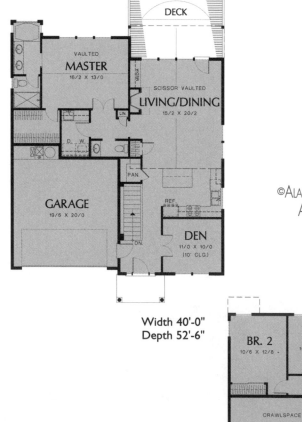

DECK

VAULTED
MASTER
16/2 X 13/0

SCISSOR VAULTED
LIVING/DINING
15/2 X 20/2

GARAGE
19/6 X 20/0

PAN.

DEN
11/0 X 10/0
(10' CLG.)

REF.

DN.

Width 40'-0"
Depth 52'-6"

Design by
©ALAN MASCORD DESIGN
ASSOCIATES, INC.

BR. 2
10/6 X 12/8

BR. 3
10/8 X 11/0

REC. RM.
14/10 X 12/8

CRAWLSPACE

UP

STORAGE

64

Design 9543

Main Level: 2,188 square feet
Lower Level: 1,049 square feet
Total: 3,237 square feet

Carriage lamps and brick columns provide a dramatic element to the impressive entry on this hillside traditional home. This well-designed floor plan flows very well. The den is ideally located for use as an office if the need arises. To the left rests the formal living and dining rooms, which provide nearby access to the step-saving kitchen. The family room is separated from the kitchen only by the breakfast nook, which provides access to the rear deck. The master suite, with its tray ceiling and luxurious master bath, completes the first floor. The basement contains a recreation room, two secondary bedrooms (one with access to the rear grounds) and a full bath.

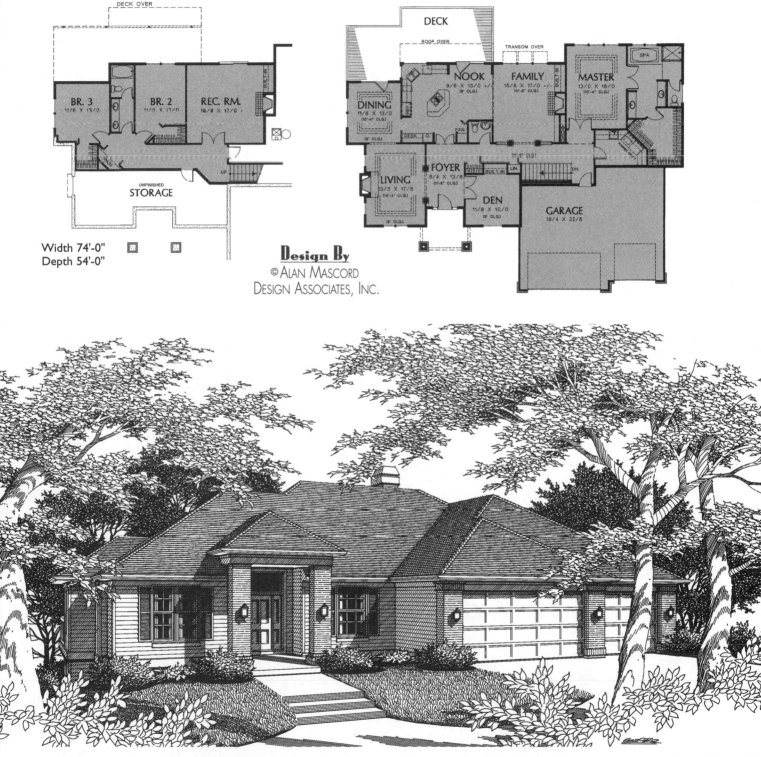

Width 74'-0"
Depth 54'-0"

Design By
© Alan Mascord
Design Associates, Inc.

Design Q518

First Floor: 792 square feet
Second Floor: 573 square feet
Total: 1,365 square feet

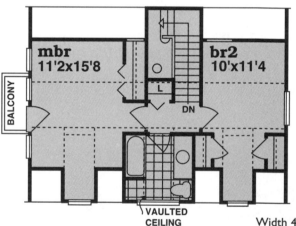

mbr
11'2x15'8

br2
10'x11'4

BALCONY

DN

L

VAULTED
CEILING

Width 42'-0"
Depth 32'-0"

This distinctive vacation home is designed ideally for a gently sloping lot, which allows for a daylight basement. It can, however, accommodate a flat lot nicely. An expansive veranda sweeps around two sides of the exterior and is complemented by full-height windows. Decorative woodwork and traditional multi-pane windows belie the contemporary interior. An open living/dining room area, with wood stove and two bay windows, is complemented by a galley-style kitchen. A bedroom, or den, on the first floor has the use of a full bath. The second floor holds a master bedroom with balcony and one family bedroom. Both bedrooms have dormer windows and they share a full bath with vaulted ceiling. Choose a basement or a crawlspace foundation—plans include details for both.

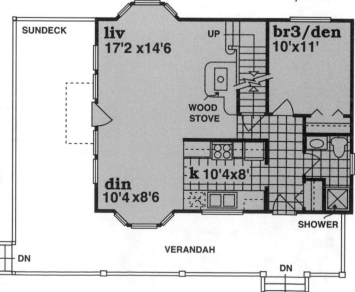

SUNDECK

liv
17'2 x14'6

UP

br3/den
10'x11'

WOOD
STOVE

din
10'4 x8'6

k 10'4x8'

SHOWER

DN

VERANDAH

DN

Side View

Rear View

DESIGN Q223

Square Footage: 1,530
Unfinished Basement: 1,440 square feet

Rustic in nature, this hillside home offers a surrounding deck and upper level balcony on the exterior to complement its horizontal siding and stone detailing. The entry opens to a staircase leading up to the main level or down to finish-later space in the basement. The kitchen is at the heart of the home and has miles of counter space and a pass-through bar to the dining room. Both the living and dining rooms have sliding glass doors to the deck. A corner fireplace warms and lights both areas. One large bedroom sits to the right of the plan and has a private bath and deck access. Two additional bedrooms with a shared bath sit to the left of the plan. One of these bedrooms has deck access. Unfinished lower-level space adds 1,440 square feet to the total for future development.

Design By
© SELECT HOME DESIGNS

DECK   DECK

DINING   —28'-6"(8.7m)—   LIVING
—27'-7"—

12'

BEDROOM
11' X 11'-3"

KITCHEN

MASTER
BEDROOM
13'-3" X 11'

BEDROOM
11' X 9'-1"

BALCONY

GARAGE

Width 77'-7"
Depth 61'-0"

© American Home Gallery, Ltd.

DESIGN T105

First Floor: 2,565 square feet
Second Floor: 1,375 square feet
Total: 3,940 square feet
Unfinished Lower Level: 1,912 square feet

A symmetrical facade with twin chimneys makes a grand statement. A covered porch welcomes visitors and provides a pleasant place to spend a mild evening. The entry foyer is flanked by formal living areas: a dining room and a living room, each with a fireplace. A third fireplace is the highlight of the expansive great room to the rear. An L-shaped kitchen offers a work island and a walk-in pantry as amenities and easily serves the nearby breakfast and sun rooms. The deck is accessible through the great room, the sun room or the master bedroom. The first-floor master bedroom suite is lavish in its luxuries: His and Hers walk-in closets, a sunny bay window and a sumptuous bath. The second floor offers three bedrooms, two full baths and plenty of storage space. This home is designed with a walkout basement foundation.

Design By
STEPHEN FULLER

Rear View

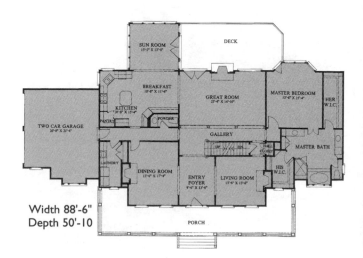

Width 88'-6"
Depth 50'-10

© American Home Gallery, Ltd.

Width 61'-0"
Depth 70'-6"

MASTER
BATH

MASTER BEDRDOOM
16'-4" X 13'-6"

PORCH

BREAKFAST
13'-4" X 9'-0"

BEDROOM/
OFFICE
10'-4" X 11'-0"

GREAT ROOM
17'-0" X 17'-8"

BEDROOM NO. 2
10'-4" X 12'-0"

KITCHEN
13'-4" X 10'-6"

BATH

LAUNDRY

DN

BATH

TWO CAR GARAGE
20'-6" X 19'-6"

DINING ROOM
11'-4" X 12'-10"

FOYER
5'-4" X
12'-10"

BEDROOM/
STUDY
11'-2" X 12'-0"

PORCH

Design By
STEPHEN FULLER

Design T052

Square Footage: 2,090
Unfinished Lower Level:
1,384 square feet

This traditional home features board-and-batten and cedar shingle in an attractively proportioned exterior. Finishing touches include a covered entrance and porch with column detailing and an arched transom, flower boxes and shuttered windows. The foyer opens to both the dining room and the great room beyond with French doors opening onto the porch. Through the double doors to the right of the foyer is the combination bedroom/study. A short hallway leads to a full bath and a secondary bedroom with ample closet space. The master bedroom is spacious, with walk-in closets on both sides of the entrance to the master bath. With separate vanities, a shower and toilet, the master bath forms a private retreat at the rear of the home. Convenient to both the great room and dining room, the kitchen opens to an attractive breakfast area featuring a bay window. An additional room is remotely located off the kitchen, providing a retreat for today's at-home office or guest. This home is designed with a walkout basement foundation.

DESIGN T179

Design By
STEPHEN FULLER

First Floor: 2,496 square feet
Second Floor: 1,373 square feet
Total: 3,869 square feet
Unfinished Lower Level: 1,620 square feet

Classical symmetry prevails inside in same-size living and dining rooms that open off either side of the entrance foyer. The less formal living spaces beyond flow easily into one another from a central stair hall. Dormers bathe interior spaces in natural light. A dramatic vaulted great room with three dormers, a window-wrapped breakfast area and a master suite in the right wing all open onto a private rear porch. Five dormers on the front elevation distinguish a second story that includes three bedrooms, two baths and an optional linen closet or cozy seating area. This home is designed with a walkout basement.

Breakfast Room 15³x11⁰

Deck

Two Car Garage 22⁰x22³

Kitchen 15³x13⁰

Family Room 23³x17⁰

Master Bedroom 15³x18⁰

Master Bath

W.I.C.

Dining Room 15⁶x13³

Living Room 15⁶x13³

Width 78'-0"
Depth 53'-3"

Future Recreation Room 15⁶x24⁶

Future Family Room 23³x17⁰

Future Bedroom 15⁶x20⁶

Storage

Storage

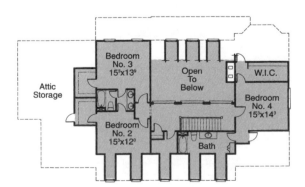

Bedroom No. 3 15³x13⁰

Open To Below

W.I.C.

Attic Storage

Bedroom No. 4 15³x14³

Bedroom No. 2 15³x12⁰

Bath

© American Home Gallery, Ltd.

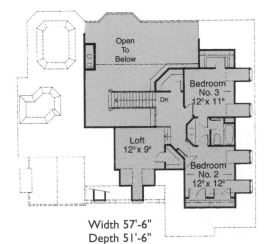

Width 57'-6"
Depth 51'-6"

Open To Below

Bedroom No. 3
12⁰ x 11⁶

Loft
12⁰ x 9⁹

Dn

Bedroom No. 2
12⁰ x 12⁰

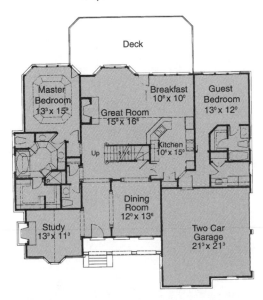

Deck

Master Bedroom
13³ x 15⁰

Breakfast
10⁶ x 10⁰

Guest Bedroom
13⁰ x 12⁰

Great Room
15⁹ x 16⁸

Kitchen
10⁶ x 15⁰

Up

Study
13³ x 11³

Dining Room
12⁰ x 13⁶

Two Car Garage
21³ x 21³

DESIGN T201

First Floor: 2,076 square feet
Second Floor: 843 square feet
Total: 2,919 square feet
Unfinished Lower Level: 984 square feet

Elegant arches and columns and a classic brick exterior resonate with a simple, natural theme. The pride of a place of one's own begins with an inviting entry—a sunburst fanlight and a box-paneled front door create a warm welcome. The foyer opens to a formal dining room, defined by decorative columns, and leads to a two-story great room with a fireplace, a bay window and access to the rear deck. The kitchen and breakfast areas overlook this casual space and share its natural light. The master bedroom suite to the left of the main floor includes a spacious bedroom with a coffered ceiling, a sumptuous bath with a whirlpool tub and a walk-in closet. A study with its own hearth completes this level. Two family bedrooms share the upper level with a loft that offers space for computers and books. This home is designed with a walkout basement foundation.

Design By
STEPHEN FULLER

Rear View

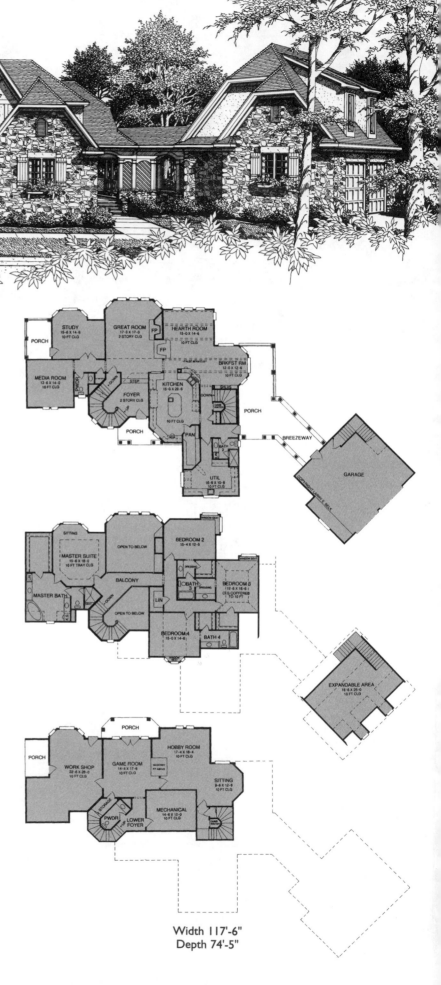

COPYRIGHT LARRY E. BELK

DESIGN 8147

Main Level: 2,340 square feet
Upper Level: 1,806 square feet
Lower Level: 1,608 square feet
Total: 5,754 square feet

Design By
© LARRY E. BELK DESIGNS

Full of amenities for the owner, this country estate includes a media room and a study. The two-story great room is perfect for formal entertaining. Family and friends will enjoy gathering in the large kitchen, the hearth room and the breakfast room. The luxurious master suite is located upstairs. Bedrooms 2 and 3 share a bath that includes dressing areas for both bedrooms. Bedroom 4 features a private bath. The detached garage is equipped with stairs to the expandable area above. The home features a rear stair complete with a dumbwaiter, which goes down to a walk-out basement, where you'll find an enormous workshop, a game room and a hobby room. This home may also be built with a slab foundation. Please specify your preference when ordering.

Width 117'-6"
Depth 74'-5"

DESIGN 3360

Main Level: 2,673 square feet
Lower Level: 1,389 square feet
Total: 4,062 square feet

L

This plan has the best of both worlds—a traditional exterior and a modern, multi-level floor plan. The central foyer routes traffic effectively to all areas: the kitchen, gathering room, sleeping area and media room. The lower level can be developed later. Plans include space for a summer kitchen, activities room and bedroom with full bath. The master suite features a luxurious bath with a whirlpool tub.

Design By
© HOME PLANNERS

QUOTE ONE®
Cost to build? See page 214 to order complete cost estimate to build this house in your area!

Rear View

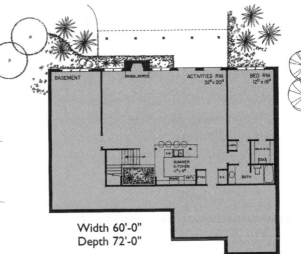

Width 60'-0"
Depth 72'-0"

DESIGN T051

First Floor: 1,840 square feet
Second Floor: 950 square feet
Total: 2,790 square feet
Unfinished Lower Level: 1,840 square feet

Design By
STEPHEN FULLER

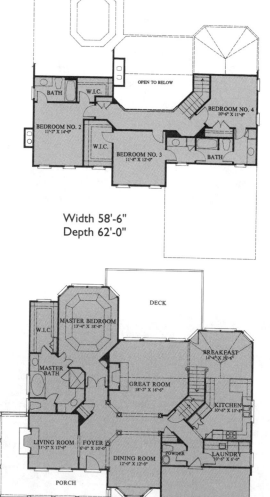

Width 58'-6"
Depth 62'-0"

The appearance of this Early American home brings the past to mind with its wraparound porch, wood siding and flower-box detailing. The uniquely shaped foyer leads to the dining room accented by columns. Nearby, columns frame the great room as well, while a ribbon of windows creates a wall of glass at the back of the house from the great room to the breakfast area. The asymmetrical theme continues through the kitchen as it leads back to the hallway, accessing the laundry and two-car garage. Left of the foyer lies the living room with a warming fireplace. The master suite begins with double doors that open to a large bedroom with an octagonal tray ceiling and a bay window. The spacious master bath and walk-in closet complete the suite. Stairs to the second level lead from the breakfast area to an open landing overlooking the great room. Three additional bedrooms with large walk-in closets and a variety of bath arrangements complete this level. This home is designed with a walkout basement foundation.

Rear View

Rear View

DESIGN T068

First Floor: 1,475 square feet
Second Floor: 1,460 square feet
Total: 2,935 square feet
Unfinished Lower Level:
911 square feet

QUOTE ONE®
Cost to build? See page 214
to order complete cost estimate
to build this house in your area!

Quaint keystones and shutters offer charming accents to the stucco-and-stone exterior of this stately English country home. The two-story foyer opens through decorative columns to the formal living room, which offers a wet bar. The nearby media room shares a through-fireplace with the two-story great room, which has double doors that lead to the rear deck. A bumped-out bay holds a breakfast area that shares its light with an expansive gourmet kitchen with an angled cooktop counter. This area opens to the formal dining room through a convenient butler's pantry. One wing of the second floor is dedicated to the rambling master suite, which boasts unusual amenities: the bedroom features angled walls, a tray ceiling and a bumped-out bay with a sitting area. This home is designed with a walkout basement foundation.

Design By
STEPHEN FULLER

Width 57'-6"
Depth 46'-6"

Design T155

First Floor: 1,567 square feet
Second Floor: 1,895 square feet
Total: 3,462 square feet
Unfinished Lower Level: 1,567 square feet

Rear View

This home's fine proportions contain formal living areas, including a dining room and a living room. At the back of the first floor you'll find a fine kitchen that serves a breakfast nook. A great room with a fireplace and a bumped-out window makes everyday living very comfortable. A rear porch allows for outdoor dining and relaxation.

Upstairs, four bedrooms include a master suite with lots of notable features. A boxed ceiling, a lavish bath, a large walk-in closet and a secluded sitting room (which will also make a nice study or exercise room) assure great livability. One of the secondary bedrooms contains a full bath. This home is designed with a walkout basement.

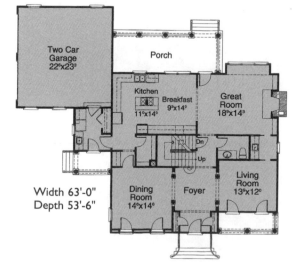

Width 63'-0"
Depth 53'-6"

Design By
Stephen Fuller

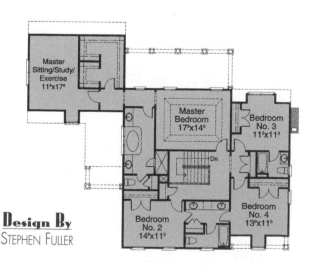

© American Home Gallery, Ltd.

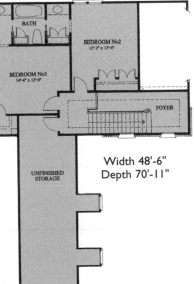

Width 48'-6"
Depth 70'-11"

Quote One®

Cost to build? See page 214
to order complete cost estimate
to build this house in your area!

Design T013

First Floor: 1,580 square feet
Second Floor: 595 square feet
Total: 2,175 square feet
Unfinished Lower Level: 1,373 square feet

This home is a true Southern original. Inside, the spacious foyer leads directly to a large vaulted great room with its handsome fireplace. The dining room, just off the foyer, features a dramatic vaulted ceiling. The spacious kitchen offers both storage and large work areas opening up to the breakfast room. At the rear of the home, you will find the master suite with its garden bath, His and Hers vanities and oversized closet. The second floor provides two additional bedrooms with a shared bath and a balcony overlook to the foyer below. Storage space or a fourth bedroom may be placed over the garage area. This home is designed with a walkout basement foundation.

Design By
STEPHEN FULLER

Design T244

First Floor: 2,963 square feet
Second Floor: 1,308 square feet
Total: 4,271 square feet
Unfinished Lower Level:
1,521 square feet
Bonus Room: 358 square feet

Design By
Stephen Fuller

A design of the times, this classic home offers a bonus room and space on the lower level for future development. The main level is sweeping in its appeal with a wide foyer that opens to both the formal dining room and the central great room. A keeping room connects to both the great room and the breakfast room. An island kitchen is nearby. The master suite is on the first floor and has a sitting area that opens to the rear porch. The master bath features His and Hers closets. The second floor holds three family bedrooms—or two and an office—and three full baths, plus a media room. The bonus space has two dormer windows. This home is designed with a walkout basement foundation.

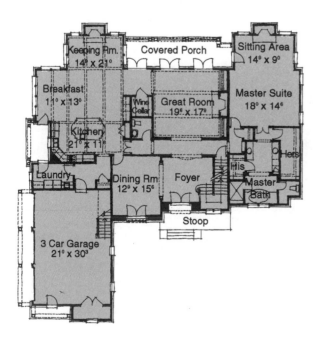

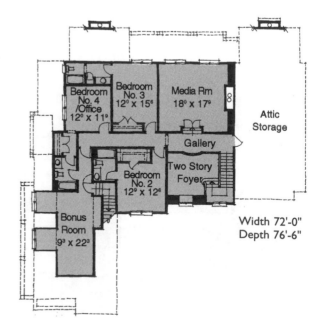

Width 72'-0"
Depth 76'-6"

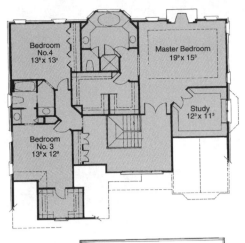

Bedroom No.4
13⁸ x 13⁰

Master Bedroom
19⁹ x 15³

Study
12³ x 11³

Bedroom No. 3
13⁸ x 12⁹

Rear View

Width 52'-0"
Depth 50'-6"

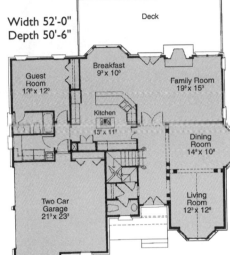

Deck

Breakfast
9³ x 10⁰

Family Room
19⁹ x 15³

Guest Room
13⁸ x 12⁰

Kitchen
15⁰ x 11⁰

Dining Room
14⁹ x 10⁸

Two Car Garage
21³ x 23³

Living Room
12³ x 12⁶

DESIGN T198

Design By
STEPHEN FULLER

First Floor: 1,621 square feet
Second Floor: 1,766 square feet
Total: 3,387 square feet
Unfinished Lower Level: 1,079 square feet

All-American charm springs from the true Colonial style of this distinguished home. Formal living areas are set off from the entrance foyer with pairs of columns. Double French doors partition the casual region of the home, headlined with the comfortable family room and its lovely fireplace. The oversized kitchen features a cooktop island and a work counter that's open to the breakfast and family rooms. A guest room is located behind the kitchen area, making it a perfect maid's or nurse's room. Upstairs, the master suite has a private study, fireplace and an amenity-laden bath with extended walk-in closet. This home is designed with a walkout basement foundation.

© American Home Gallery, Ltd.

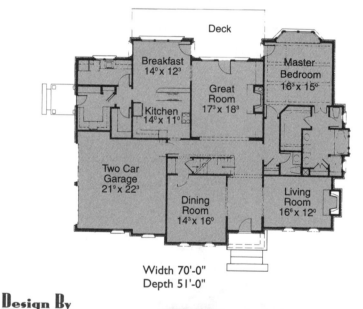

© American Home Gallery, Ltd.

DESIGN T197

First Floor: 2,302 square feet
Second Floor: 1,177 square feet
Total: 3,479 square feet
Unfinished Lower Level: 1,494 square feet

Classic quoins set off a stately pediment on this noble brick exterior. The heart of this home is the great room, which offers a focal-point fireplace and a private door to the rear deck. The formal living room opens from the foyer and features its own hearth. A corner master suite boasts a lavish bath with a spa tub, as well as a bay window and a door to the rear deck. Upstairs, three additional bedrooms enjoy a balcony hall with overlooks to the foyer and to the great room. Two share a full bath. This home is designed with a walkout basement foundation.

Design By
STEPHEN FULLER

Deck

Breakfast
14⁰ x 12³

Master
Bedroom
16³ x 15⁰

Great
Room
17³ x 18³

Kitchen
14⁰ x 11⁰

Two Car
Garage
21⁹ x 22³

Living
Room
16⁶ x 12⁰

Dining
Room
14³ x 16⁰

Width 70'-0"
Depth 51'-0"

Bedroom
No. 4
14⁰ x 15⁹

Open
To
Below

Bedroom
No. 3
15⁹ x 13³

Bedroom
No. 2
14³ x 15⁹

Open
To
Below

Rear View

80

Width 61'-6"
Depth 51'-0"

Deck

Solarium
11⁹x12⁶

Screened
Porch
10⁶x12⁶

Family
Room
15⁹x15⁹

Kitchen
16⁶x13⁰

Two Car
Garage
20⁹x25⁹

Living
Room
13⁹x12⁰

Dining
Room
14⁹x12⁰

Up
Foyer

Master
Bedroom
16⁹x13⁰

Bedroom
No. 4
15⁹x120³

Bedroom
No. 2
13⁹x12⁰

Open
To
Below

Bedroom
No. 3
14⁹x12⁰

Design By
STEPHEN FULLER

DESIGN T167

First Floor: 1,698 square feet
Second Floor: 1,542 square feet
Total: 3,240 square feet
Unfinished Lower Level: 1,207 square feet

Make your mark with this brick traditional. With a walkout basement, there's lots of room to grow. On the first floor, such attributes as informal/formal zones, a gourmet kitchen and a solarium, deck and screened porch are immediate attention getters. In the kitchen, meal preparation is a breeze with an island work station and plenty of counter space. Four bedrooms make up the second floor of this plan. One of the family bedrooms possesses a personal bath. The master bedroom has its own bath and a giant walk-in closet. This home is designed with a walkout basement.

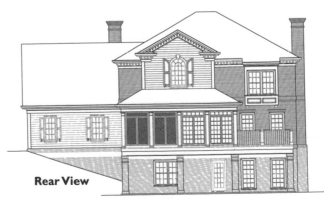

Rear View

DESIGN T169

First Floor: 1,828 square feet
Second Floor: 1,552 square feet
Total: 3,380 square feet
Unfinished Lower Level:
1,828 square feet

A stately appearance and lots of living space give this home appeal. The foyer introduces formal living and dining rooms. For more humble occasions, a great room opens to the back. The breakfast room has convenient proximity to these formal areas. The kitchen has plenty of work space. Four bedrooms on the second floor enjoy complete privacy. In the master bedroom suite, a short hallway flanked by closets leads to a lovely bath with a spa tub, a compartmented toilet, a separate shower and dual lavatories. This home is designed with a walkout basement

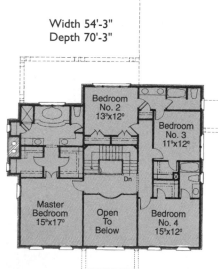

Width 54'-3"
Depth 70'-3"

Rear View

Design By
STEPHEN FULLER

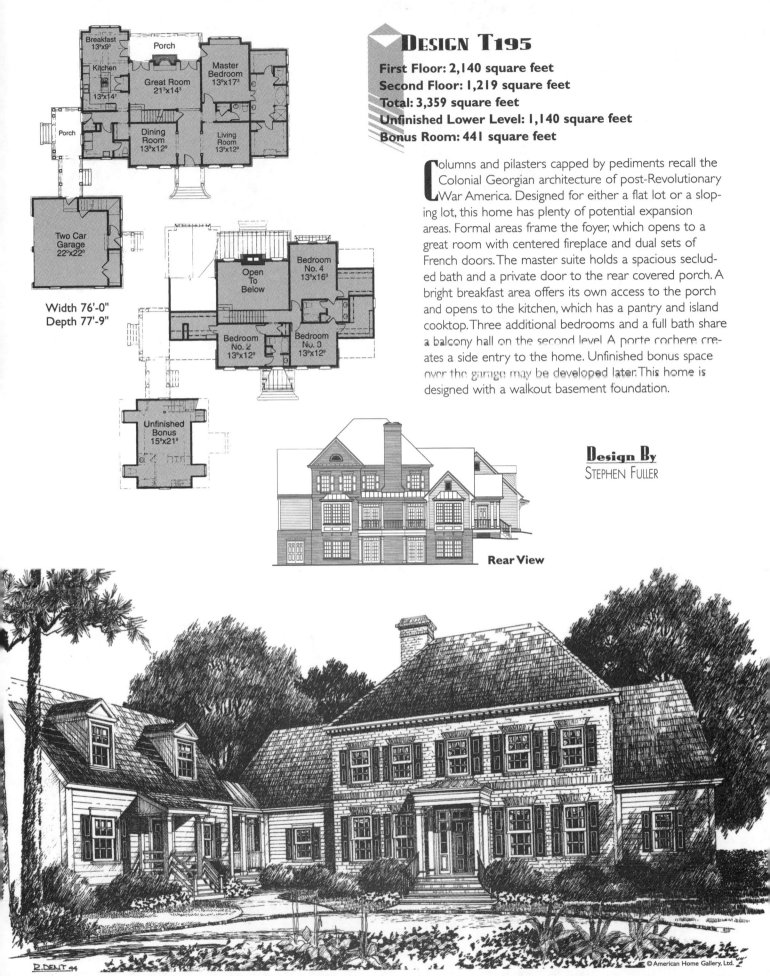

DESIGN T195

First Floor: 2,140 square feet
Second Floor: 1,219 square feet
Total: 3,359 square feet
Unfinished Lower Level: 1,140 square feet
Bonus Room: 441 square feet

Columns and pilasters capped by pediments recall the Colonial Georgian architecture of post-Revolutionary War America. Designed for either a flat lot or a sloping lot, this home has plenty of potential expansion areas. Formal areas frame the foyer, which opens to a great room with centered fireplace and dual sets of French doors. The master suite holds a spacious secluded bath and a private door to the rear covered porch. A bright breakfast area offers its own access to the porch and opens to the kitchen, which has a pantry and island cooktop. Three additional bedrooms and a full bath share a balcony hall on the second level. A porte cochere creates a side entry to the home. Unfinished bonus space over the garage may be developed later. This home is designed with a walkout basement foundation.

Breakfast 13'x9'³
Kitchen 13'x14'³
Great Room 21'x14'³
Master Bedroom 13'x17'³
Porch
Porch
Dining Room 13'x12'⁹
Living Room 13'x12'⁹
Two Car Garage 22'x22'⁰

Width 76'-0"
Depth 77'-9"

Open To Below
Bedroom No. 4 13'x16'³
Bedroom No. 2 13'x12'⁹
Bedroom No. 3 13'x12'⁹
Unfinished Bonus 15'x21'⁹

Rear View

Design By
STEPHEN FULLER

R. DENT 94

© American Home Gallery, Ltd.

Design T023

First Floor: 1,960 square feet

Second Floor: 905 square feet

Total: 2865 square feet

Unfinished Lower Level: 1,243 square feet

Bonus Room: 297 square feet

The classical styling of this Colonial home will be appreciated by traditionalists. The foyer opens to both a banquet-sized dining room and formal living room with fireplace. Just beyond is the two-story great room. The entire right side of the main level is taken up by the master suite. The other side of the main level includes a large kitchen and breakfast room just steps away from the detached garage. Upstairs, each bedroom features ample closet space and direct access to bathrooms. The detached garage features an unfinished office or studio on its second level. This home is designed with a walkout basement.

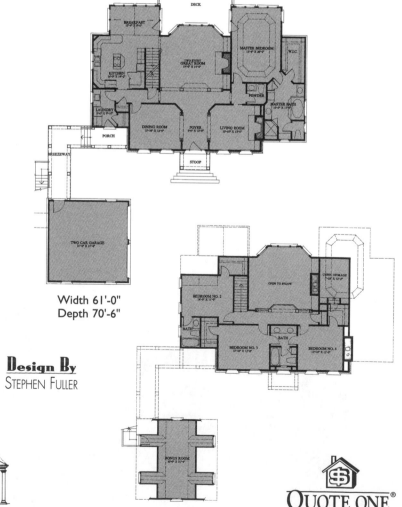

Width 61'-0"
Depth 70'-6"

Design By
STEPHEN FULLER

Rear View

Quote One®
Cost to build? See page 214
to order complete cost estimate
to build this house in your area!

© American Home Gallery, Ltd.

Design By
STEPHEN FULLER

DESIGN T049

First Floor: 2,078 square feet
Second Floor: 896 square feet
Total: 2,974 square feet
Unfinished Lower Level:
1,243 square feet
Unfinished Storage:
300 square feet

Width 69'-8"
Depth 59'-0"

This Georgian country-style home displays an impressive appearance. Textures of brick and wood are used to reflect this architectural period perfectly. Georgian symmetry balances the living room and dining room to the right and left of the foyer. Both are framed by columns, while the living room features its own fireplace. The foyer opens onto the two-story great room with built-in cabinetry, a fireplace and a large bay window that overlooks the rear deck. A dramatic tray ceiling, a wall of glass and access to the rear deck complete the master bedroom. The master bath features a large walk-in closet. Upstairs are three bedrooms and an open railing overlooking the great room below. Each bedroom features ample closet space and direct access to a bathroom. This home is designed with a walkout basement foundation.

Rear View

© American Home Gallery, Ltd.

Design By
Stephen Fuller

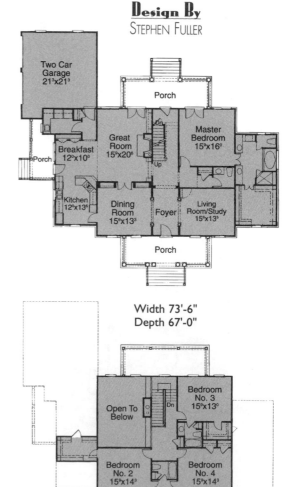

Two Car Garage 21³x21³

Porch

Porch

Breakfast 12⁰x10⁰

Great Room 15⁵x20⁶

Master Bedroom 15⁰x16⁰

Kitchen 12⁰x13⁶

Dining Room 15⁵x13³

Foyer

Living Room/Study 15⁵x13³

Porch

Design T170

First Floor: 2,174 square feet
Second Floor: 1,113 square feet
Total: 3,287 square feet
Unfinished Lower Level: 2,174 square feet

Front and back porches and old Southern charm give this home extra appeal. The foyer is flanked by a dining room and a living room (or a study). You'll find a great room with a fireplace for family livability. The kitchen and breakfast room are not far away from here. The master suite is contained on the first floor. It contains porch access, a private bath and a large walk-in closet. Upstairs, secondary bedrooms accommodate the children or guests. This home's walkout basement plan increases the overall square footage.

Width 73'-6"
Depth 67'-0"

Open To Below

Bedroom No. 3 15⁵x13⁰

Bedroom No. 2 15⁵x14³

Bedroom No. 4 15⁵x14³

Rear View

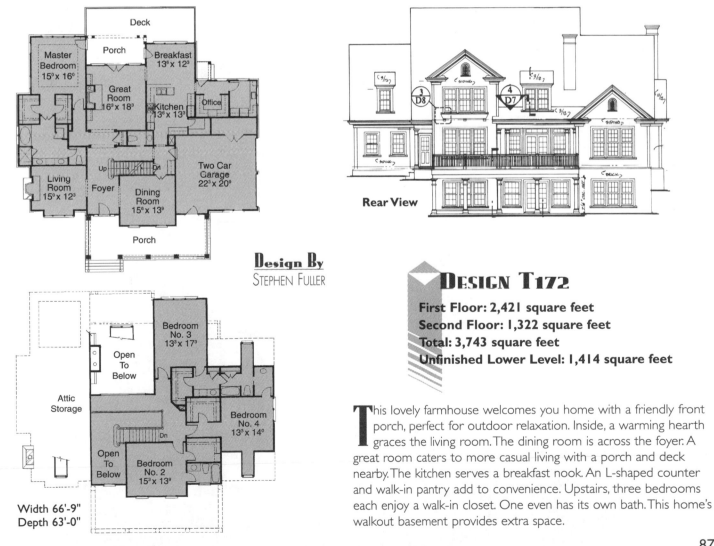

Rear View

Design By
STEPHEN FULLER

Width 66'-9"
Depth 63'-0"

DESIGN T172

First Floor: 2,421 square feet
Second Floor: 1,322 square feet
Total: 3,743 square feet
Unfinished Lower Level: 1,414 square feet

This lovely farmhouse welcomes you home with a friendly front porch, perfect for outdoor relaxation. Inside, a warming hearth graces the living room. The dining room is across the foyer. A great room caters to more casual living with a porch and deck nearby. The kitchen serves a breakfast nook. An L-shaped counter and walk-in pantry add to convenience. Upstairs, three bedrooms each enjoy a walk-in closet. One even has its own bath. This home's walkout basement provides extra space.

© American Home Gallery, Ltd.

DESIGN T022

First Floor: 1,944 square feet
Second Floor: 954 square feet
Total: 2,898 square feet
Unfinished Lower Level:
1,216 square feet

This story-and-a-half home combines warm informal materials with a modern livable floor plan to create a true Southern classic. The dining room, study and great room work together to create one large, exciting space. Just beyond the open rail, the breakfast room is lined with windows. Plenty of counter space and storage make the kitchen truly usable. The master suite, with its tray ceiling and decorative niche, is a gracious and private owner's retreat. Upstairs, two additional bedrooms each have their own vanity within a shared bath, while the third bedroom or guest room has its own bath and walk-in closet. This home is designed with a walkout basement foundation.

Design By
STEPHEN FULLER

Width 51'-6"
Depth 73'-0"

Rear View

QUOTE ONE®

Cost to build? See page 214
to order complete cost estimate
to build this house in your area!

88

© American Home Gallery, Ltd.

Width 52'-6"
Depth 43'-6"

MASTER BATH

MASTER BEDROOM
19'-2" X 13'-8"

W.I.C.

UNFIN.
BEDROOM NO. 4
13'-0" X 13'-0"

W.I.C. BATH

DN

W.I.C. W.I.C.

BATH

BEDROOM NO. 3
11'-8" X 13'-0"

OPEN TO BELOW

BEDROOM NO. 2
11'-4" X 13'-0"

Design By
STEPHEN FULLER

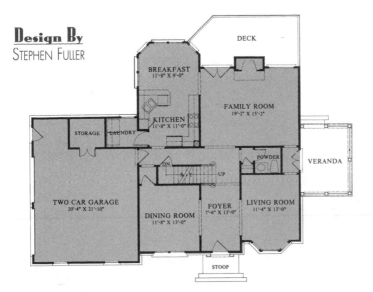

DECK

BREAKFAST
11'-8" X 9'-0"

FAMILY ROOM
19'-2" X 15'-2"

KITCHEN
11'-8" X 11'-0"

STORAGE LAUNDRY

POWDER

VERANDA

DN UP

TWO CAR GARAGE
20'-4" X 21'-10"

DINING ROOM
11'-8" X 13'-0"

FOYER
7'-6" X 13'-0"

LIVING ROOM
11'-4" X 13'-0"

STOOP

DESIGN T088

First Floor: 1,205 square feet
Second Floor: 1,160 square feet
Total: 2,365 square feet
Unfinished Lower Level: 924 square feet

This charming exterior conceals a perfect family plan. The formal dining and living rooms are located to either side of the foyer. At the rear of the home is a family room with a fireplace and access to a deck and a side veranda. The modern kitchen features a sunlit breakfast area. The second floor provides room for four bedrooms, one of which may be finished at a later date and used as a guest suite. The master bedroom includes a pampering bath and a walk-in closet. Note the extra storage space in the garage. This home is designed with a walkout basement foundation.

Quote One®

Cost to build? See page 214
to order complete cost estimate
to build this house in your area!

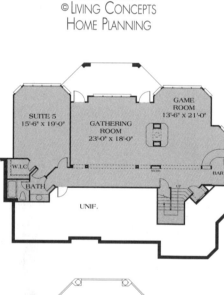

Design By
© LIVING CONCEPTS
HOME PLANNING

DESIGN A215

Main Level: 2,450 square feet
Upper Level: 1,675 square feet
Lower Level: 1,568 square feet
Total: 5,693 square feet

This stately home is characterized by its hip roof, stucco detailing and beautiful lines. Designed for a rear sloping lot, this plan is filled with amenities for any family. Columns define the formal dining room as well as the spacious great room. Here, a through-fireplace is shared with the bayed breakfast nook and island kitchen. Located for privacy on the main level, the master bedroom suite is sure to please with a large walk-in closet and a pampering bath. Upstairs, three secondary bedrooms—each with walk-in closets—have direct access to a loft for studying or relaxing. The basement level consists of a fourth secondary bedroom, also with walk-in closet, and a spacious gathering room that shares a through-fireplace with a games room.

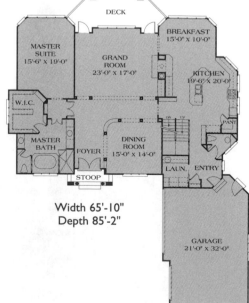

Width 65'-10"
Depth 85'-2"

Rear View

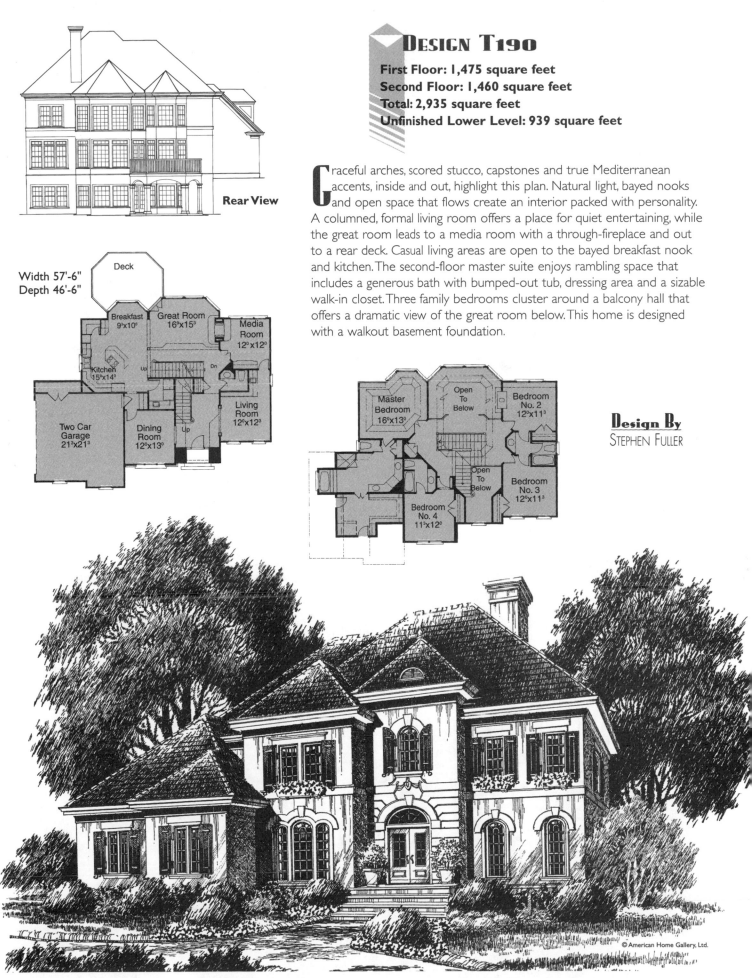

Rear View

DESIGN T190

First Floor: 1,475 square feet
Second Floor: 1,460 square feet
Total: 2,935 square feet
Unfinished Lower Level: 939 square feet

Graceful arches, scored stucco, capstones and true Mediterranean accents, inside and out, highlight this plan. Natural light, bayed nooks and open space that flows create an interior packed with personality. A columned, formal living room offers a place for quiet entertaining, while the great room leads to a media room with a through-fireplace and out to a rear deck. Casual living areas are open to the bayed breakfast nook and kitchen. The second-floor master suite enjoys rambling space that includes a generous bath with bumped-out tub, dressing area and a sizable walk-in closet. Three family bedrooms cluster around a balcony hall that offers a dramatic view of the great room below. This home is designed with a walkout basement foundation.

Width 57'-6"
Depth 46'-6"

Deck

Breakfast 9⁹x10⁰
Great Room 16⁹x15³
Media Room 12⁰x12⁰

Kitchen 15'x14⁰

Two Car Garage 21³x21³
Dining Room 12⁰x13⁰
Living Room 12⁰x12³

Master Bedroom 16⁰x13⁰
Open To Below
Bedroom No. 2 12⁰x11³
Open To Below
Bedroom No. 3 12⁰x11³
Bedroom No. 4 11³x12⁰

Design By
STEPHEN FULLER

© American Home Gallery, Ltd.

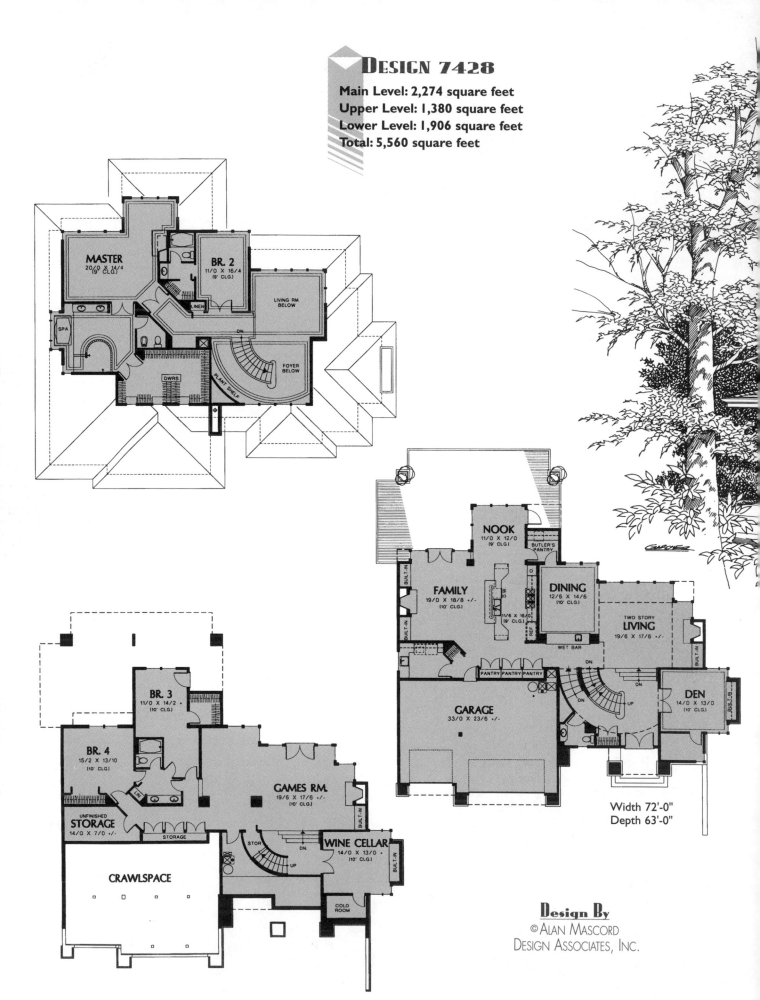

DESIGN 7428

Main Level: 2,274 square feet
Upper Level: 1,380 square feet
Lower Level: 1,906 square feet
Total: 5,560 square feet

MASTER
20/0 X 14/4
(9' CLG.)

BR. 2
11/0 X 16/4
(9' CLG.)

LIVING RM.
BELOW

SPA

LINEN

DN

FOYER
BELOW

DWRS

PLANT SHELF

NOOK
11/0 X 12/0
(9' CLG.)

BUTLER'S
PANTRY

BUILT-IN

FAMILY
19/0 X 18/8 +/-
(10' CLG.)

11/6 X 16/0
(9' CLG.)

DINING
12/6 X 14/6
(10' CLG.)

REF

DW

TWO STORY
LIVING
19/6 X 17/6 +/-

WET BAR

BUILT-IN

PANTRY PANTRY PANTRY

GARAGE
33/0 X 23/6 +/-

DN

DN

UP

DEN
14/0 X 13/0
(10' CLG.)

BUILT-IN

Width 72'-0"
Depth 63'-0"

BR. 3
11/0 X 14/2
(10' CLG.)

BR. 4
15/2 X 13/10
(10' CLG.)

LIN

GAMES RM.
19/6 X 17/6 +/-
(10' CLG.)

BUILT-IN

UNFINISHED
STORAGE
14/0 X 7/0 +/-

STORAGE

STOR

DN

UP

WINE CELLAR
14/0 X 13/0
(10' CLG.)

BUILT-IN

CRAWLSPACE

COLD
ROOM

Design By
© ALAN MASCORD
DESIGN ASSOCIATES, INC.

This multi-level contemporary offers an array of winning combinations to make it truly unique and enjoyable. On the main level, the living and dining rooms are open to each other, creating ample space for entertaining, and feature a fireplace and a shared wet bar. The informal area combines a large family room, boasting another fireplace and outdoor access, with a sunny breakfast nook and an efficient kitchen. A secluded den and a powder room complete the main level. On the upper level, the master bedroom includes a separate sitting space, a spa bath and an immense walk-in closet. It shares space with a guest suite that could also be used as an office or study. On the lower level, two family bedrooms share a full bath and enjoy a game room (with a third fireplace) and a wine cellar.

DESIGN T199

First Floor: 1,383 square feet
Second Floor: 1,576 square feet
Total: 2,959 square feet
Unfinished Lower Level: 903 square feet

Design By
STEPHEN FULLER

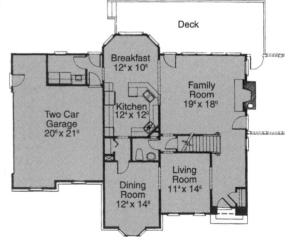

Deck

Breakfast
12⁶ x 10⁶

Family Room
19⁶ x 18⁰

Two Car Garage
20⁶ x 21⁰

Kitchen
12⁴ x 12⁰

Living Room
11⁴ x 14⁶

Dining Room
12⁴ x 14⁶

Arches, gables and multi-pane windows decorate the charming facade of this European cottage, but the real beauty lies within. An extensive foyer opens to both formal and casual living areas. Guests may want to linger in the stylish bayed dining room, but coax them back to the warmth of the fireplace in the family room, which offers views to the rear deck. The nearby kitchen offers an angled counter and a breakfast nook that promises a warm bath of sunshine in the morning. The plan upstairs affords privacy to the master suite—a comfortable retreat for the home-owner, with His and Her walk-in closets, dual vanities and a whirlpool tub. Three family bedrooms share a generous hall bath and complete this floor. This home is designed with a walkout basement foundation.

Rear View

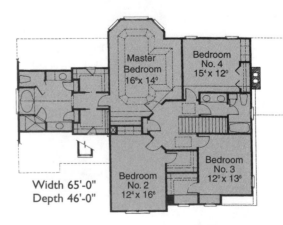

Master Bedroom
16⁶ x 14⁰

Bedroom No. 4
15⁴ x 12⁰

Bedroom No. 2
12⁴ x 16⁶

Bedroom No. 3
12⁰ x 13⁶

Width 65'-0"
Depth 46'-0"

DESIGN 2894

Main Level: 1,490 square feet
Lower Level: 1,357 square feet
Total: 2,847 square feet

L

Contemporary, bi-level living will be enjoyed in this home. The foyer is complemented by skylights and an open staircase that leads to the upper and lower levels. The gathering room is up just a few steps and is graced by a fireplace, a sloped ceiling and large size. To the left is a study (or guest bedroom) with a full bath and a walk-in closet. The efficient kitchen and breakfast room benefit from a nearby wet bar. The lower level holds two bedrooms and a bath on one side and the master suite on the other. Centered here is a large activity room with raised-hearth fireplace. All rooms to the rear of the plan have outdoor access.

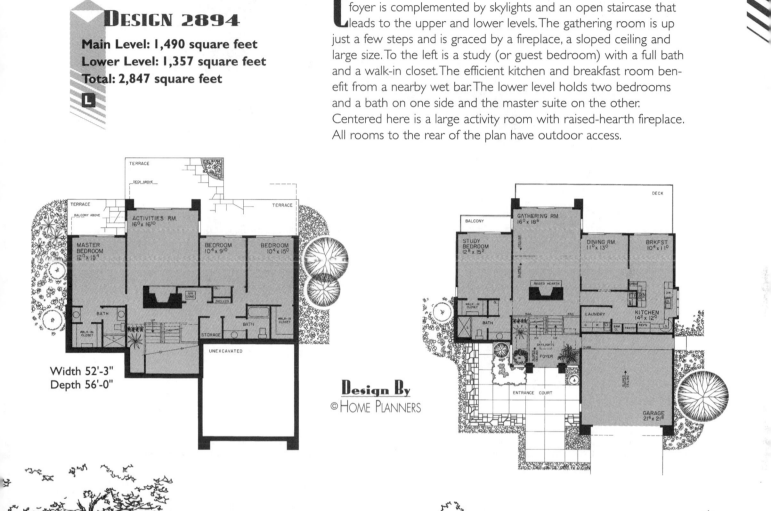

Width 52'-3"
Depth 56'-0"

Design By
© HOME PLANNERS

DESIGN 2926

Main Level: 1,570 square feet
Upper Level: 598 square feet
Lower Level: 1,080 square feet
Total: 3,248 square feet

Design By
© HOME PLANNERS

An incredible combination of curving lines and circles in this ultramodern design makes for an interesting floor plan. The dramatic use of balconies and overlooks highlights a first-floor gathering room with a fireplace open to the study, a formal dining room and a kitchen with a circular breakfast room. A goblet-shaped bedroom on this floor has a balcony and a full bath. Reached by a curved stair, the upper level is dominated by the master suite. A lower-level activities room with a bar and a fireplace, and an exercise room with an attached sauna, a hot tub and a bath overlook the lower terrace. Take special note of the generous use of skylights throughout.

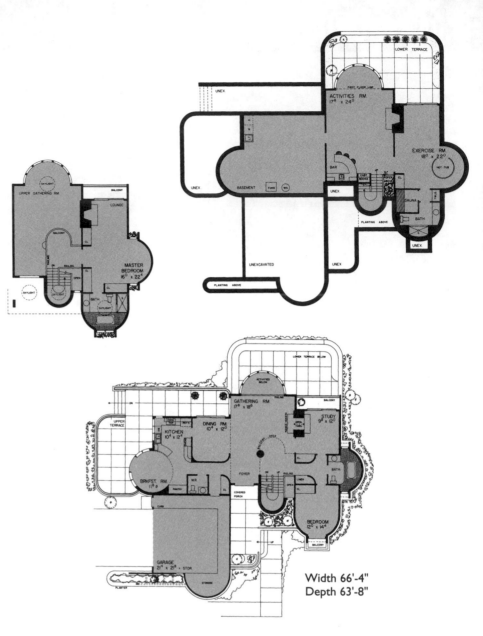

Width 66'-4"
Depth 63'-8"

Design By
© Home Planners

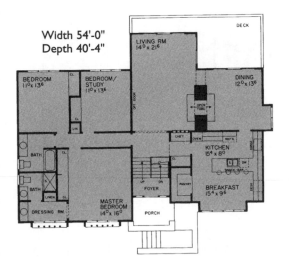

Width 54'-0"
Depth 40'-4"

Design 2843

Main Level: 1,861 square feet
Lower Level: 1,181 square feet
Total: 3,042 square feet

L

A Spanish-style bi-level? Why not? This one has lots going for it upstairs and down. Up top, note the living room and formal dining room; they share a fireplace, and each leads to a comfy deck out back. In addition, the kitchen and breakfast area are centers of attention; the latter has a wonderful, over-sized pantry. Zoned to the left of the entry are three bedrooms (two if you make one a study). Down below is a potpourri of space: family room, lounge with raised-hearth fireplace, large laundry room (note the bay window), another bedroom, full bath and plenty of storage in the garage.

Rear View

DESIGN 7546

Main Level: 2,300 square feet
Lower Level: 1,114 square feet
Total: 3,414 square feet

Looking for all the world like a one-story plan, this elegant hillside design has a surprise on the lower level. The main level is reached through an arched, recessed entry that opens to a twelve-foot ceiling. The formal dining room is on the right, next to a cozy den or Bedroom 3. Columns decorate the hall and separate it from the dining room and great room, which has a tray ceiling and fireplace flanked by built-ins. The breakfast nook and kitchen are just steps away; the nook accesses a rear deck. A master suite and one additional bedroom are on the left. Note the fine master bath. Lower-level space includes another great room with built-ins and two family bedrooms sharing a full bath.

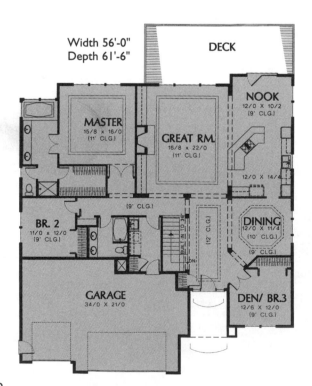

Width 56'-0"
Depth 61'-6"

DECK

NOOK
12/0 X 10/2
(9' CLG.)

MASTER
15/8 x 16/0
(11' CLG.)

GREAT RM.
16/8 x 22/0
(11' CLG.)

12/0 X 14/4

(9' CLG.)

BR. 2
11/0 x 12/0
(9' CLG.)

DINING
12/0 X 11/4
(10' CLG.)

(9' CLG.)

GARAGE
34/0 X 21/0

DEN/ BR.3
12/6 x 12/0
(9' CLG.)

Design By
© ALAN MASCORD
DESIGN ASSOCIATES, INC.

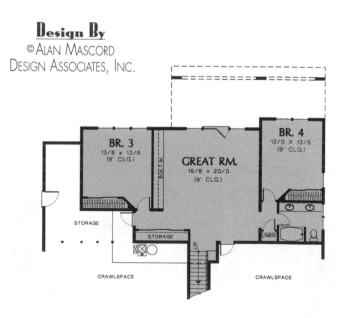

BR. 3
13/8 x 13/6
(9' CLG.)

GREAT RM.
16/8 x 20/0
(9' CLG.)

BR. 4
12/0 x 13/8
(9' CLG.)

STORAGE

STORAGE

LINEN

CRAWLSPACE

CRAWLSPACE

Width 87'-6"
Depth 56'-0"

BR. 3
10/8 X 14/8

BR. 2
14/0 X 14/8

STORAGE

PATIO

LINEN

12/10 X 22/4

UP

BUILT-INS

STORAGE
9/2 X 13/8

MEDIA RM.
18/8 X 12/4

BUILT-INS

SPA

SKYLITE

MASTER
14/0 X 18/0
(10' CLG.)

DECK

GREAT RM.
20/0 X 16/4
(13'-4" CLG.)

KIT./NOOK
13/6 X 23/0
(10' CLG.)

SHELVES

SKYLITE

PANTRY

GARAGE
30/0 X 25/0

GALLERY
8/6 X 20/6
(13'-4" CLG.)

DN

DINING
11/0 X 15/0
(13'-4" CLG.)

D REF

Design 7529

Main Level: 1,854 square feet
Lower Level: 1,703 square feet
Total: 3,557 square feet

There's room to spare in this grand hillside design. And the plan is made to seem even larger than it is, due to a high roofline that allows for extended ceilings in the main-level rooms. Beyond the columned gallery are a dining room with tray ceiling and a great room with tray ceiling and corner fireplace. The kitchen/nook area has deck access and an island work counter with space for casual dining. The master suite is on the main level and is reached through a skylit hall. The master bath is also skylit and offers a spa tub, walk-in closet and double sinks. Family bedrooms are on the lower level along with a media room and an additional space that may be used as a family room or den. Two large storage areas—one accessed from inside, the other from outside—are also found on the lower level. Note the large covered patio.

Design By
© Alan Mascord
Design Associates, Inc.

DESIGN 9539

Main Level: 2,219 square feet
Lower Level: 1,324 square feet
Total: 3,543 square feet

Sleek lines define the contemporary feel of this home. Double entry doors lead to a columned gallery and an expansive great room. It showcases a fireplace, built-ins and a curving wall of windows. The nearby kitchen utilizes efficient zoning. A nook here opens to a wraparound deck. A dining room and a den finish the first-floor living areas. In the master bedroom suite, large proportions and an elegant bath with a see-through fireplace aim to please. The two bedrooms on the lower level have in-room vanities; one has direct access to the compartmented bath. A games room with a fireplace and built-ins leads to outdoor livability.

Design By
© ALAN MASCORD
DESIGN ASSOCIATES, INC.

Width 80'-0"
Depth 54'-6"

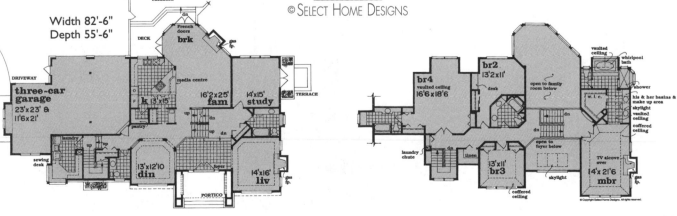

DESIGN Q606

Main Level: 2,201 square feet
Upper Level: 2,034 square feet
Lower Level: 1,882 square feet
Total: 6,117 square feet

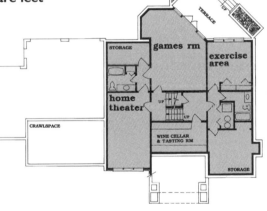

Three full levels of livability are contained within the floor plan of this design. The main level features formal living and dining areas, a family room with vaulted ceiling, a breakfast nook and a study with private terrace. The three-car garage is on this level and opens to the back of the plan. The upper level holds the bedrooms—three family bedrooms and a master suite. Bedroom 4 has a private bath, as does the master suite. Lower-level livability includes a games room, a home theater and an exercise area, plus a wine cellar for your private collection. A terrace at this level opens off the games room. Two large storage areas will be welcome.

Design By
© SELECT HOME DESIGNS

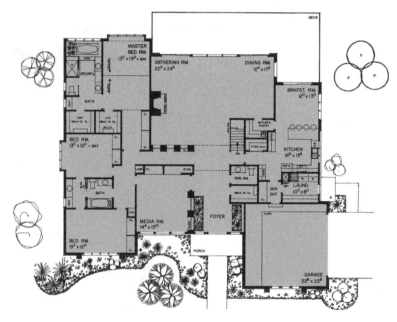

DESIGN 3361

Main Level: 3,548 square feet
Lower Level: 1,036 square feet
Total: 4,584 square feet

Here's a dandy hillside home that can easily accommodate the largest of families and is perfect for both formal and informal entertaining. Straight back from the foyer is a grand gathering room/dining room combination. It is complemented by the breakfast room and a front-facing media room. The sleeping wing contains three bedrooms and two full baths. On the lower level is an activities room with summer kitchen and a fourth bedroom that makes the perfect guest room.

QUOTE ONE®

Cost to build? See page 214
to order complete cost estimate
to build this house in your area!

Design By
© HOME PLANNERS

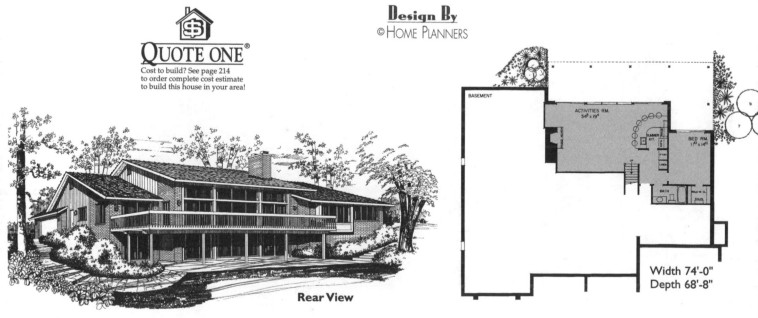

Rear View

Width 74'-0"
Depth 68'-8"

Design 2761

Main Level: 1,242 square feet
Lower Level: 1,242 square feet
Total: 2,484 square feet

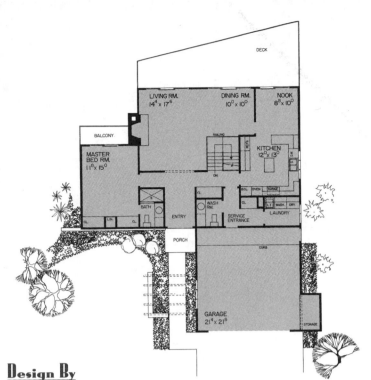

This one-story home doubles its livability by exposing the lowest level at the rear. Formal living on the main level and informal living in an activity room and study on the lower level create the best of floor plans. Decks and terraces provide wonderful outdoor livability. The master suite is on the main level for complete privacy. Two family bedrooms reside on the lower level and share a bath with dual sinks.

Design By
© Home Planners

Rear View

Width 50'-0"
Depth 52'-0"

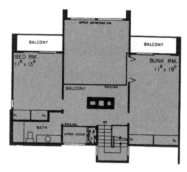

DESIGN 2511

Main Level: 1,043 square feet
Upper Level: 703 square feet
Lower Level: 794 square feet
Total: 2,540 square feet

L D

Design By
© HOME PLANNERS

This outstanding multi-level home comes complete with outdoor deck and balconies. The entry level provides full living space: gathering room with fireplace, study (or optional bedroom) with bath, dining room and U-shaped kitchen. A huge deck area wraps around the gathering room and dining room for outdoor enjoyment. A bedroom and bunk room on the upper level are joined by a wide balcony area and full bath. Lower-level space includes a large activities room with fireplace, an additional bunk room and a full bath. Built-ins and open window areas abound throughout the plan.

QUOTE ONE®
Cost to build? See page 214
to order complete cost estimate
to build this house in your area!

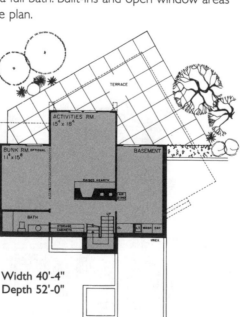

Width 40'-4"
Depth 52'-0"

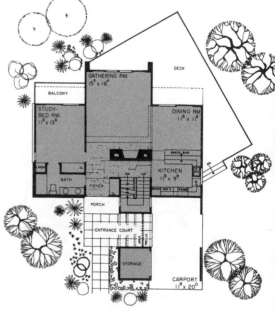

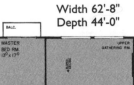

DESIGN 3362

Main Level: 1,327 square feet
Upper Level: 887 square feet
Lower Level: 1,197 square feet
Total: 3,411 square feet

This attractive multi-level home benefits from the comfort and ease of open planning. The entry foyer leads straight into a large gathering room with fireplace and is open to the dining room and kitchen. A perfect arrangement for the more informal demands of today! A media room features a built-in area for your TV, VCR and stereo. The sleeping area features two bedrooms on the upper level—one a master suite with His and Hers walk-in closets. The lower level includes an activities room, a wet bar and a third bedroom with a full bath.

Design By
© HOME PLANNERS

Width 62'-8"
Depth 44'-0"

QUOTE ONE®
Cost to build? See page 214
to order complete cost estimate
to build this house in your area!

Rear View

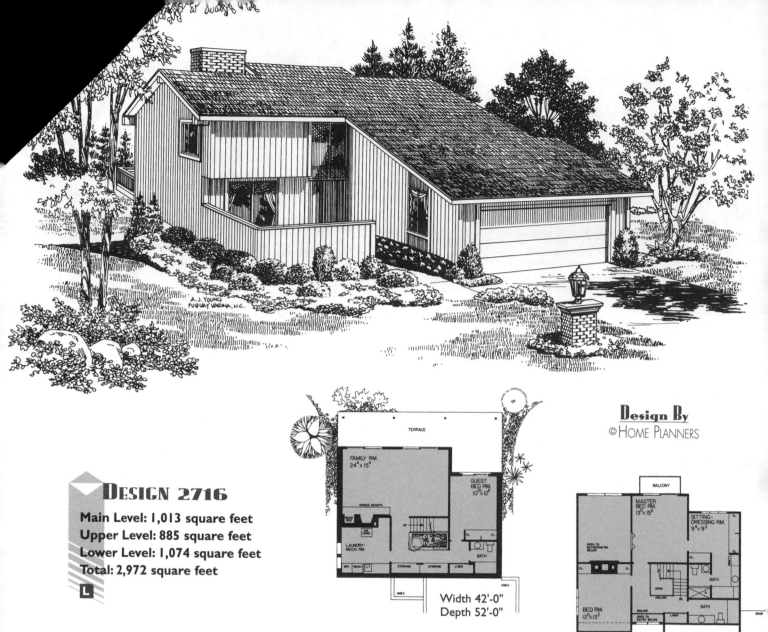

DESIGN 2716

Main Level: 1,013 square feet
Upper Level: 885 square feet
Lower Level: 1,074 square feet
Total: 2,972 square feet

L

Width 42'-0"
Depth 52'-0"

Design By
© HOME PLANNERS

A genuine master suite! It overlooks the gathering room through the shuttered windows and includes a private balcony, a 9' x 9' sitting/dressing room and a full bath. There's more—a two-story gathering room with a raised-hearth fireplace, sloped ceiling and sliding glass doors onto the main balcony. Plus, a family room and a study both have fireplaces. A kitchen with lots of built-ins and a separate dining nook finish out this comfortable plan.

Rear View

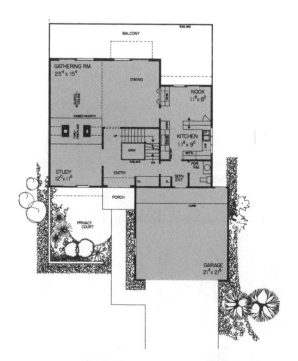

Design By
© HOME PLANNERS

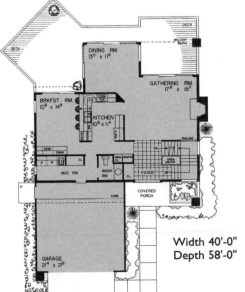

Width 40'-0"
Depth 58'-0"

Rear View

DESIGN 2937

Main Level: 1,096 square feet
Upper Level: 1,115 square feet
Lower Level: 1,104 square feet
Total: 3,315 square feet

A splendidly symmetrical plan, this clean-lined, open-planned contemporary home is a great place for the outdoor minded. A gathering room (with fireplace), dining room and breakfast room all lead out to a deck off the main level. Similarly, the lower-level activity room (another fireplace), hobby room and guest bedroom contain separate doors to the backyard terrace. Upstairs are three bedrooms, including a suite with through-fireplace, private balcony, walk-in closet, dressing room and whirlpool tub.

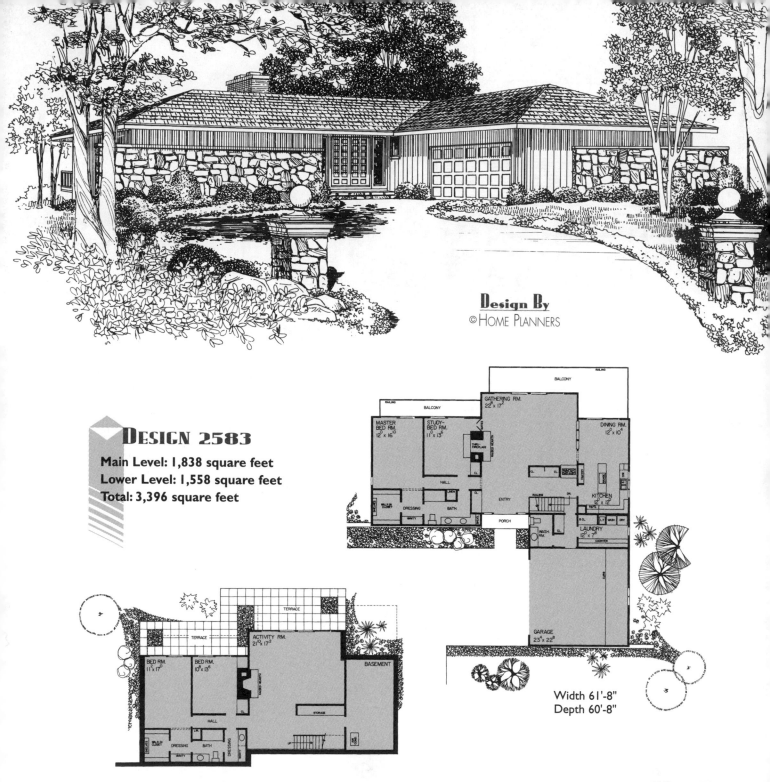

Design By
©Home Planners

Design 2583

Main Level: 1,838 square feet
Lower Level: 1,558 square feet
Total: 3,396 square feet

Width 61'-8"
Depth 60'-8"

Four bedrooms! Or three plus a study. It's your choice. A fireplace in the study/bedroom guarantees a cozy atmosphere. The warmth of a fireplace will also be enjoyed in the gathering room and the activities room. There's lots of living space too, including an exceptionally large gathering room with sliding glass doors that open onto the main terrace to enjoy the scenic outdoors. Nearby are a formal dining room and kitchen that promises to turn a novice cook into a pro. Check out the counter space, the pantry and island range. This house is designed to make living pleasant.

Rear View

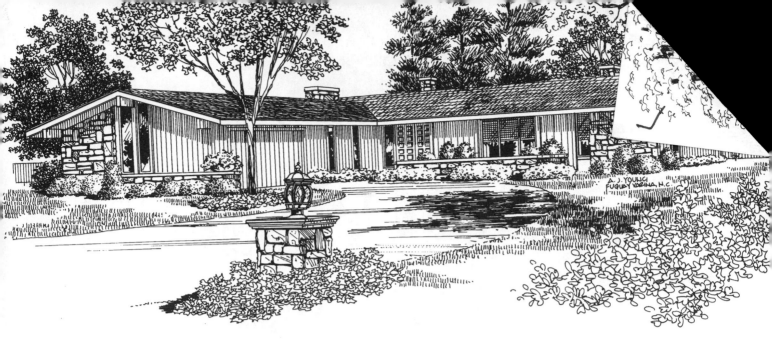

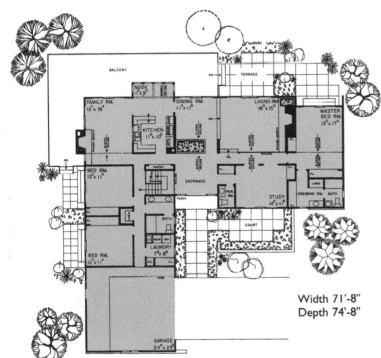

Width 71'-8"
Depth 74'-8"

DESIGN 2502

Main Level: 2,606 square feet
Lower Level: 1,243 square feet
Total: 3,849 square feet

This sleek contemporary home has two faces. From the street this design gives all the appearances of being a one-story, L-shaped home. When viewed from the rear, a whole new countenance is shown off by the sloping terrain. Inside, formal and informal living are both accommodated, as well as sleeping arrangements, which include two family bedrooms and a deluxe master suite.

Design By
© HOME PLANNERS

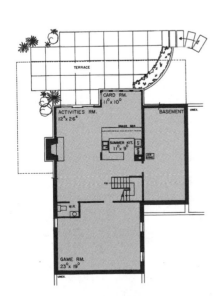

Rear View

DESIGN 3366

Main Level: 1,638 square feet
Upper Level: 650 square feet
Lower Level: 934 square feet
Total: 3,222 square feet

There is much more to this design than meets the eye. While it may look like a 1½-story plan, bonus recreation and hobby space in the walkout basement adds almost 1,000 square feet. The first floor holds living and dining areas as well as the deluxe master bedroom suite. Two family bedrooms share a full bath on the second floor and are connected by a balcony that overlooks the gathering room below. Notice the covered porch beyond the breakfast and dining rooms.

Rear View

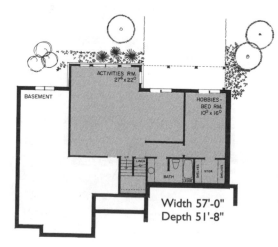

Width 57'-0"
Depth 51'-8"

Design By
© HOME PLANNERS

QUOTE ONE®

Cost to build? See page 214
to order complete cost estimate
to build this house in your area!

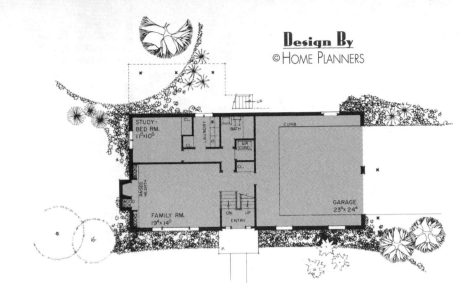

Design By
© Home Planners

Design 1850

Main Level: 1,456 square feet
Lower Level: 728 square feet
Total: 2,184 square feet

A perfect rectangle, this split-level home is comparatively inexpensive to build and very appealing to live in. It features a large upper-level living room with a fireplace, a formal dining room, three bedrooms (with two full baths nearby), and an outdoor deck. Another fireplace warms the family room on the lower level, which also has a full bath and room for a study or a fourth bedroom.

Quote One®

Cost to build? See page 214
to order complete cost estimate
to build this house in your area!

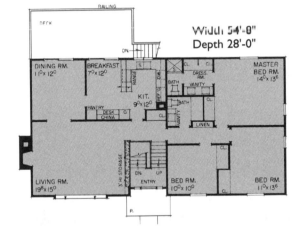

Width 54'-0"
Depth 28'-0"

Design 3713

Main Level: 1,028 square feet
Lower Level: 442 square feet
Total: 1,470 square feet

This home offers a living room, a dining room, a kitchen, two full baths and three bedrooms. The lower level, with a two-car garage, can be finished in the future to include a family room, a powder room and a utility room. The basic plan may be enhanced with a fireplace in the living room, a brick veneer front, decorative louvers and a rear deck. The blueprints for this house show how to build both the basic, low-cost version and the enhanced, upgraded version.

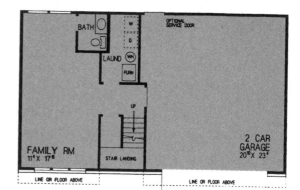

Rear View

Design By
© Home Planners

Width 40'-0"
Depth 26'-0"

DESIGN 1378

Main Level: 1,040 square feet
Lower Level: 1,040 square feet
Total: 2,080 square feet

The popularity of the bi-level can be traced to the tremendous amount of livable space that such a design provides per construction dollar. While the lower level is partially below grade, it enjoys plenty of natural light and, hence, provides a bright, cheerful atmosphere for total livability. Two family bedrooms are found on this level along with a family room. The second floor holds the master suite, the living and dining rooms and two additional bedrooms.

Design By
©HOME PLANNERS

MASTER BED RM. 12⁰ x 11⁸
BATH
EATING
RANGE
DINING RM. 9⁰ x 11⁰
GARAGE 12⁰ x 22⁰
KIT. 10⁰ x 10⁸
BATH
REF'G
CL.
CL.
CL.
CL.
BED RM. 11⁸ x 11⁰
BED RM. 9⁰ x 11⁰
DN. UP
LIVING RM. 15⁰ x 14⁴
P

Width 52'-0"
Depth 26'-0"

BED RM. 11⁰ x 12⁶
CL.
BATH
CL.
FAMILY RM. 16⁰ x 25⁴
CL.
D.
W.
LIN CL.
UP
BED RM. HOBBIES 18⁸ x 11⁶
STORAGE
UNEX.

DESIGN Q469

Square Footage: 1,363
Unfinished Lower Level:
848 square feet

A columned, covered entry charms the exterior of this three-bedroom split-entry home. Inside, a 1½-story foyer boasts a dual staircase—one up to the main floor living area and the other down to the basement. The living area includes a gas fireplace and windows on all walls, ensuring natural light. The adjacent dining room with an alcove for a buffet exits through a sliding glass door to the rear patio. The roomy kitchen has a raised snack bar, built-in pantry and is open to a bayed eating area surrounded by windows. A skylight brightens the hall to the three bedrooms. Look for His and Hers closets and a private bath in the master suite. Future expansion is reserved for space on the lower level.

Design By
© SELECT HOME DESIGNS

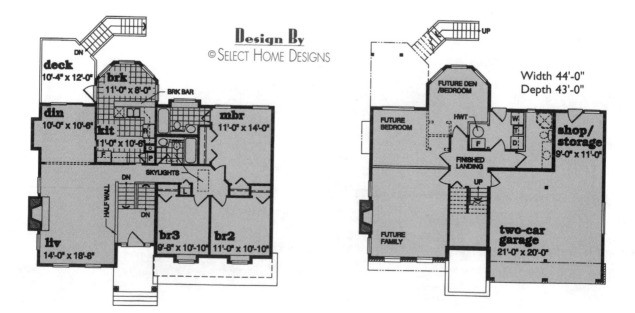

deck 10'-4" x 12'-0"
brk 11'-0" x 8'-0"
BRK BAR
din 10'-0" x 10'-6"
kit 11'-0" x 10'-6"
mbr 11'-0" x 14'-0"
SKYLIGHTS
HALF WALL
br3 9'-8" x 10'-10"
br2 11'-0" x 10'-10"
liv 14'-0" x 18'-8"

UP
FUTURE DEN/BEDROOM
Width 44'-0"
Depth 43'-0"
FUTURE BEDROOM
HWT
shop/storage 9'-0" x 11'-0"
FINISHED LANDING
FUTURE FAMILY
two-car garage 21'-0" x 20'-0"

Design Q268

Square Footage: 1,282

Unfinished Lower Level: 1,122 square feet

Design By

© Select Home Designs

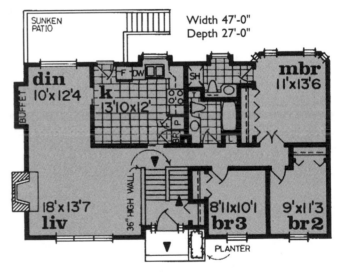

Width 47'-0"
Depth 27'-0"

SUNKEN PATIO

din 10'x12'4

k 13'10x12'

mbr 11'x13'6

18'x13'7 liv

36" HIGH WALL

8'11x10'1 br3

9'x11'3 br2

PLANTER

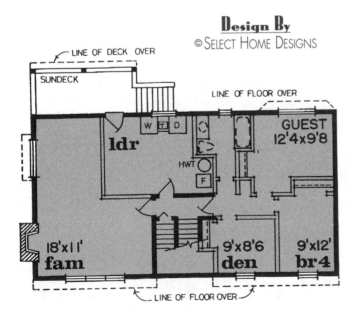

LINE OF DECK OVER

SUNDECK

LINE OF FLOOR OVER

ldr

HWT

GUEST 12'4x9'8

18'x11' fam

9'x8'6 den

9'x12' br4

LINE OF FLOOR OVER

Bold horizontal siding and clean lines make a pleasing exterior for this hillside home. The living room and dining room flow together for a spacious entertaining area. The living room is warmed by a hearth; the dining room has buffet space. The country kitchen is an ideal gathering spot and allows access to a rear deck. The master bedroom is tucked into a window bay and features a private bath. Two additional bedrooms share a full bath. The suggested lower level holds laundry space, plus two additional bedrooms, a den and a large family room with fireplace—an additional 1,122 square feet—when finished. A warm sun deck graces the lower level.

Design Q216

Square Footage: 1,033
Unfinished Lower Level:
1,000 square feet

Unpretentious, but appealing, this home is attractive in its contemporary styling and exterior details. Unfinished space on the lower level adds 1,000 square feet to the floor plan of this design. Use it for an activities room or additional bedrooms as needed in the future. The laundry area is also located here. The main level is complete with a living room with fireplace, family room with rear access, L-shaped kitchen and three bedrooms. The master suite has a half bath, while family bedrooms share a full bath in the hall. A covered carport at the left side of the plan protects your vehicle.

Design By
© Select Home Designs

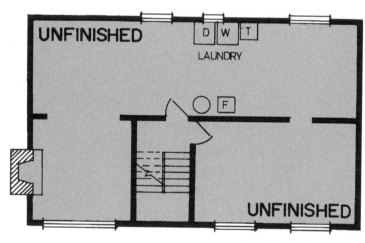

Width 52'-6"
Depth 26'-0"

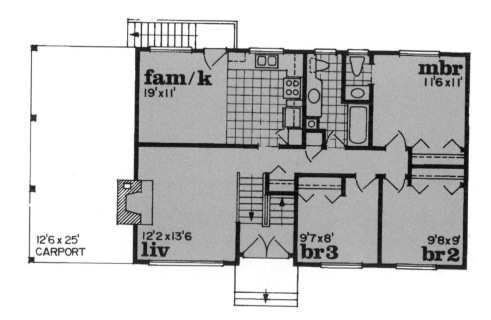

Design By
© DESIGN BASICS, INC.

Width 44'-0"
Depth 30'-8"

DESIGN 7279

Square Footage: 1,201

Hilly sites are easily accommodated by this efficient home. The entry opens to a volume great room with a fireplace and a large boxed window. The conveniently located laundry room is only a half-flight down on the garage level. The well-planned kitchen features a wrapping counter, a corner sink with windows, a pantry, a Lazy Susan and a snack bar serving the sunny dining area. The master bedroom, with walk-in closet space and a compartmented toilet and shower, provides comfort and convenience. Two secondary bedrooms share a full hall bath and enjoy lots of privacy.

Design Q289

Square Footage: 1,299
Unfinished Lower Level:
617 square feet

This elegant split-level home is made even more so with columns at the front entry, further adorned by a half-circular transom window. Railings in the living room overlook the cathedral entry. The living room connects to a formal dining room and is warmed by a fireplace. Look for handy buffet space in the dining room. Sliding glass doors lead out to a deck in the dining room and the breakfast room. The kitchen is U-shaped and holds abundant counter space. Two family bedrooms with box-bay windows join a master suite on the left side of the plan. The master has a private bath, while family bedrooms share a full bath. Space on the lower level—617 square feet—can be developed into a family room with fireplace and sliding glass doors to a covered patio. The laundry is also found on this level and includes a full bath. Note the great storage area in the two-car garage.

Design By
© SELECT HOME DESIGNS

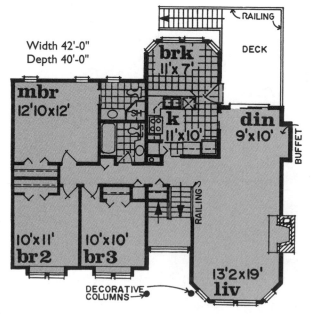

Width 42'-0"
Depth 40'-0"

RAILING

DECK

brk 11'x 7'

mbr 12'10x12'

k 11'x10'

din 9'x10'

BUFFET

SH

RAILING

10'x11' **br 2**

10'x10' **br3**

DECORATIVE COLUMNS

13'2x19' **liv**

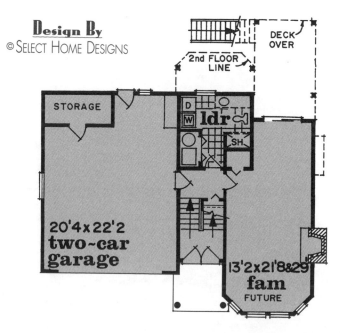

2nd FLOOR LINE

DECK OVER

STORAGE

D W **ldr**

SH

20'4x22'2 **two-car garage**

13'2x21'8&29 **fam** FUTURE

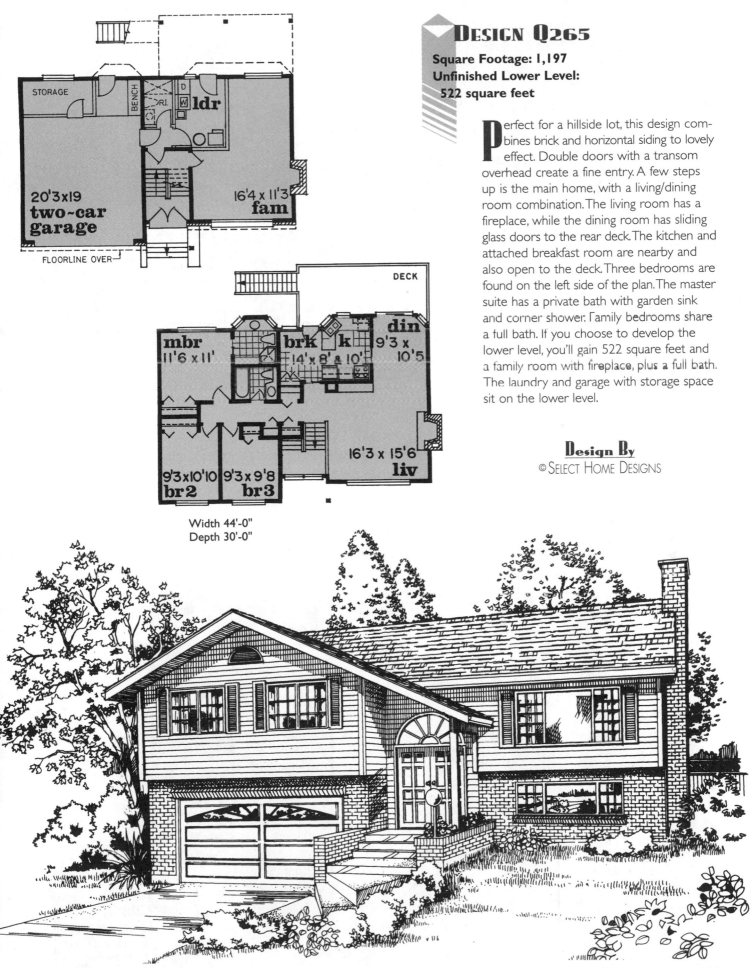

DESIGN Q265

Square Footage: 1,197
Unfinished Lower Level:
522 square feet

STORAGE

BENCH

ldr

D
W

20'3x19
**two-car
garage**

16'4 x 11'3
fam

FLOORLINE OVER

DECK

mbr
11'6 x 11'

brk
14' x 8'

k
& 10'

din
9'3 x
10'5

9'3x10'10
br2

9'3 x 9'8
br3

16'3 x 15'6
liv

Width 44'-0"
Depth 30'-0"

Perfect for a hillside lot, this design combines brick and horizontal siding to lovely effect. Double doors with a transom overhead create a fine entry. A few steps up is the main home, with a living/dining room combination. The living room has a fireplace, while the dining room has sliding glass doors to the rear deck. The kitchen and attached breakfast room are nearby and also open to the deck. Three bedrooms are found on the left side of the plan. The master suite has a private bath with garden sink and corner shower. Family bedrooms share a full bath. If you choose to develop the lower level, you'll gain 522 square feet and a family room with fireplace, plus a full bath. The laundry and garage with storage space sit on the lower level.

Design By
© SELECT HOME DESIGNS

Design Q339

Square Footage: 1,007
Unfinished Lower Level:
1,007 square feet

To accommodate a very narrow lot, this plan can be built without the deck and the garage, though the plan includes the options for both. The lower floor can be finished later into a family room and additional bedrooms and a bath, if you choose. The cathedral entry offers steps up to the main living areas. The living room has a fireplace and leads to the L-shaped kitchen. Here you'll find abundant counter and cupboard space and room for a breakfast table. Sliding glass doors open to the optional deck. Bedrooms include a master suite and two family bedrooms.

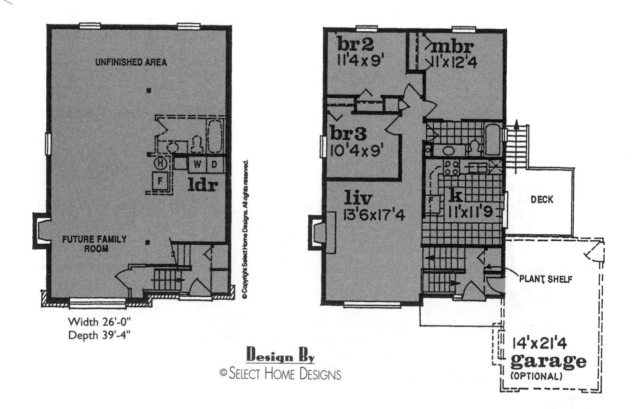

UNFINISHED AREA

ldr

FUTURE FAMILY ROOM

Width 26'-0"
Depth 39'-4"

br2 11'4 x 9'   mbr 11' x 12'4

br3 10'4 x 9'

liv 13'6 x 17'4   k 11' x 11'9   DECK

PLANT SHELF

14' x 21'4 garage (OPTIONAL)

Design By
© SELECT HOME DESIGNS

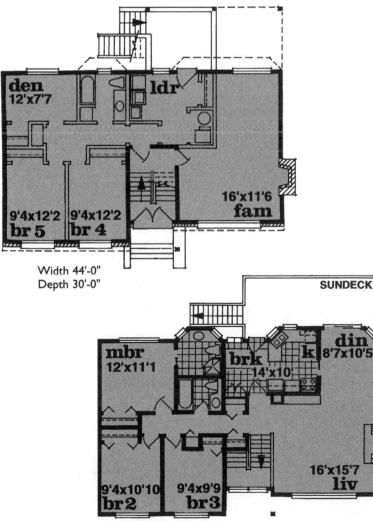

den
12'x7'7

ldr

br 5
9'4x12'2

br 4
9'4x12'2

fam
16'x11'6

Width 44'-0"
Depth 30'-0"

mbr
12'x11'1

brk
14'x10

k

din
8'7x10'5

SUNDECK

br 2
9'4x10'10

br 3
9'4x9'9

liv
16'x15'7

Design Q264

Square Footage: 1,194
Unfinished Lower Level:
1,156 square feet

This traditional design offers not only a great exterior, but plenty of room for expansion in the future. The main level contains an open living room and dining room, warmed by a fireplace and open to the rear deck through sliding glass doors. The kitchen and breakfast room are reached easily from either the living room or dining room and also have access to the deck. The master bedroom and two family bedrooms are on the left side of the plan. The master has its own bath, while family bedrooms share a full bath. The lower level offers 1,156 square feet of unfinished space for two additional bedrooms, a den, a full bath and a family room with fireplace. The laundry room is also on this level.

Design By
© Select Home Designs

DESIGN Q245

Square Footage: 1,047
Unfinished Lower Level:
712 square feet

Design By
© SELECT HOME DESIGNS

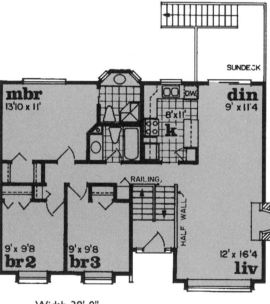

mbr
13'10 x 11'

din
9' x 11'4

SUNDECK

k
8'x11'

RAILING

HALF WALL

br2
9' x 9'8

br3
9' x 9'8

liv
12' x 16'4

Width 38'-0"
Depth 28'-6"

This split-level design offers a single-car garage on the lower level along with space for a family room, extra bedrooms or an in-law suite. The main level has a living room with fireplace that overlooks the vaulted foyer and stretches to a dining area. Sliding glass doors lead out to a sun deck at the back. The kitchen features a counter pass-through to the dining room. Bedrooms are on the left side of the plan. They include a master bedroom with full bath and two bedrooms with a shared bath.

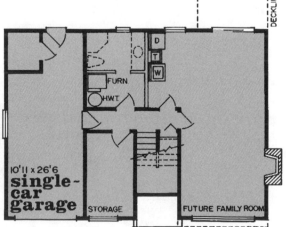

DECKLINE OVER

D
T
W

FURN

HWT

single-car garage
10'11 x 26'6

STORAGE

FUTURE FAMILY ROOM

FLOORLINE OVER

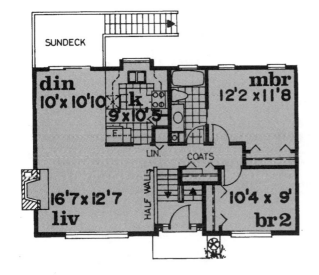

SUNDECK

din
10' x 10'10"

k
9 x 10'5

LIN.

mbr
12'2 x 11'8

COATS

HALF WALL

16'7 x 12'7
liv

10'4 x 9'
br 2

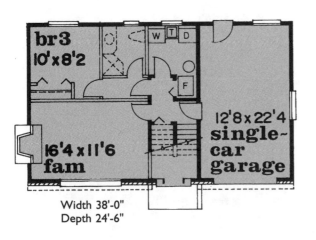

br 3
10' x 8'2

W T D

F

16'4 x 11'6
fam

12'8 x 22'4
single-car garage

Width 38'-0"
Depth 24'-6"

DESIGN Q262

Square Footage: 924
Unfinished Lower Level:
646/736 square feet

This home comes with a choice of two elevations—one has a single-car garage. Finish both with horizontal wood siding and brick for a comfortable, traditional look. The entry opens to a cathedral entry with a half wall separating it from the living room. A fireplace warms this living space. The dining room is attached and has sliding glass doors to a sun deck. The kitchen features a box window over the sink and a U-shaped work area. Two bedrooms sit at the right side of the plan. They share a full bath. If you choose to finish the lower level, you'll gain 646 square feet with the garage or 736 without the garage. One option allows for a bedroom, full bath and family room with fireplace. The other adds another bedroom and a workshop.

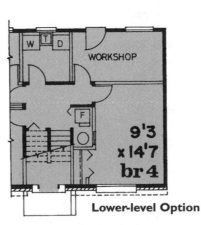

W T D

WORKSHOP

F

9'3 x 14'7
br 4

Lower-level Option

Design By
© SELECT HOME DESIGNS

123

DESIGN 9345

Main Level: 1,499 square feet
Lower Level: 57 square feet
Total: 1,556 square feet

A high-impact entry defines the exterior of this special multi-level home design. A formal dining room with interesting ceiling detail and a boxed window is open to the entry. In the volume great room, homeowners will enjoy a handsome brick fireplace and large windows to the back. Wrapping counters, a corner sink, Lazy Susan and pantry add convenience to the thoughtful kitchen. The adjoining bayed breakfast area has a sloped ceiling and arched transom window. The three bedrooms in this home provide privacy from the main living areas. Two secondary bedrooms share the hall bath. Last, but not least, the master suite offers a vaulted ceiling, skylit dressing/bath area with double vanity, walk-in closet and whirlpool tub.

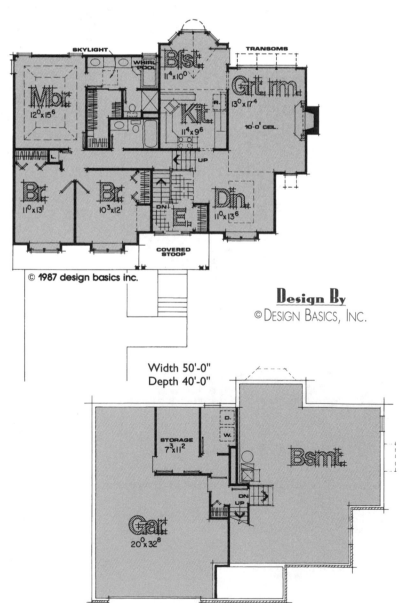

© 1987 design basics inc.

Design By
© DESIGN BASICS, INC.

Width 50'-0"
Depth 40'-0"

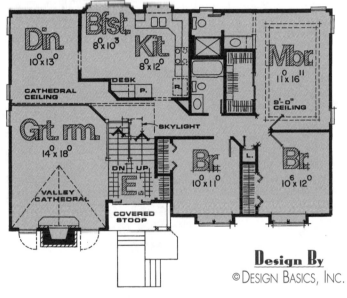

Design By
© DESIGN BASICS, INC.

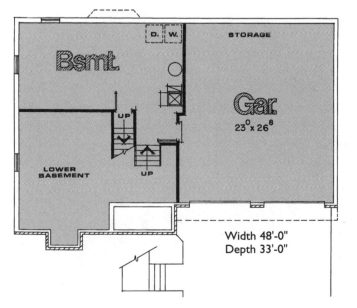

Width 48'-0"
Depth 33'-0"

DESIGN 9291

Square Footage: 1,458

From the volume entry, expansive views of the great room and dining room captivate homeowners and guests. The great room, with a fireplace centered under the valley cathedral ceiling, beckons. An efficient kitchen, which serves the bright dinette, has a pantry and planning desk. The cathedral ceiling in the dining room adds to elegant meals and entertaining. Two secondary bedrooms with boxed windows are accessed by the corridor hallway. Comfort abounds in the master suite with a nine-foot tiered ceiling plus mirrored bi-pass doors for the walk-in closet and a private bath. A garage and basement storage are found on the lower level.

Design Q360

Square Footage: 1,449
Unfinished Lower Level:
1,222 square feet

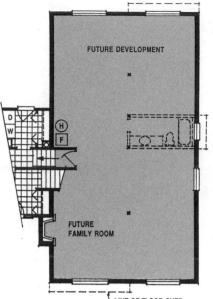

This lovely split-level home offers full livability on one floor with the possibility of expanding to the lower level at a future time. The main living level includes a large living room with optional bay window and a fireplace. The connecting dining room has access directly to the L-shaped kitchen (note that there is space for a breakfast table in the kitchen). Bedrooms are to the rear of the plan and include a master suite with private bath and two family bedrooms sharing a full bath. All three bedrooms have ample wall closets. The laundry is at the entry level, where there are stairs to the lower level as well. When developed, the lower level will include a family room with fireplace, additional bedrooms and a full bath.

FUTURE DEVELOPMENT

D W

H F

FUTURE FAMILY ROOM

LINE OF FLOOR OVER

Design By
© SELECT HOME DESIGNS

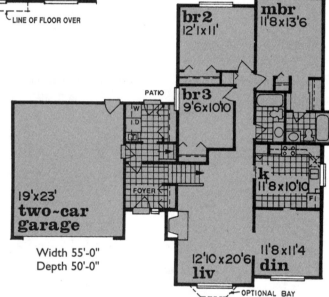

br2
12'1x11'

mbr
11'8x13'6

PATIO

br3
9'6x10'10

W D

19'23'
two-car garage

FOYER

k
11'8x10'10

Width 55'-0"
Depth 50'-0"

12'10x20'6
liv

11'8x11'4
din

OPTIONAL BAY

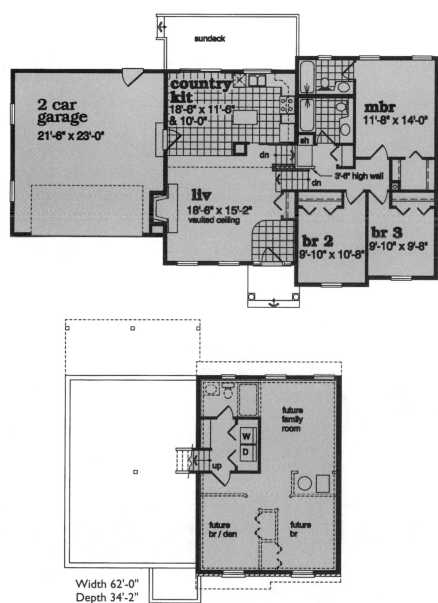

sundeck

country kit
18'-6" x 11'-6" & 10'-0"

2 car garage
21'-6" x 23'-0"

mbr
11'-8" x 14'-0"

liv
18'-6" x 15'-2"
vaulted ceiling

dn

dn

sh

3'-6" high wall

br 2
9'-10" x 10'-8"

br 3
9'-10" x 9'-8"

future family room

W D

up

future br / den

future br

Width 62'-0"
Depth 34'-2"

DESIGN Q467

Square Footage: 1,215

The main entry to this home is well protected by a columned front porch. The living room is vaulted and has a warming fireplace. The vaulted ceiling carries over to the country-style kitchen, which features a work island and a generously sized eating area. A deck just beyond is the perfect spot for outdoor dining. The bedrooms are up a few stairs and include a master suite with walk-in closet and full bath. Two additional bedrooms have wall closets and share the use of a main bath in the hallway. Space on the lower level may be developed later as needs grow. It features area for a family room, and two bedrooms or one bedroom and a den. The laundry room and a full bath are also on this level.

Design By
© Select Home Designs

DESIGN 2608

Main Level: 728 square feet
Upper Level: 874 square feet
Lower Level: 310 square feet
Total: 1,912 square feet

Tri-level living could hardly ask for more than this rustic design has to offer. Not only can you enjoy the three levels but there is also a fourth basement level for bulk storage and, perhaps, a shop area. The interior livability is outstanding. The main level has an L-shaped formal living/dining area with a fireplace in the living room, sliding glass doors in the dining room leading to the upper terrace, a U-shaped kitchen and an informal eating area. Down a few steps to the lower level is the family room with another fireplace and sliding doors to the lower terrace, a washroom and a laundry room. The upper level houses all of the sleeping facilities including three bedrooms, a bath and the master suite.

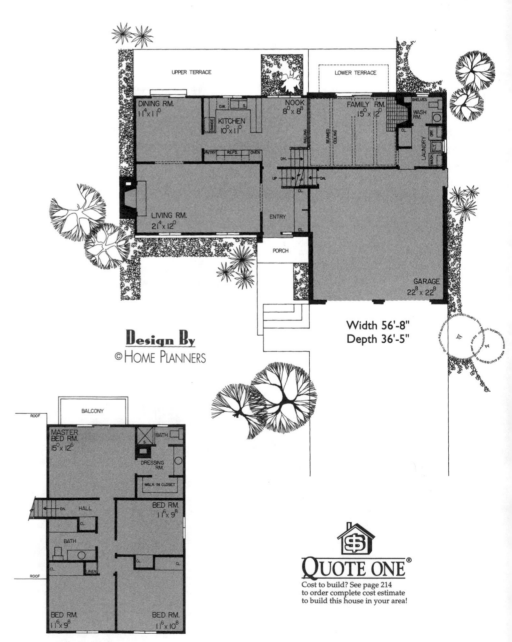

Design By
© HOME PLANNERS

Width 56'-8"
Depth 36'-5"

QUOTE ONE®

Cost to build? See page 214
to order complete cost estimate
to build this house in your area!

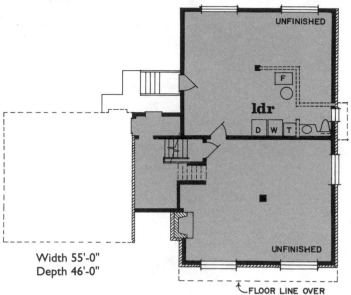

UNFINISHED

F

ldr

D W T

UNFINISHED

Width 55'-0"
Depth 46'-0"

FLOOR LINE OVER

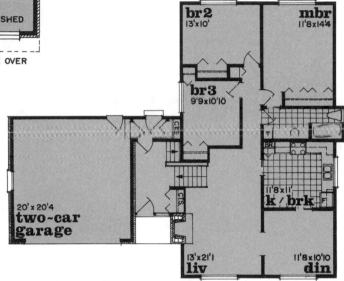

DESIGN Q218

**Square Footage: 1,328
Unfinished Lower Level:
1,081 square feet**

br2
13'x10'

mbr
11'8x14'4

br3
9'9x10'10

11'8x11'

k / brk F

two-car garage
20' x 20'4

13'x21'1
liv

11'8x10'10
din

Design By
© SELECT HOME DESIGNS

Classic split-level design makes this traditional home a perennial favorite in any neighborhood. A weather-protected entry opens to a split staircase leading to main- and lower-level spaces. The lower level remains unfinished until you are ready to turn it into a family room and additional bedrooms. The main level holds a living room with fireplace and a formal dining room near the convenient L-shaped kitchen. Three bedrooms on this level include a master bedroom and two family bedrooms. The two-car garage is connected to the main house via a service entrance that also leads out to the rear yard.

Design Q230

Square Footage: 1,211 square feet
Unfinished Lower Level:
742 square feet

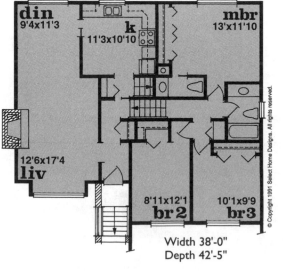

din
9'4x11'3

k
11'3x10'10

mbr
13'x11'10

12'6x17'4
liv

8'11x12'1
br2

10'1x9'9
br3

Width 38'-0"
Depth 42'-5"

PATIO

UNFINISHED AREA

FAM RM

H.W.T.

FURNACE

R.I. FIREPLACE

STOR.

D W

COOLER

20'6x20'6
two~car
garage

Design By
© Select Home Designs

Adorned with horizontal siding and brick, the exterior of this home sports details for a rustic, country appeal. The entry is deep-set for weather protection and opens directly to the open living and dining room area of the home. A fireplace and box-bay window here are added features. The kitchen is also at this level. Its L-shaped configuration is made for convenience and allows space for a breakfast table. Up a few steps are the bedrooms—two family bedrooms and a master suite with full bath. One family bedrooms boasts a walk-in closet. Space on the lower level can be developed into a family room with double-door access to a rear patio, a den or recreation room with fireplace and bedrooms, if you choose. Rough-in plumbing is included for a half bath and the laundry room.

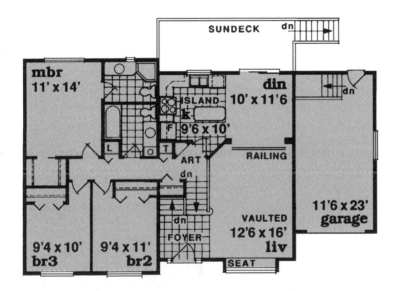

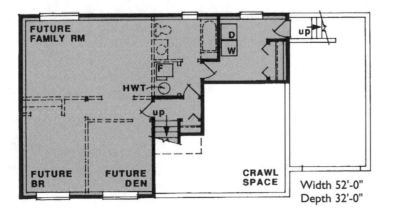

Width 52'-0"
Depth 32'-0"

DESIGN Q423

Square Footage: 1,200
Unfinished Lower Level:
858 square feet

This well-planned split-level home leaves room for expansion in the future. The foyer opens to steps leading both up and down—up to the main level, down to expansion space. The main level holds a living room with window seat and railing that separates it from the dining room. Reach the sun deck through sliding glass doors in the dining room. The L-shaped kitchen is nearby and has an island workspace. Three bedrooms include a master suite with full bath and walk-in closet and two family bedrooms with shared bath. The lower level has 858 square feet of unfinished space that may be developed into a family room, a full bath, a den and a bedroom. The laundry is also found on this level.

Design By
© SELECT HOME DESIGNS

131

DESIGN Q349

Square Footage: 1,257
Unfinished Lower Level: 1,092 square feet

Brick and siding grace the exterior of this split-level design. The recessed entry leads to a skylit foyer that directs traffic to all areas of the plan. The living room has a bay window and fireplace and connects to a formal dining room with kitchen access. The kitchen is L-shaped and saves space for a breakfast table. Bedrooms revolve around a full hall bath with soaking tub. The unfinished lower level can be developed later into a family room, additional bedrooms, a bathroom and a laundry.

Design By
© SELECT HOME DESIGNS

UNFINISHED AREA

ldr

W   D

FUTURE FAMILY ROOM

◄── LINE OF BAY WINDOW OVER

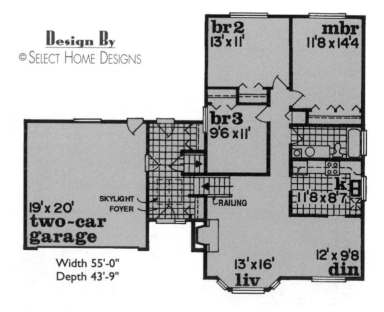

br 2
13'x11'

mbr
11'8 x 14'4

br 3
9'6 x 11'

19'x20'
**two~car
garage**

SKYLIGHT
FOYER

RAILING

k
11'8 x 8'7

Width 55'-0"
Depth 43'-9"

13'x16'
liv

12' x 9'8
din

DESIGN Q266

Square Footage: 1,247 square feet
Unfinished Lower Level:
745 square feet

Design By
© SELECT HOME DESIGNS

The stylish good looks of this traditional split-level home make it a wonderful choice for any family. The front veranda opens to a spacious living and dining room. The living features a fireplace; the dining room has hutch space and double doors to a rear deck. An L-shaped kitchen is nearby. Three bedrooms on this level include a master suite with private bath and walk-in closet. Two family bedrooms share a full hall bath. The lower level has a family room with fireplace, a laundry area with half bath and additional unfinished space for more bedrooms or a home office. The two-car garage sits at the lower level.

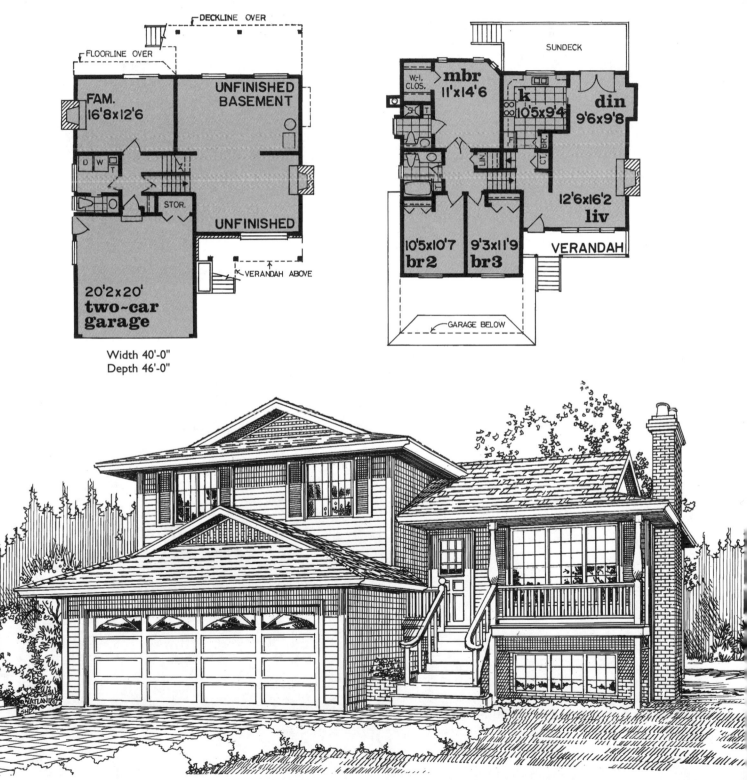

DECKLINE OVER

FLOORLINE OVER

FAM.
16'8x12'6

UNFINISHED BASEMENT

D W

STOR.

UNFINISHED

VERANDAH ABOVE

20'2x20'
two-car garage

Width 40'-0"
Depth 46'-0"

SUNDECK

W-I. CLOS.

mbr
11'x14'6

k
10'5x9'4

din
9'6x9'8

LIN.

CT. BR.

12'6x16'2
liv

10'5x10'7
br2

9'3x11'9
br3

VERANDAH

GARAGE BELOW

© American Home Gallery, Ltd.

Design T109

Square Footage: 1,770
Lower-Level Storage: 516 square feet

Design By
Stephen Fuller

Perfect for sloping sites, this European-style plan includes living areas on one level and bedrooms on another. The great room contains a fireplace and access to the rear deck. Close by are the U-shaped kitchen and breakfast room with a boxed window. The formal dining room completes the living area and is open to the entry foyer. Bedrooms are a few steps up from the living area and include a master suite with two walk-in closets and a sumptuous bath with a compartmented toilet. Secondary bedrooms share a full bath with a double-bowl vanity. On the lower level is garage and bonus space that may be used later for additional bedrooms or casual gathering areas. This home is designed with a basement foundation.

Width 48'-0"
Depth 47'-5"

DECK   DN

BREAKFAST
11'-4" X 7'-4"

GREAT ROOM
14'-0" X 19'-6"

MASTER
BEDROOM
12'-6" X 16'-0"

W.I.C.

MASTER
BATH

KITCHEN
11'-4" X 12'-0"

W.I.C.

W.I.C.

UP

DN

DINING ROOM
11'-4" X 12'-6"

FOYER
5'-0" X 8'-8"

POWDER

COAT

LAUNDRY

BEDROOM NO. 3
12'-0" X 11'-0"

STOOP

BATH

BEDROOM NO. 2
12'-9" X 11'-9"

Quote One®

Cost to build? See page 214
to order complete cost estimate
to build this house in your area!

134

© American Home Gallery, Ltd.

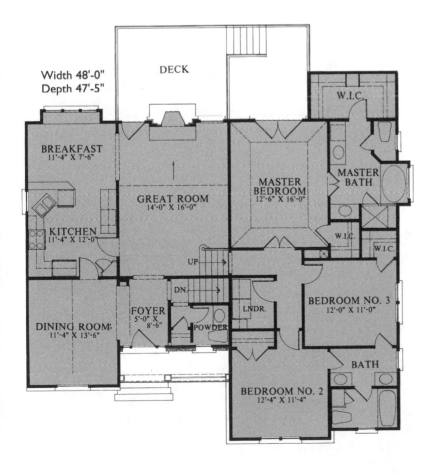

Width 48'-0"
Depth 47'-5"

DECK

BREAKFAST
11'-4" X 7'-6"

GREAT ROOM
14'-0" X 16'-0"

MASTER
BEDROOM
12'-6" X 16'-0"

MASTER
BATH

W.I.C.

KITCHEN
11'-4" X 12'-0"

W.I.C.

W.I.C.

UP

DN

FOYER
5'-0" X
8'-6"

LNDR.

BEDROOM NO. 3
12'-0" X 11'-0"

POWDER

DINING ROOM
11'-4" X 13'-6"

BATH

BEDROOM NO. 2
12'-4" X 11'-4"

DESIGN T137

Square Footage: 1,770
Lower-Level Storage: 516 square feet

Design By
STEPHEN FULLER

Wood frame, weatherboard siding and stacked stone give this home its country cottage appeal. The concept is reinforced by the double elliptical arched front porch, the Colonial balustrade and the roof-vent dormer. Inside, the foyer leads to the great room and the dining room. The well-planned kitchen easily serves the breakfast room. A rear deck makes outdoor living extra enjoyable. The bi-level nature of the home puts three bedrooms upstairs. They include a master suite with a tray ceiling and a luxurious bath. The two secondary bedrooms share a compartmented bath. A basement foundation provides extra storage.

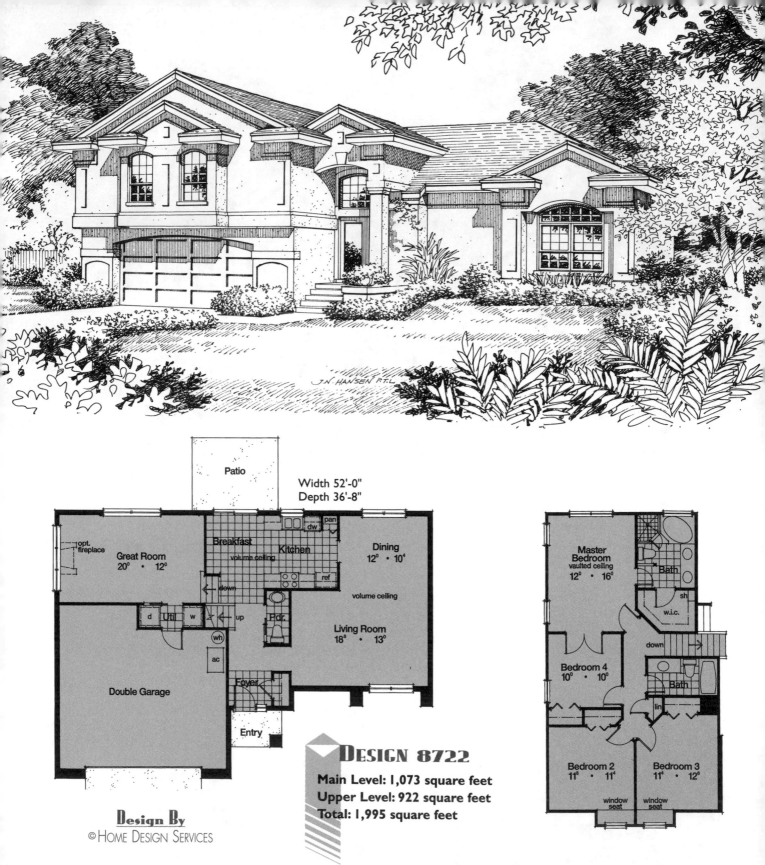

Width 52'-0"
Depth 36'-8"

Patio

Great Room
20⁰ • 12⁰

opt. fireplace

Breakfast
volume ceiling

Kitchen

pan
dw

Dining
12⁰ • 10⁴

ref

volume ceiling

Living Room
18⁸ • 13⁰

down

Uti
d   w

up

Pdr.

wh

ac

Double Garage

Foyer

Entry

Master Bedroom
vaulted ceiling
12⁰ • 16⁰

Bath

sh

w.i.c.

down

Bedroom 4
10⁰ • 10⁰

Bath

lin

Bedroom 2
11⁸ • 11⁴

Bedroom 3
11⁴ • 12⁶

window seat

window seat

DESIGN 8722

Main Level: 1,073 square feet
Upper Level: 922 square feet
Total: 1,995 square feet

Design By
© HOME DESIGN SERVICES

This efficient plan offers ample living spaces, with an L-shaped formal living/dining room. The kitchen is well designed for the frugal gourmet and the nook has a view of the rear yard and family room below. Just off the foyer is a convenient powder room and staircase up to the bedroom wing, while a set of stairs also leads down to the family room that can have a fireplace. An efficient laundry room design leads into the generous two-car garage. Once upstairs, the

three- or-four bedroom version can be chosen to suit your family's needs, and both designs are thoughtful and make the best use of space. Note the two front bedrooms with their window seats, which not only add thoughtful space but also create a distinctive elevation treatment. Both master bedroom configurations are big on luxury, especially in their respective bath layouts.

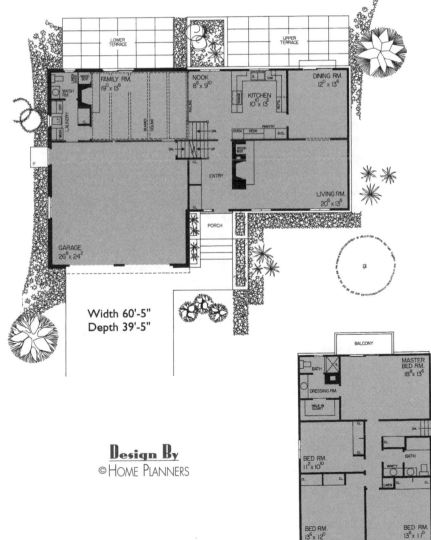

Width 60'-5"
Depth 39'-5"

Design By
© HOME PLANNERS

DESIGN 2624

Main Level: 904 square feet
Upper Level: 1,120 square feet
Lower Level: 404 square feet
Total: 2,428 square feet

L D

This is tri-level living at its best. The exterior is that of the most popular Tudor styling—a facade that will hold its own for many a year to come. Livability will be achieved to its maximum on the four (including basement) levels. The occupants of the master bedroom can enjoy the outdoors on their private balcony. Additional outdoor enjoyment can be gained on the two terraces. That family room is more than 19' x 13' and includes a beamed ceiling and fireplace with wood box. Its formal companion, the living room, is similar in size and also will have the added warmth of a fireplace.

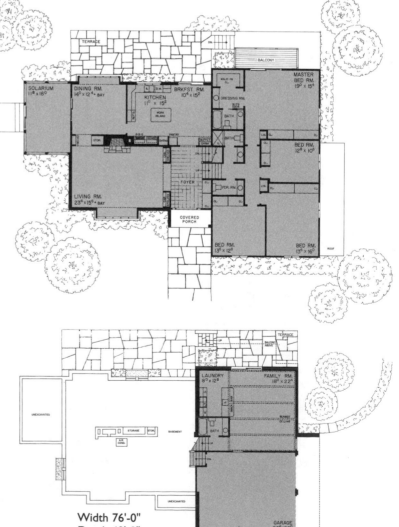

Design 2254

Main Level: 1,220 square feet
Upper Level: 1,344 square feet
Lower Level: 659 square feet
Total: 3,223 square feet

Tudoresque down to the curved half timbers and diamond-paned windows, this multi-level is a classic design with a thoroughly modern floor plan. Centers of attention include a large foyer, a big kitchen and breakfast area, a splendidly large living room with a fireplace and a bay window, a formal dining room and a sun room. Upstairs are four bedrooms—one a master suite with a private balcony. The lower level has a family room, a built-in snack bar and access to a terrace out back.

Design By
© Home Planners

Width 76'-0"
Depth 48'-0"

DESIGN 2788

Main Level: 1,795 square feet
Lower Level: 866 square feet
Total: 2,661 square feet

Design By
© HOME PLANNERS

This pleasing Tudor design accommodates the sloping site well. On the upper level, a large living room with a fireplace will make gatherings a real pleasure. The formal dining room is easily served by the efficient kitchen. Three bedrooms include a master bedroom suite with two closets, a private bath and a dressing room. On the lower level, a family room and a study further livability. The two-car garage opens to the side.

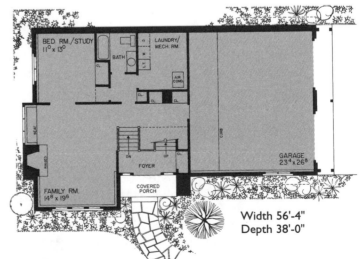

Width 56'-4"
Depth 38'-0"

Design By
© ALAN MASCORD
DESIGN ASSOCIATES, INC.

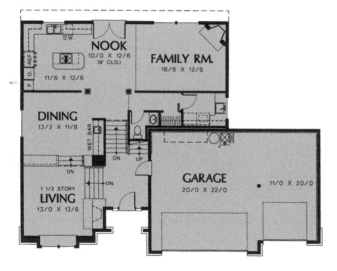

Width 45'-0"
(56'-0" with 3-car garage)
Depth 45'-0"

DESIGN 7421

Main Level: 1,255 square feet
Upper Level: 982 square feet
Total: 2,237 square feet

This Mediterranean-flavored contemporary is sure to please with its many amenities. From the raised foyer, a living room with the option for a fireplace and a 1½-story ceiling flows into the formal dining room. A spacious family room, with a corner fireplace and windows to the rear yard, works well with the island kitchen and eating nook. Upstairs, three family bedrooms share a full bath. A master bedroom suite features a walk-in closet and a private bath. A three-car garage shelters the family fleet.

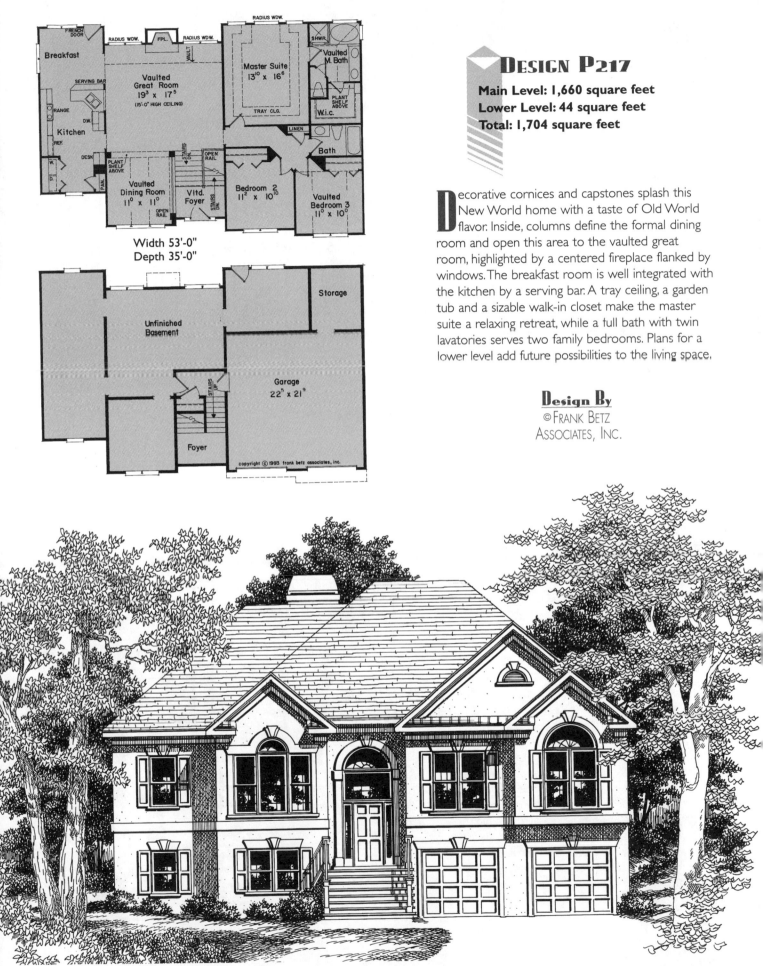

DESIGN P217

Main Level: 1,660 square feet
Lower Level: 44 square feet
Total: 1,704 square feet

Decorative cornices and capstones splash this New World home with a taste of Old World flavor. Inside, columns define the formal dining room and open this area to the vaulted great room, highlighted by a centered fireplace flanked by windows. The breakfast room is well integrated with the kitchen by a serving bar. A tray ceiling, a garden tub and a sizable walk-in closet make the master suite a relaxing retreat, while a full bath with twin lavatories serves two family bedrooms. Plans for a lower level add future possibilities to the living space.

Design By
© FRANK BETZ
ASSOCIATES, INC.

Width 53'-0"
Depth 35'-0"

Breakfast

Vaulted Great Room
19³ x 17⁵
(15'-0" HIGH CEILING)

Kitchen

Master Suite
13¹⁰ x 16⁶

Vaulted M. Bath

W.i.c.

Bath

Vaulted Dining Room
11⁰ x 11⁰

Vltd. Foyer

Bedroom 2
11² x 10¹⁰

Vaulted Bedroom 3
11⁰ x 10⁰

Unfinished Basement

Storage

Garage
22⁵ x 21⁹

Foyer

copyright © 1993 frank betz associates, inc.

Design T093

Square Footage: 1,770
Lower-Level Storage: 517 square feet

Design By
Stephen Fuller

Perfect for a hillside lot, this split-level plan has three distinct levels: basement, sleeping and living. The basement is undeveloped space but could be used for any number of activities if needed. The sleeping level holds two family bedrooms and a master suite with plenty of amenities. Its bath is truly opulent with a corner tub, double vanity, walk-in closet and separate shower. The family bedrooms each have a walk-in closet and share a full bath. The living areas include a formal dining room, family room and kitchen with breakfast nook. Special items include the fireplace in the family room and the columns that separate the dining and family rooms. This home is designed with a basement foundation.

BREAKFAST
10'-10" X 9'-4"

MASTER BATH

FAMILY ROOM
14'-0" X 19'-0"

KITCHEN
0'-10" X 11'-0"

MASTER BEDROOM
13'-0" X 15'-6"

W.I.C.

DINING ROOM
13'-6" X 10'-6"

FOYER
7'-6" X 18'-0"

BATH

BEDROOM NO.2
12'-0" X 10'-6"

Width 49'-6"
Depth 47'-0"

STOOP

BEDROOM NO.1
12'-0" X 10'-0"

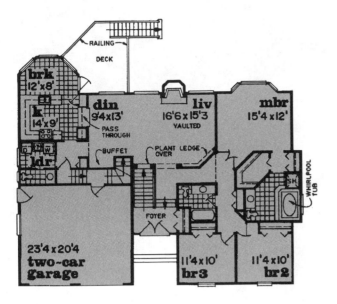

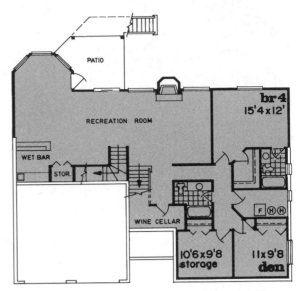

Width 58'-4"
Depth 48'-0"

Design By
© SELECT HOME DESIGNS

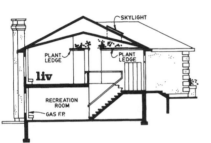

DESIGN Q324

Square Footage: 1,816
Unfinished Lower Level:
1,725 square feet

This design works perfectly for a lot that slopes to the rear— you can finish the walk-out basement at a later time to include extra living and sleeping space. The main level begins with a skylit foyer, with planter ledge, stepping up to the spacious living and dining rooms. A pass-through in the dining room separates it from the U-shaped kitchen and attached breakfast nook. A door in the nook leads out to the rear deck. Three bedrooms on the right side of the plan include a master suite with bay window, walk-in closet and full bath with whirlpool tub. Family bedrooms share a full hall bath. If you choose, you may also build this home on one level with a crawlspace foundation.

DESIGN 9576

Main Level: 1,894 square feet
Upper Level: 1,544 square feet
Total: 3,438 square feet

Sleek, contemporary lines define the exterior of this home. Steps lead up a front-sloping lot to the bright entry. A front-facing den is brightly lit by a curving wall of windows. Built-ins enhance the utility of this room. A two-story living room offers a fireplace and lots of windows. The nearby dining room is capped by an elegant ceiling. The kitchen serves a sunny breakfast nook and an oversized family room. The family will find plenty of sleeping space with four bedrooms on the second level. The master bedroom suite is a real attention-getter. Its roomy bath includes a spa tub and a separate shower.

Design By
© ALAN MASCORD
DESIGN ASSOCIATES, INC.

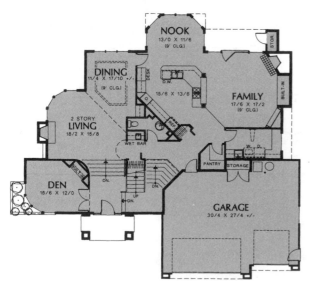

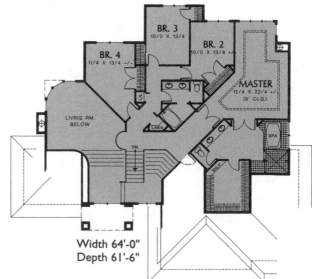

Width 64'-0"
Depth 61'-6"

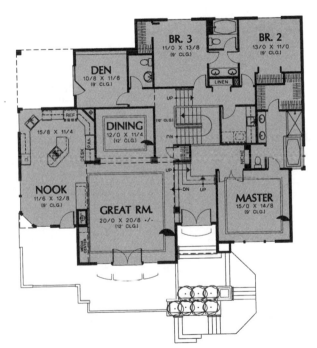

DEN
10/8 X 11/8
(9' CLG.)

BR. 3
11/0 X 13/8
(9' CLG.)

BR. 2
13/0 X 11/0
(9' CLG.)

LINEN

REF

15/8 X 11/4

DINING
12/0 X 11/4
(12' CLG.)

UP

DESK

PAN.

NICHE

NOOK
11/6 X 12/8
(9' CLG.)

GREAT RM.
20/0 X 20/8 -/-
(12' CLG.)

MASTER
15/0 X 14/8
(9' CLG.)

MEDIA
CENTER

UP

DN   UP

DESIGN 7412

Main Level: 2,412 square feet
Lower Level: 130 square feet
Total: 2,542 square feet

Design By
© ALAN MASCORD
DESIGN ASSOCIATES, INC.

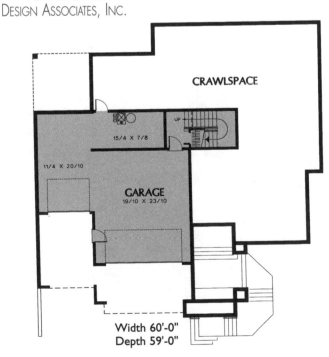

CRAWLSPACE

15/4 X 7/8

UP

11/4 X 20/10

GARAGE
19/10 X 23/10

Width 60'-0"
Depth 59'-0"

A grand great room sets the tone for this fabulous floor plan, with an elegant tray ceiling and French doors to a private front balcony. With windows and glass panels to take in the view, this design would make an exquisite seaside resort. The formal dining room is off the center of the plan for privacy, and is served by a nearby gourmet kitchen. Three steps up from the foyer, the sleeping level includes a spacious master suite with a sizable private bath. Each of two additional bedrooms has private access to a shared bath with two vanities.

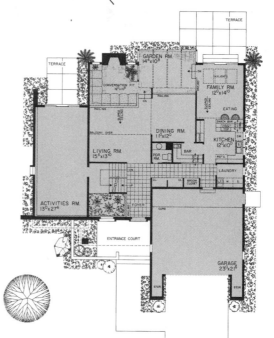

DESIGN 2901

Main Level: 2,114 square feet
Upper Level: 419 square feet
Total: 2,533 square feet

L

This luxurious three-bedroom home offers comfort on many levels. Its modern design incorporates a rear garden room and conversation pit off a living and dining room plus skylights in an adjacent family room with high sloped ceiling. Other features include an entrance court, an activities room, a convenient kitchen, an upper lounge and a master bedroom.

Design By
© HOME PLANNERS

Rear View

Width 54'-0"
Depth 63'-8"

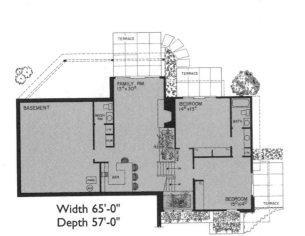

Rear View

Width 65'-0"
Depth 57'-0"

Design By
© Home Planners

Design 2679

Main Level: 1,860 square feet
Lower Level: 1,323 square feet
Total: 3,183 square feet

This spacious modern contemporary home offers plenty of livability on many levels. The main level includes a breakfast room in addition to a dining room. Adjacent is a sloped-ceilinged living room with raised hearth. The upper level features an isolated master bedroom suite with adjoining study or sitting room and a balcony. The family room level includes a long rectangular family room with an adjoining terrace on one end and a bar with a washroom at the other end. A spacious basement is included. Two other bedrooms are positioned in the lower level with their own view of the terrace. The rear deck provides lots of space for outdoor entertaining and relaxation.

DESIGN
HPTHH20006

First Floor: 897 square feet
Second Floor: 740 square feet
Total: 1,637 square feet

Clever use of space puts the two-car garage on the lower level of this home, but allows access to living and sleeping areas above. A combination living/dining room is found on the main level and is warmed by a fireplace flanked by built-in bookcases. The island kitchen has an attached nook surrounded by glass to overlook the rear yard. Bedrooms are on the upper level and include an owners suite and two family bedrooms. The owners suite has a full bath and two walk-in closets. Family bedrooms share a full bath.

Width 30'-0"
Depth 42'-6"

Design by
©ALAN MASCORD DESIGN
ASSOCIATES, INC.

DESIGN 4308

Main Level: 1,494 square feet
Upper Level: 597 square feet
Lower Level: 1,035 square feet
Total: 3,126 square feet

L

You can't help but feel spoiled by this design. Downstairs from the entry is a large living room with sloped ceiling and fireplace. Nearby is the U-shaped kitchen with a pass-through to the dining room. Also on this level, the master suite boasts a fireplace and a sliding glass door onto the deck. The living and dining rooms also feature deck access. Upstairs are two bedrooms and a shared bath. A balcony sitting area overlooks the living room. Finish the lower level when your budget and space needs allow. It includes a play room with a fireplace, a half bath, a large bar and sliding glass doors onto the patio.

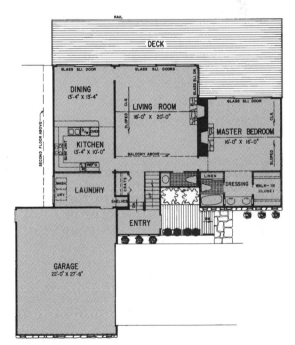

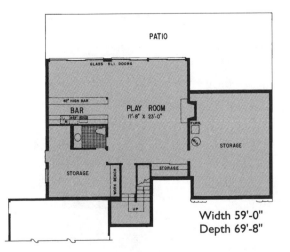

Width 59'-0"
Depth 69'-8"

Design By
© HOME PLANNERS

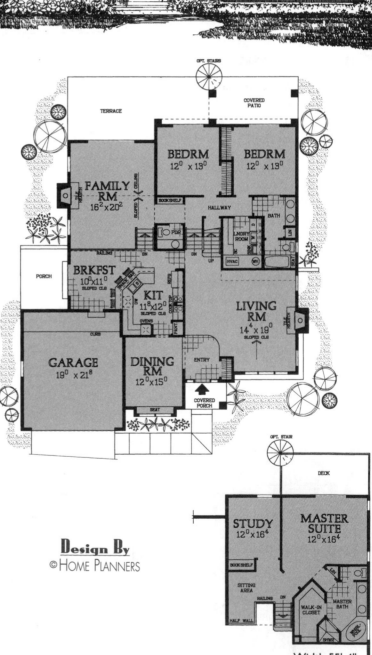

DESIGN 3493

Main Level: 2,024 square feet
Upper Level: 717 square feet
Total: 2,741 square feet

L

As you enter this charming country home, you are greeted with warmth and livability. The dining room, to the left of the entry, includes a window seat and connects to the kitchen with its snack bar to the breakfast area and to the sunken family room beyond. The family room features a central fireplace and access to the back terrace. Beyond the formal living room are two family bedrooms with access to the terrace, a covered patio and a shared full bath. The luxurious master bedroom is located on the second floor for privacy and features a separate study and sitting area, a private deck and an amenity-filled master bath.

QUOTE ONE®

Cost to build? See page 214
to order complete cost estimate
to build this house in your area!

Design By
© HOME PLANNERS

Width 55'-4"
Depth 57'-8"

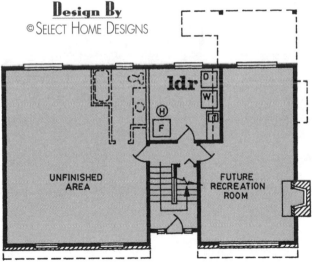

ldr

UNFINISHED
AREA

FUTURE
RECREATION
ROOM

DESIGN Q312

Main Level: 1,235 square feet
Entry: 93 square feet
Total: 1,328 square feet
Unfinished Lower Level:
1,161 square feet

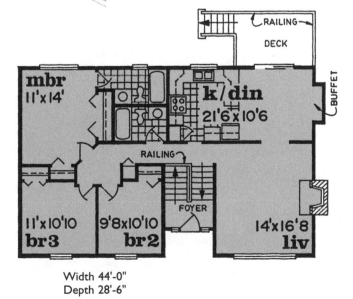

RAILING

DECK

BUFFET

mbr
11' x 14'

k/din
21'6 x 10'6

RAILING

br3
11'x10'10

br2
9'8x10'10

FOYER

liv
14'x16'8

Width 44'-0"
Depth 28'-6"

Horizontal siding and brick lead to an entry that boasts a half-round window over its door. A cathedral ceiling is found in the foyer, leading upstairs to the main living level. Amenities include a living room with masonry fireplace, a dining room with buffet space and sliding glass doors to the rear terrace, and a U-shaped kitchen open to the dinette. The master bedroom features a large wall closet and private bath. Family bedrooms sit to the front and share a bath. The lower level has 1,161 square feet of unfinished space for a recreation room with fireplace, additional bedrooms, a full bath or even a home office. The laundry is also found here.

Design By
© Select Home Designs

Quote One®

Cost to build? See page 214
to order complete cost estimate
to build this house in your area!

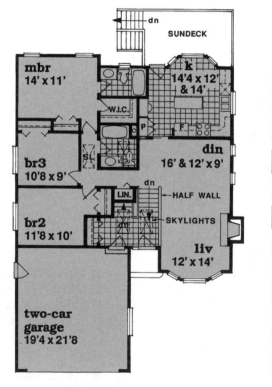

mbr
14' x 11'

W.I.C.

br3
10'8 x 9'

br2
11'8 x 10'

two-car
garage
19'4 x 21'8

dn

SUNDECK

k
14'4 x 12'
& 14'

P

F

din
16' & 12' x 9'

LIN.

HALF WALL

SKYLIGHTS

liv
12' x 14'

dn

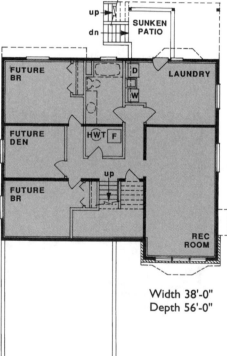

up

dn

SUNKEN
PATIO

FUTURE
BR

LAUNDRY

D

W

FUTURE
DEN

HWT F

FUTURE
BR

up

REC
ROOM

Width 38'-0"
Depth 56'-0"

Design Q426

Square Footage: 1,325
Unfinished Lower Level:
1,272 square feet

A lovely bay window and a recessed entry, complemented
by vertical wood siding enhance the exterior of this
split level. Skylights brighten the entry foyer and staircase to the main level. A half wall separates the staircase
and the living room—note the fireplace in the living
room. The dining area connects to an L-shaped kitchen
with breakfast bay and access to the rear sun deck. Three

bedrooms line the left side of the plan. The master suite
has a full bath and walk-in closet. Family bedrooms share
a full bath just off a skylit hall. The lower level contains
1,272 square feet of unfinished space that can be developed into two additional bedrooms, a full bath, a den and
a recreation room. The laundry is also on this level and
offers access to a sunken patio.

Br.3
10⁷ x 10⁰

Br.4
11⁰ x 10⁰

UNFINISHED
STORAGE

D.   W.

**Fam.
rm.**
15⁹ x 18³

UP

STORAGE

DESIGN 7277

Main Level: 962 square feet
Lower Level: 668 square feet
Total: 1,630 square feet

Design By
© DESIGN BASICS, INC.

Br.2
10⁰ x 10⁰

Mbr.
12⁶ x 14⁰

Kit.
9⁰ x 10¹

Din.

SNACK
BAR

SHELVES

SLOPED
CEILING

Gar.
11³ x 21³

Grt.
16⁴ x 21⁰

DN   UP

COVERED
STOOP

Width 32'-0"
Depth 46'-0"

© design basics inc.

Ideal for a mountain or lakeside retreat, this efficient plan gives an elegant touch to vacation living. In the expansive great room, a sloped ceiling and a warming hearth combine for the best in both formal and informal living. The kitchen forms a snack bar for impromptu dining. The master bedroom views the rear grounds through two windows. A second bedroom shares a full hall bath with the master bedroom. Downstairs, a family room is ready to house fun and games. Bedrooms 3 and 4 share a full bath. A laundry room and a one-car garage with built-in shelves finish the plan.

DESIGN Q342

Square Footage: 1,184
Unfinished Lower Level:
902 square feet

This affordable home is not only appealing, but is well suited to a narrow lot. The entry level hosts a skylit foyer and a spacious living room with box-bay window, fireplace and multi-paned windows. Up a few steps is the L-shaped kitchen with pantry, breakfast room, island work center and French doors to a rear patio. The master bedroom at the rear of the plan has a private bath and linen closet, while the two family bedrooms share a full bath. Lower-level space can be developed to include a recreation room or games room, an additional bedroom and a full bath. Note the large storage area here, as well as laundry space. A two-car garage sits in front of the bedrooms to protect them from street noise.

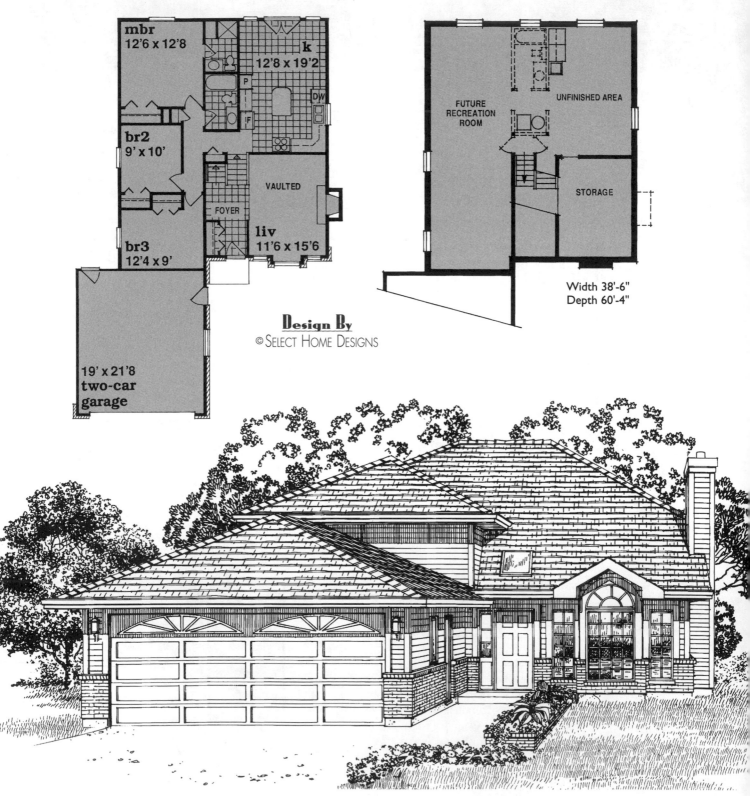

mbr
12'6 x 12'8

k
12'8 x 19'2

P

DW

F

br2
9' x 10'

VAULTED

FOYER

liv
11'6 x 15'6

br3
12'4 x 9'

19' x 21'8
**two-car
garage**

**FUTURE
RECREATION
ROOM**

UNFINISHED AREA

STORAGE

Width 38'-6"
Depth 60'-4"

Design By
© Select Home Designs

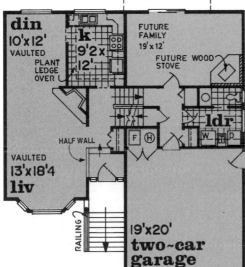

din		
10'x12'		FUTURE FAMILY
VAULTED	**k**	19' x 12'
PLANT LEDGE OVER	9'2 x 12'	FUTURE WOOD STOVE

HALF WALL

VAULTED
13'x18'4
liv

ldr
W D

F H

RAILING

19'x20'
two-car garage

Width 40'-0"
Depth 45'-0"

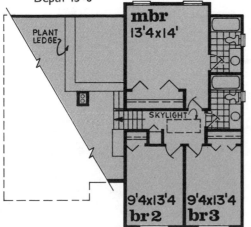

PLANT LEDGE

mbr
13'4x14'

SKYLIGHT

9'4x13'4
br2

9'4x13'4
br3

DESIGN Q315

Main Level: 634 square feet
Upper Level: 749 square feet
Total: 1,383 square feet
Bonus Room: 435 square feet

Finished in brick and horizontal siding, this split-level design is as appealing on the outside as it is livable on the inside. Begin with a foyer beyond the entry that spills over into a living room with bay window and dining room. Both formal rooms have vaulted ceilings. The L-shaped kitchen has a double sink with window. To the rear is space for a family room in the future, if desired. It has a corner wood stove and rear-deck access. The upper level holds bedrooms—two family bedrooms and a master suite. The master bedroom has a private bath, while family bedrooms share a hall bath. Space on the lower level may be developed later for even more living space.

Design By
© SELECT HOME DESIGNS

DESIGN P451

Main Level: 1,440 square feet
Lower Level: 118 square feet
Total: 1,558 square feet

This unique split-level design features its livability on a level above the ground-level basement and opens with a split staircase at the entry. Take steps down to the lower level where there is a two-car garage, storage and an unfinished area that could become additional bedrooms or activity rooms. The main level holds vaulted dining and great rooms on one side and bedrooms on the other. The great room has a fireplace and is separated from the dining room by a plant ledge. The kitchen sits in the middle of the home and has a large breakfast nook with windows overlooking the rear yard. The master suite is luxurious with a tray ceiling, walk-in closet and bath with separate tub and shower and dual sinks. Two family bedrooms are nearby and share a full bath.

Design By
© FRANK BETZ
ASSOCIATES, INC.

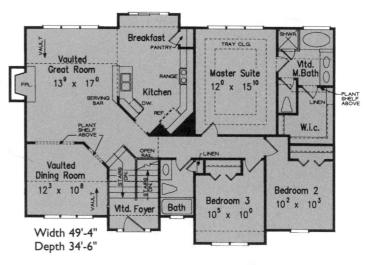

Width 49'-4"
Depth 34'-6"

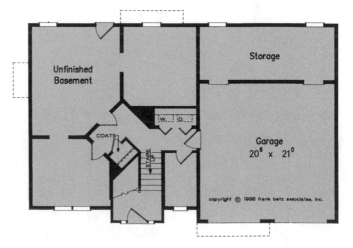

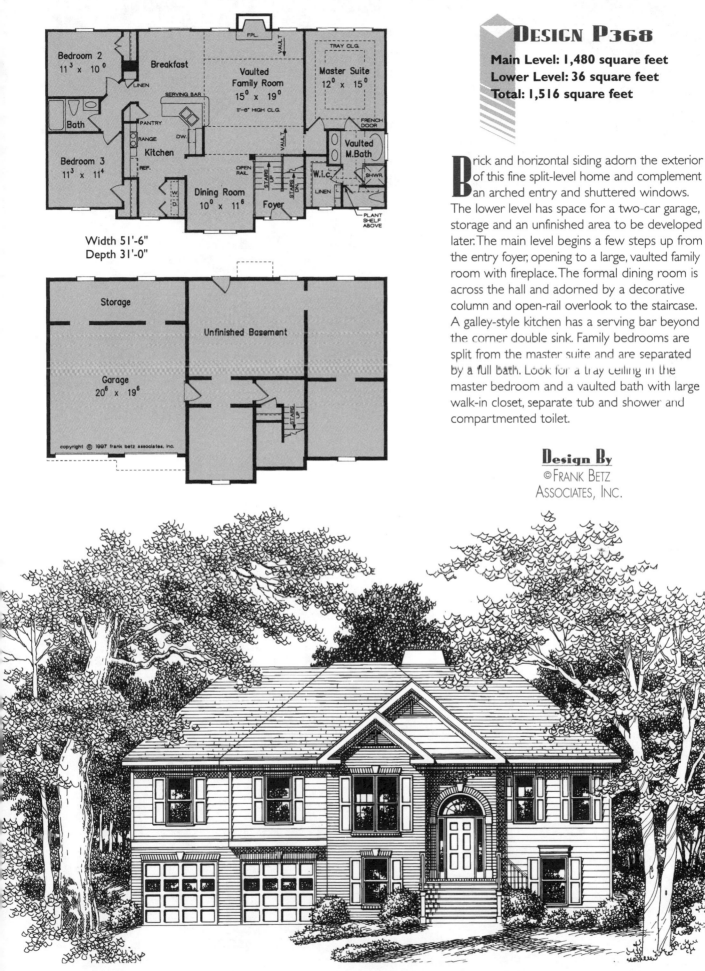

Bedroom 2
11³ x 10⁰

Breakfast

FPL.

VAULT

Vaulted Family Room
15⁰ x 19⁰
11'-8" HIGH CLG.

TRAY CLG.

Master Suite
12⁰ x 15⁰

LINEN

SERVING BAR

Bath

PANTRY

RANGE

DW.

FRENCH DOOR

VAULT

Vaulted M.Bath

Bedroom 3
11³ x 11⁴

Kitchen

REF.

OPEN RAIL

STAIRS UP

STAIRS DN

W.I.C.

LINEN

SHWR.

W
D

Dining Room
10⁰ x 11⁶

Foyer

PLANT SHELF ABOVE

Width 51'-6"
Depth 31'-0"

Storage

Unfinished Basement

Garage
20⁶ x 19⁶

STAIRS UP

copyright © 1997 frank betz associates, inc.

DESIGN P368

Main Level: 1,480 square feet
Lower Level: 36 square feet
Total: 1,516 square feet

Brick and horizontal siding adorn the exterior of this fine split-level home and complement an arched entry and shuttered windows. The lower level has space for a two-car garage, storage and an unfinished area to be developed later. The main level begins a few steps up from the entry foyer, opening to a large, vaulted family room with fireplace. The formal dining room is across the hall and adorned by a decorative column and open-rail overlook to the staircase. A galley-style kitchen has a serving bar beyond the corner double sink. Family bedrooms are split from the master suite and are separated by a full bath. Look for a tray ceiling in the master bedroom and a vaulted bath with large walk-in closet, separate tub and shower and compartmented toilet.

Design By
© FRANK BETZ
ASSOCIATES, INC.

Design P415

Main Level: 1,365 square feet
Lower Level: 20 square feet
Total: 1,385 square feet

Design By
© Frank Betz
Associates, Inc.

With unfinished space on the lower level of this traditional split-level home, you can expand the livability to include additional bedrooms or living areas. The two-car garage is also found at this level. Reach the main level via stairs in the lower level or through the arched, raised entry in the front. The vaulted family room is defined by an arched opening with a plant shelf above. French doors near the family-room hearth lead to the rear yard. The kitchen and vaulted dining room combine to create one large area. Note the pass-through from the kitchen to the family room. Bedrooms are clustered to the left of the plan and include a master suite and two family bedrooms. Besides a tray ceiling in the master bedroom, this retreat features His and Hers walk-in closets and a bath with vaulted ceiling, separate tub and shower and compartmented toilet.

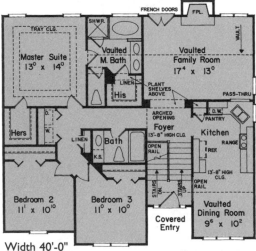

Width 40'-0"
Depth 38'-4"

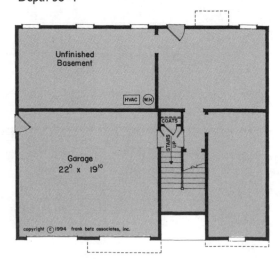

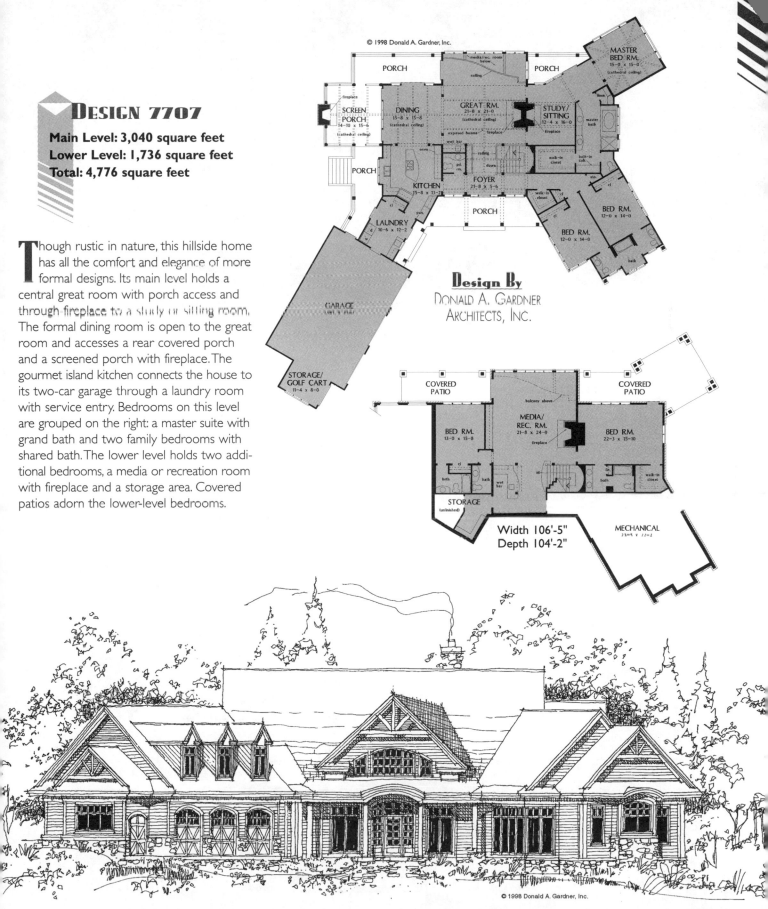

DESIGN 7707

Main Level: 3,040 square feet
Lower Level: 1,736 square feet
Total: 4,776 square feet

Though rustic in nature, this hillside home has all the comfort and elegance of more formal designs. Its main level holds a central great room with porch access and through fireplace to a study or sitting room. The formal dining room is open to the great room and accesses a rear covered porch and a screened porch with fireplace. The gourmet island kitchen connects the house to its two-car garage through a laundry room with service entry. Bedrooms on this level are grouped on the right: a master suite with grand bath and two family bedrooms with shared bath. The lower level holds two additional bedrooms, a media or recreation room with fireplace and a storage area. Covered patios adorn the lower-level bedrooms.

© 1998 Donald A. Gardner, Inc.

Design By
DONALD A. GARDNER
ARCHITECTS, INC.

Width 106'-5"
Depth 104'-2"

© 1998 Donald A. Gardner, Inc.

159

COPYRIGHT LARRY E. BELK

DESIGN 8160

Main Level: 1,709 square feet
Lower Level: 1,051 square feet
Total: 2,760 square feet

Designed for a sloping lot, this home, complete with a roomy front porch, evokes a Southern character. Nine-foot ceilings throughout the main floor provide an aura of spacious hospitality. A covered balcony is located off the breakfast room and makes a perfect place to sit and view the lake or woods beyond. Double closets and vanities are among the luxuries found in the master suite. The basement offers two bedrooms, each with a private bath. A large den completes the downstairs plan. Please specify slab or basement foundation when ordering.

Width 60'-10"
Depth 69'-3"

Design By
© LARRY E. BELK DESIGNS

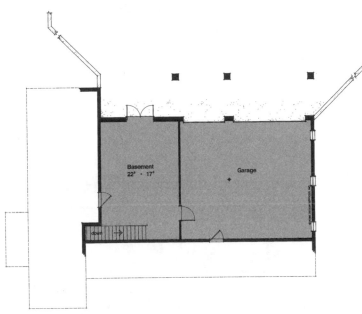

Width 64'-0"
Depth 52'-0"

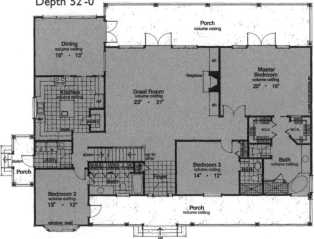

Design By
© HOME DESIGN SERVICES

DESIGN 8648

Square Footage: 2,500
Unfinished Lower Level:
492 square feet

This Florida "Cracker"-style home is warm and inviting. Unpretentious space is the hallmark of the Florida Cracker. This design shows the style at its best. Private baths for each of the bedrooms are a fine example of this. The huge great room, which sports a volume ceiling, opens to the expansive rear back porch for extended entertaining. Traditional Cracker homes had sparse master suites. Not this one! It has a lavish bed chamber and a luxurious bath with His and Hers closets and a corner soaking tub. Perfect for a sloping lot, this home can be expanded with a lower garage and bonus space in the basement.

DESIGN 2847

Main Level: 1,874 square feet
Lower Level: 1,131 square feet
Total: 3,005 square feet

QUOTE ONE®
Cost to build? See page 214
to order complete cost estimate
to build this house in your area!

Width 78'-10"
Depth 43'-5"

Think Tudors are only two stories? Think again. This is a magnificent hillside plan, complete with a main-level fireplace, easy-to-reach rear deck (four different rooms lead to it), and plenty of storage space. The lower level is a delight. Note the fireplace, second kitchen with snack bar, rear terrace, space for an extra bedroom (or two), built-ins galore, and lots of bonus space that could easily be a workroom, exercise room or both.

Design By
© HOME PLANNERS

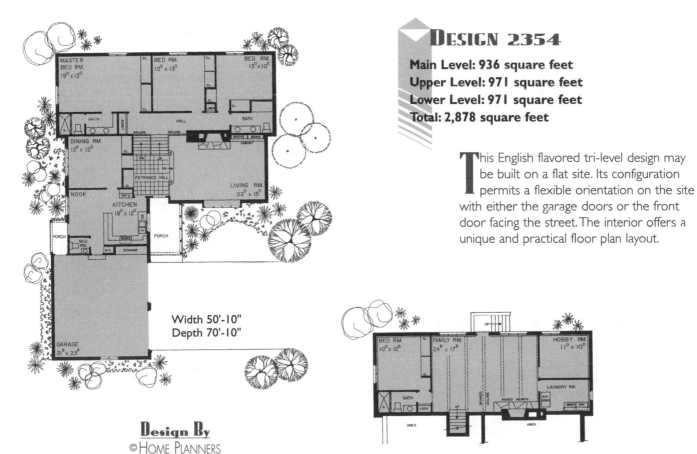

Width 50'-10"
Depth 70'-10"

Design By
© HOME PLANNERS

DESIGN 2354

Main Level: 936 square feet
Upper Level: 971 square feet
Lower Level: 971 square feet
Total: 2,878 square feet

This English flavored tri-level design may be built on a flat site. Its configuration permits a flexible orientation on the site with either the garage doors or the front door facing the street. The interior offers a unique and practical floor plan layout.

DESIGN Q341

Square Footage: 1,120
Unfinished Lower Level:
1,056 square feet

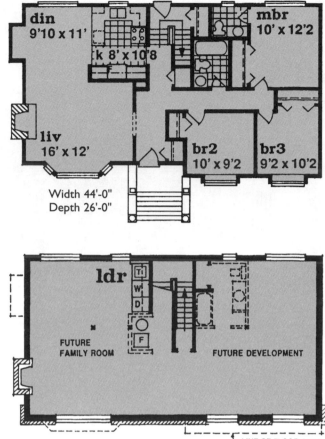

din
9'10 x 11'

k 8' x 10'8

mbr
10' x 12'2

liv
16' x 12'

br2
10' x 9'2

br3
9'2 x 10'2

Width 44'-0"
Depth 26'-0"

ldr

FUTURE
FAMILY ROOM

FUTURE DEVELOPMENT

LINE OF FLOOR OVER

This economical three-bedroom split-level home offers an efficient floor plan that can be expanded. Brick veneer and siding grace the outside, further enhanced by two box-bay windows and a bay window. The living and dining rooms are on the left side of the plan and offer a fireplace and buffet alcove. The U-shaped kitchen has loads of cupboards and counter space and connects directly to the dining room. Bedrooms are on the right side and are comprised of a master suite with half bath and two family bedrooms sharing a full bath. The lower level is reached via a staircase at the rear. It includes space for a family room with fireplace, one or two bedrooms and a full bath. The laundry is also located here.

Design By
© SELECT HOME DESIGNS

DESIGN Q213

Main Level: 1,048 square feet
Lower Level: 480 square feet
Total: 1,528 square feet

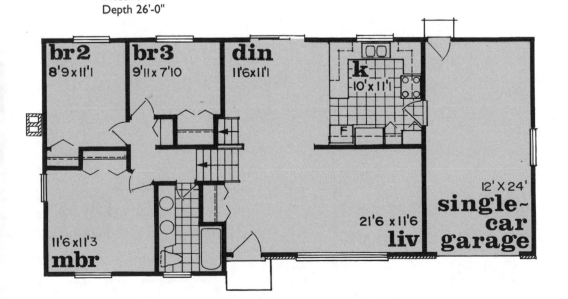

fam
19' x 11'

CRAWLSPACE

F

UTILITY &
STORAGE   D W T

Width 54'-0"
Depth 26'-0"

br2
8'9 x 11'1

br3
9'11 x 7'10

din
11'6 x 11'1

k
10' x 11'1

F

11'6 x 11'3
mbr

21'6 x 11'6
liv

12' X 24'
**single-
car
garage**

In traditional split-level styling, this simple design makes an efficient use of space in a smaller footprint. The main level features living and dining spaces that include a large living room, a dining room with sliding glass doors to the rear yard and a U-shaped kitchen. The single-car garage is accessed through the kitchen. Bedrooms are a few steps up: a master bedroom and two family bedrooms all share a full bath. The lower level holds space for a family room with fireplace and a mechanical area where the laundry and storage space are located. For the growing family, this is a most practical plan.

Design By
© SELECT HOME DESIGNS

DESIGN 7467

Square Footage: 1,632
Unfinished Lower Level:
1,043 square feet

Lower-level space adds to the compact floor plan of this home, and gives it future possibilities. The main level opens off a covered porch to a dining room on the right and a den or bedroom on the left. The great room with attached nook is to the rear of the plan and features a corner fireplace. A door in the nook opens to the rear deck. Note the amount of counter and cabinet space in the L-shaped kitchen. Two bedrooms—a master suite and a family bedroom are on the left, as is a laundry alcove. The lower level has space for a games room, two additional bedrooms and a full bath. Develop this area as needed or finish it along with the main level for immediate use.

Design By
© ALAN MASCORD
DESIGN ASSOCIATES, INC.

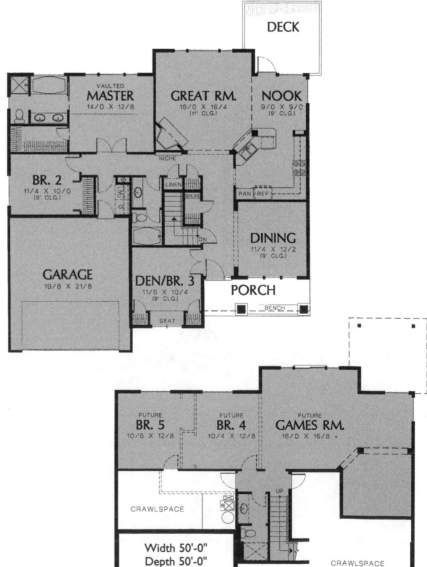

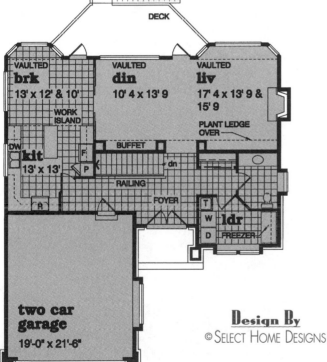

DECK

VAULTED
brk
13' x 12' & 10'

VAULTED
din
10' 4 x 13' 9

VAULTED
liv
17' 4 x 13' 9 &
15' 9

WORK
ISLAND

PLANT LEDGE
OVER

DW
kit
13' x 13'

F
BUFFET

P

dn

RAILING

FOYER

R

T
W **ldr**
D FREEZER

**two car
garage**
19'-0" x 21'-6"

Design By
© Select Home Designs

Design Q478

Main Level: 1,128 square feet
Lower Level: 1,092 square feet
Total: 2,220 square feet

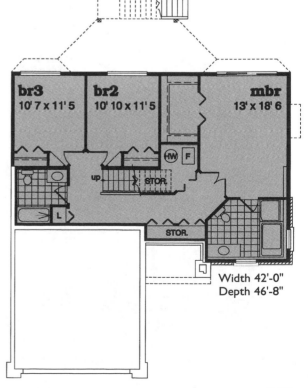

br3
10' 7 x 11' 5

br2
10' 10 x 11' 5

mbr
13' x 18' 6

HW F

up

STOR.

L

STOR.

Width 42'-0"
Depth 46'-8"

Beautiful Craftsman accents are evident in this design, perfect for a sloping lot. A double-door entry opens off a covered porch to an impressive vaulted foyer. Living areas are to the back and are manifest in vaulted living and dining rooms. The living room boasts a bay window and fireplace. Access to the deck sits between the living and dining rooms. The L-shaped kitchen features an island work space and vaulted breakfast bay with deck access. The laundry area is to the front of the house and contains a half bath. Stairs to the lower level are found in the foyer. Sleeping quarters are found below—two family bedrooms and a master suite. The master suite has a walk-in closet and bath with separate tub and shower. Family bedrooms share a full bath.

DESIGN Q571

Square Footage: 1,526
Unfinished Lower Level:
1,466 square feet

Stone and vertical siding lend a country touch to the exterior of this design. A balcony with double doors to the living room inside is an interesting detail. The main level places living and dining areas to the left of the entry. The living room has a corner fireplace; the dining room has hutch space. The L-shaped kitchen is cen-trally located and has a small breakfast bay for casual dining. A master suite with rear-deck access and a full bath joins two family bedrooms and a shared bath on the right side of the plan. The lower level adds a family room, a games room, a den and an additional bedroom with full bath. A laundry at this level has access to a rear deck.

Design By
© SELECT HOME DESIGNS

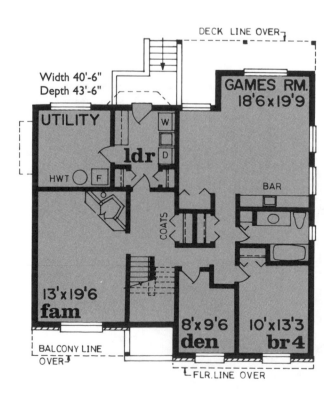

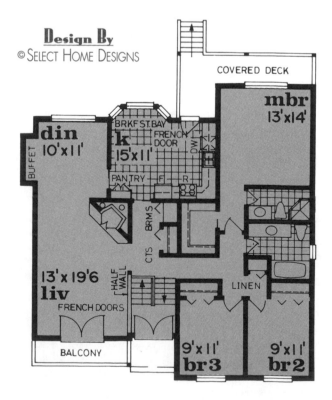

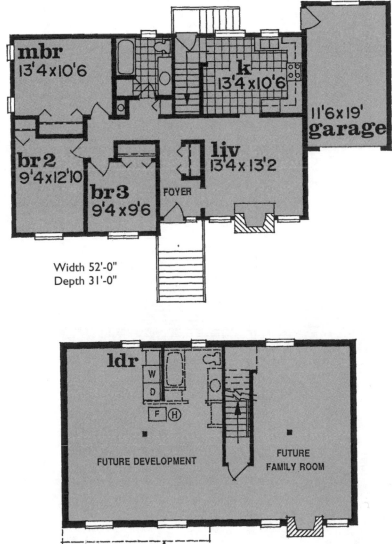

mbr
13'4 x 10'6

k
13'4 x 10'6

garage
11'6 x 19'

br 2
9'4 x 12'10

br3
9'4 x 9'6

liv
13'4 x 13'2

FOYER

Width 52'-0"
Depth 31'-0"

ldr

W
D

F H

FUTURE DEVELOPMENT

FUTURE
FAMILY ROOM

LINE OF FLOOR OVER

DESIGN Q340

Square Footage: 1,040
Unfinished Lower Level:
1,013 square feet

Affordable, yet appealing, this three-bedroom home is an ideal starter home. Unfinished space in the lower level adds a family room and additional bedrooms with a full bath. The main level includes all the right spaces—a living room with fireplace, a U-shaped kitchen with room for a table and chairs, and three bedrooms with a full bath. The single-car garage is accessed from the outside and may be built as a detached garage if needed for a narrow lot. Special features include a hall coat closet, a linen closet and abundant windows in all the rooms.

Design By
© SELECT HOME DESIGNS

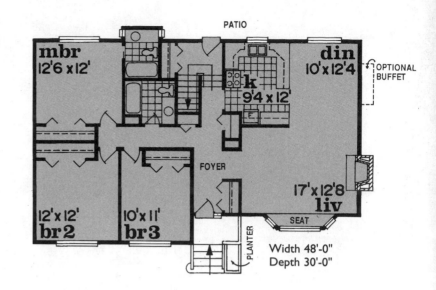

Design Q355

Square Footage: 1,352
Unfinished Lower Level: 1,341 square feet

Designed as a starter or retirement home, this compact design has ample space on the lower level for future development. Besides a laundry on this level, there is room for three additional bedrooms, a full bath and a recreation room with fireplace. The main level maintains full livability in a living room with window seat and fireplace, a dining area with optional buffet space and a U-shaped kitchen. The three main-level bedrooms include two family bedrooms with a shared bath and a master suite with private bath. A rear patio area is reached via a door in the stair landing.

Design By
©Select Home Designs

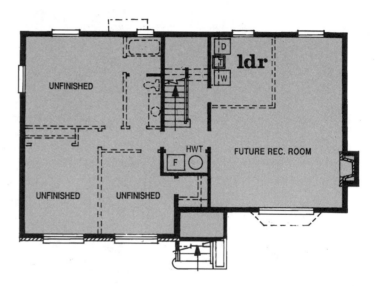

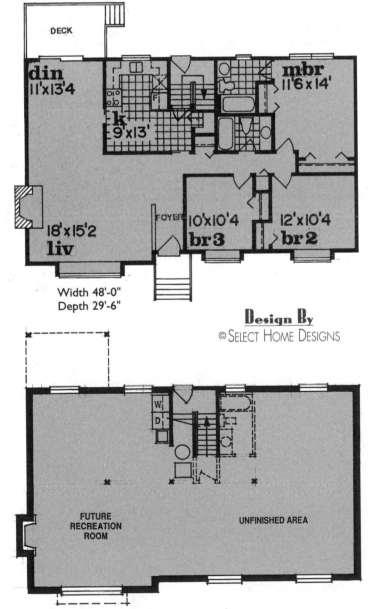

din
11'x13'4

k
9'x13'

DECK

mbr
11'6 x 14'

F

liv
18'x15'2

FOYER

br3
10'x10'4

br2
12'x10'4

Width 48'-0"
Depth 29'-6"

Design By
© SELECT HOME DESIGNS

W
D

FUTURE
RECREATION
ROOM

UNFINISHED AREA

DESIGN Q356

Square Footage: 1,373

Though smaller in square footage, this home has space on the lower level that can be developed in the future. The main level has three bedrooms and two baths—or make one of the family bedrooms into a den, if you prefer. Twin wall closets in the master bedroom add to its appeal. The spacious living room has a box-bay window and masonry fireplace, and is open to the dining room with sliding glass doors to a rear sun deck. The dining room is separated from the U-shaped kitchen by a pocket door. The lower level allows for a recreation room with fireplace and for additional bedrooms and a bath to be finished as more space is needed.

DESIGN 8273

First Floor: 3,413 square feet
Second Floor: 2,076 square feet
Total: 5,489 square feet
Bonus Room: 430 square feet

Classic design combined with dynamite interiors make this executive home a real gem. Inside, a free-floating curved staircase rises majestically to the second floor. The enormous living room, great for formal entertaining, features a dramatic two-story window wall. The family room, breakfast room and kitchen are conveniently grouped. A large pantry and a companion butler's pantry serve both the dining room and kitchen. Privately located, the master suite includes a sitting area and sumptuous master bath. The second floor includes Bedroom 2 with a private bath. Bedrooms 3 and 4 share a bath that includes two private dressing areas. A large game room is accessed from a rear stair.

Design by
©Larry E. Belk Designs

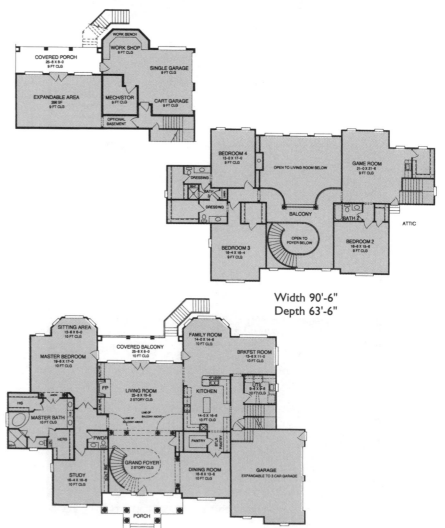

Width 90'-6"
Depth 63'-6"

© American Home Gallery, Ltd.

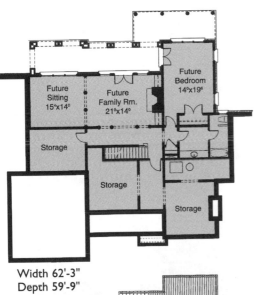

Width 62'-3"
Depth 59'-9"

Design T182

First Floor: 2,270 square feet
Second Floor: 1,128 square feet
Total: 3,398 square feet
Unfinished Lower Level: 1,271 square feet

Designed for lovers of the outdoors, this 1½ story home crafts native creek stone and rugged lap siding into a design inspired by the rambling ski lodges of the high country. Massive stone fireplaces and soaring vaulted ceilings set the scene for casual living in the living room, great room, master bedroom and breakfast area. An island kitchen provides comfortable work space while the wide rear porch invites outside entertaining. A separate vestibule leads to the elegant downstairs master bedroom with a luxurious master bath and room-sized walk-in closet. Upstairs are three more bedrooms and two full baths, one private. This home is designed with a walk-out basement.

Design By
Stephen Fuller

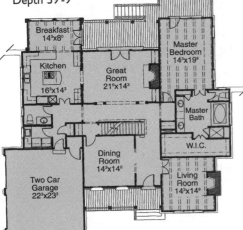

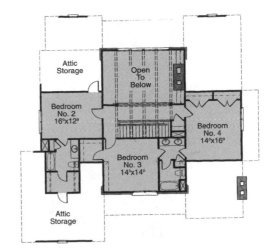

Design T180

First Floor: 1,704 square feet

Second Floor: 1,449 square feet

Total: 3,153 square feet

Unfinished Lower Level: 1,172 square feet

Bonus Room: 455 square feet

The fieldstone exterior and cupola evoke rural Southern appeal. The distinctive railed balcony, bay windows and porch arches recall Colonial detail. Inside, formal and informal spaces are separated by a graceful central stair hall that opens off the front foyer. French doors lead from the front porch into a formal dining room that links both the stair hall and the foyer. The living room, which also opens off the entrance foyer, leads to a cheerful great room that features a fireplace and built-in bookcases. An adjoining breakfast area opens onto a columned rear porch. Upstairs, a spacious master suite overlooks the rear yard. Two additional bedrooms share a convenient hall bath. A generous bonus space above the garage is also available. This home is designed with a walk-out basement.

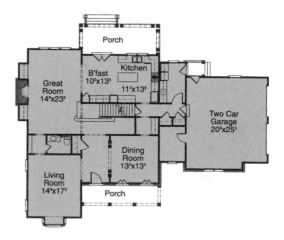

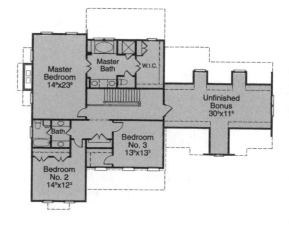

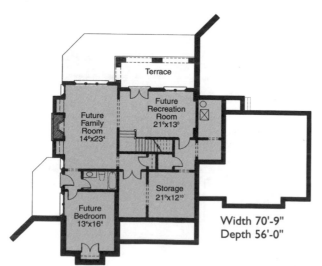

Width 70'-9"
Depth 56'-0"

Design By
Stephen Fuller

DESIGN T181

First Floor: 1,634 square feet
Second Floor: 1,598 square feet
Total: 3,232 square feet
Unfinished Lower Level: 1,018 square feet
Bonus Room: 273 square feet

Only a sloping pediment above double front windows adorns this simple, Mid-Western-style house, where a side-entry garage looks like a rambling addition. The wide porch signals a welcome that continues throughout the house. A front study doubles as a guest room with an adjacent full bath. A large dining room is ideal for entertaining and a sun-filled breakfast room off a spacious kitchen provides comfortable space for casual family meals. The open, contemporary interior plan flows from a stair hall at the heart of the house. On the private second level, the master bedroom includes a luxurious bath: two other bedrooms share a bath with dual vanities. An extra room over the kitchen makes a perfect children's play area. This home is designed with a walk-out basement.

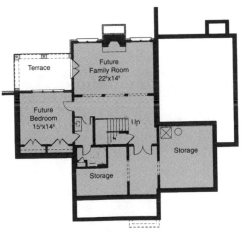

Width 62'-0"
Depth 54'-9"

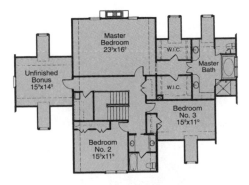

Design By
STEPHEN FULLER

175

Design 7435

Main Level: 920 square feet
Upper Level: 923 square feet
Lower Level: 730 square feet
Total: 2,573 square feet

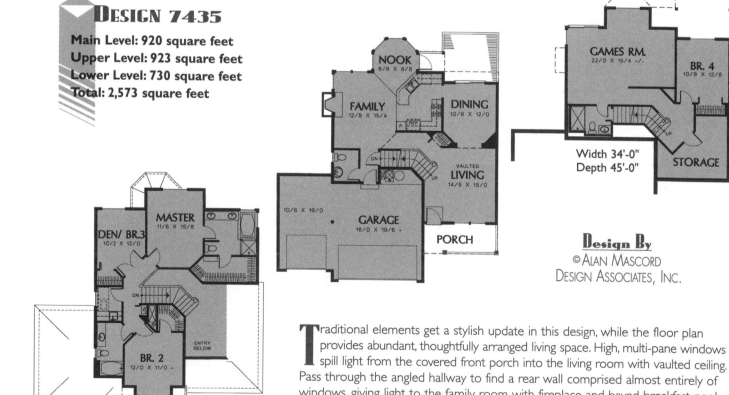

NOOK
8/8 X 8/8

FAMILY
12/8 X 15/4

DINING
10/8 X 12/0

VAULTED
LIVING
14/6 X 15/0

DN.

UP

10/6 X 19/0

GARAGE
18/0 X 19/6

PORCH

GAMES RM.
22/0 X 15/4

BR. 4
10/8 X 12/8

Width 34'-0"
Depth 45'-0"

STORAGE

UP

MASTER
11/6 X 15/8

DEN/ BR. 3
10/2 X 12/0

DN.

BR. 2
12/0 X 11/0

ENTRY BELOW

Design By
© Alan Mascord
Design Associates, Inc.

Traditional elements get a stylish update in this design, while the floor plan provides abundant, thoughtfully arranged living space. High, multi-pane windows spill light from the covered front porch into the living room with vaulted ceiling. Pass through the angled hallway to find a rear wall comprised almost entirely of windows, giving light to the family room with fireplace and bayed breakfast nook. Three roomy bedrooms, including the master suite, are secluded upstairs. The master bath features a separate tub and shower, a double vanity and a walk-in closet. The basement offers even more living space and a storage room.

DESIGN 7520

Main Level: 1,278 square feet
Lower Level: 698 square feet
Total: 1,976 square feet
Optional Den: 199 square feet

A dramatic entry introduces this hillside design and offers an arched window over the door to add light to the foyer. A split staircase leads up to the main level of the home where there are formal living and dining rooms decorated with columns. A family room with fireplace and built-in media center adjoins the island kitchen and breakfast nook at the rear. A door in the nook leads out to a rear deck. The master suite is on the main level and holds a walk-in closet and bath with spa tub and separate shower. The lower level has access to the two-car garage and allows for two additional bedrooms and a full bath. A large storage space may also be used as a den, if you choose.

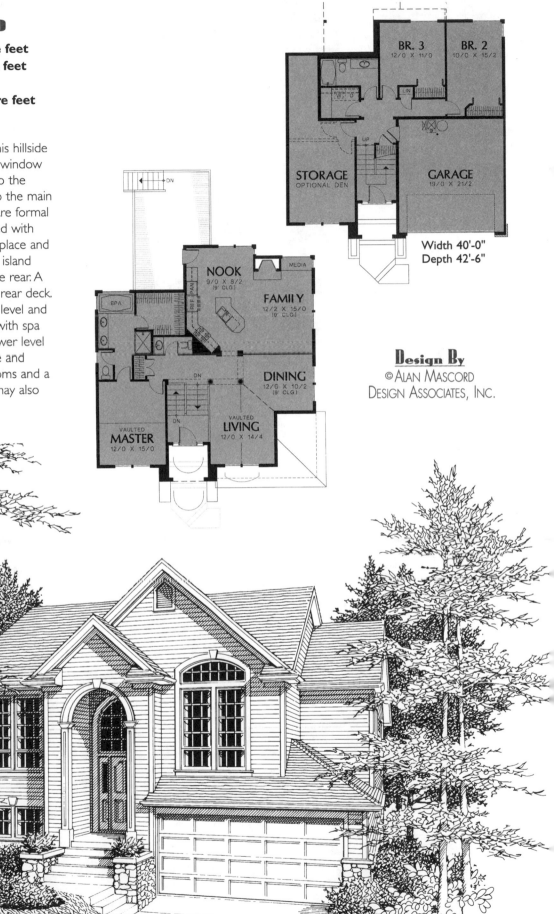

Width 40'-0"
Depth 42'-6"

Design By
© ALAN MASCORD
DESIGN ASSOCIATES, INC.

177

DESIGN 7552

Main Level: 1,158 square feet
Upper Level: 1,038 square feet
Total: 2,196 square feet
Unfinished Lower Level: 760 square feet

Design By
© ALAN MASCORD
DESIGN ASSOCIATES, INC.

Craftsman detailing adorns the exterior of this fine hillside home. Its cozy nature includes horizontal and shingle siding and a covered porch at the entry with a wide-based column. The interior is well planned and comfortable. The great room is roomy and warmed by a hearth surrounded by built-ins. The dining room is defined by columns and separates the great room and the U-shaped kitchen beyond. A wide deck at the side of the home is accessed through the dining room or the great room. A cozy den sits at the back of this level and has double doors to the rear portion of the deck. Three bedrooms on the upper level include two family bedrooms with a shared full bath and a master bedroom with sitting area and private bath with walk-in closet. The lower level has space for a games room and a guest bedroom with bath. Note the covered porch off the games room.

GUEST
12/4 X 12/2
(9' CLG.)

GAMES
12/0 X 21/6
(9' CLG.)

GARAGE
18/10 X 19/0
(9' CLG.)

STOR.

BENCH

DW

R.

14/2 X 10/0
(10' CLG.)

DEN
11/8 X 10/0
(10' CLG.)

DINING
13/0 X 11/0
(10' CLG.)

D. W.

DN

BENCH

UP

GREAT RM
17/0 X 19/0

BR. 2
12/0 X 10/0

BR. 3
10/4 X 12/8

11/0 X 9/4

LINEN

DN

MASTER
15/0 X 9/0

SEAT

OPEN TO
BELOW

Width 34'-6"
Depth 42'-0"

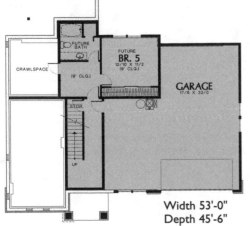

Width 53'-0"
Depth 45'-6"

DESIGN 7553

Main Level: 1,366 square feet
Upper Level: 1,159 square feet
Total: 2,525 square feet
Unfinished Lower Level: 563 square feet
Bonus Room: 465 square feet

Design By
© ALAN MASCORD
DESIGN ASSOCIATES, INC.

Three distinct levels of livability make this one of the most versatile hillside homes on the market—and all this in addition to its Craftsman-style good looks. The main level holds formal living areas as well as a cozy den and open family room with fireplace. A sunny nook and island kitchen overlook the family room. The vaulted bonus room lies overtop the two-car garage and can be finished in any way you choose. Bedrooms are on the upper level and include a master suite and two family bedrooms. The master bedroom has a tray ceiling and a bath with spa tub and separate shower. Lower-level space can be finished to include a fifth bedroom and full bath.

179

Design Q225

Square Footage: 1,161
**Unfinished Lower Level:
891 square feet**

This spacious split-level home is well-suited to a medium to narrow frontage lot. Steps lead up to a covered front porch at the entry with a single door into the foyer and double doors into the living room. The living room and dining room are part of one large open area, warmed by a fireplace. The kitchen is L-shaped and saves room for a breakfast table. The kitchen can be isolated by pocket doors at each entrance. The master bedroom sits to the back and features a walk-in closet and half bath. Family bedrooms sit to the front and share a full bath. The stairway to the lower level is found in the center of the plan. Unfinished space provides 891 square feet for future development that might include a family room with fireplace and an additional bedroom with half bath. The two-car garage offers storage and work-bench space.

Design By
© Select Home Designs

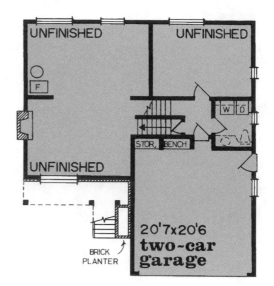

UNFINISHED

UNFINISHED

UNFINISHED

STOR. BENCH

W D

20'7x20'6
two-car garage

BRICK PLANTER

Width 38'-0"
Depth 42'-5"

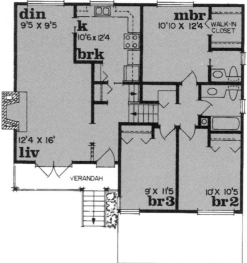

din
9'5 x 9'5

k
10'6 x 12'4

brk

mbr
10'10 x 12'4

WALK-IN CLOSET

12'4 X 16'
liv

VERANDAH

9' X 11'5
br 3

10' X 10'5
br 2

GARAGE WALL LINE BELOW

Width 44'-6"
Depth 32'-0"

DESIGN HPTHH20008

First Floor: 630 square feet
Second Floor: 1,039 square feet
Total: 1,669 square feet

Sided with cedar shakes, this home is reminiscent of beloved Craftsman style. Main living areas are found on the upper level and feature a living room with fireplace and dining room with porch access. Note that the porch extends to the side of the house. The island kitchen is nearby. The owners suite is also on the upper level. It contains a walk-in closet and well-appointed bath. The garage shares the lower level with two family bedrooms and a full bath. Bedroom 3 has access to a covered porch, which wraps around the house.

Design by
©ALAN MASCORD DESIGN ASSOCIATES, INC.

DESIGN T027

Main Level: 1,455 square feet
Upper Level: 1,649 square feet
Total: 3,104 square feet
Unfinished Lower Level:
895 square feet

The double wings, twin chimneys and center portico of this home work in concert to create a classic architectural statement. The two-story foyer is flanked by the spacious dining room and formal living room, each containing its own fireplace. A large family room with a full wall of glass beckons the outside in while it opens conveniently onto the sunlit kitchen and breakfast room. The master suite features a tray ceiling and French doors that open onto a covered porch. A grand master bath with all the amenities, including a garden tub and huge closet, completes the master suite. Two other bedrooms share a bath while another has its own private bath. The fourth bedroom also features a sunny nook for sitting or reading. This home is designed with a walkout basement foundation.

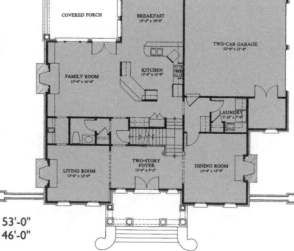

Width 53'-0"
Depth 46'-0"

Quote One®
Cost to build? See page 214
to order complete cost estimate
to build this house in your area!

Design By
STEPHEN FULLER

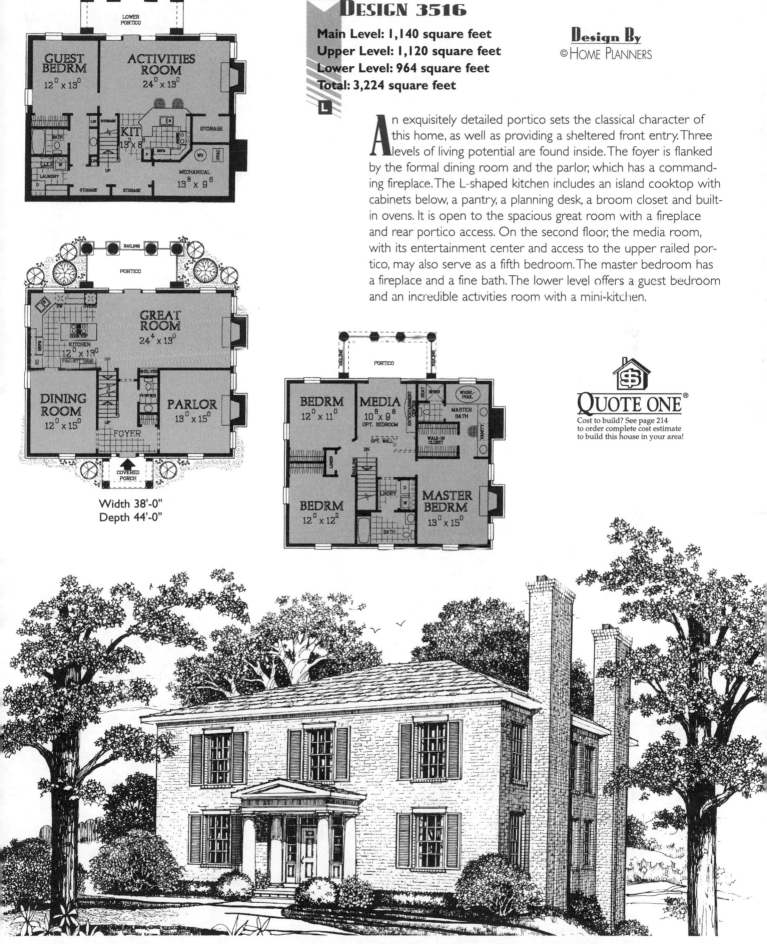

GUEST BEDRM
12⁰ x 13⁰

ACTIVITIES ROOM
24⁰ x 13⁰

LOWER PORTICO

KIT
13⁸ x 8⁰

STORAGE

BATH

LAUNDRY

UP

STORAGE   STORAGE

MECHANICAL
13⁸ x 9⁶

WH   HVAC

DESIGN 3516

Main Level: 1,140 square feet
Upper Level: 1,120 square feet
Lower Level: 964 square feet
Total: 3,224 square feet

Design By
© HOME PLANNERS

An exquisitely detailed portico sets the classical character of this home, as well as providing a sheltered front entry. Three levels of living potential are found inside. The foyer is flanked by the formal dining room and the parlor, which has a commanding fireplace. The L-shaped kitchen includes an island cooktop with cabinets below, a pantry, a planning desk, a broom closet and built-in ovens. It is open to the spacious great room with a fireplace and rear portico access. On the second floor, the media room, with its entertainment center and access to the upper railed portico, may also serve as a fifth bedroom. The master bedroom has a fireplace and a fine bath. The lower level offers a guest bedroom and an incredible activities room with a mini-kitchen.

RAILING

PORTICO

OVENS

GREAT ROOM
24⁴ x 13⁰

KITCHEN
12⁰ x 18⁰

PANTRY

COOKTOP

REFR

SHELVES

POWDER

DINING ROOM
12⁰ x 15⁰

PARLOR
13⁰ x 15⁰

UP

FOYER

COVERED PORCH

Width 38'-0"
Depth 44'-0"

PORTICO

RAILING

BEDRM
12⁰ x 11⁰

MEDIA
10⁸ x 9⁸
OPT. BEDROOM

ENTERTAINMENT CENTER

SEAT

SHWR

WHIRL-POOL

MASTER BATH

VANITY

OPT. WALL

WALK-IN CLOSET

LINEN

DN

RAILING

LNDRY

BEDRM
12⁰ x 12²

D

W

BATH

MASTER BEDRM
13⁰ x 15⁰

QUOTE ONE®

Cost to build? See page 214
to order complete cost estimate
to build this house in your area!

183

Rear View

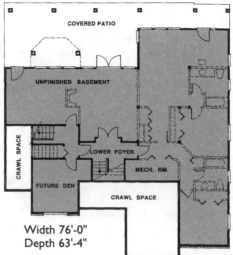

Width 76'-0"
Depth 63'-4"

Design By
© SELECT HOME DESIGNS

DESIGN Q432

Square Footage: 2,572
Unfinished Lower Level: 1,607 square feet

The lower level of this magnificent home includes unfinished space that could have a future as a den and a family room with a fireplace. This level could also house extra bedrooms or an in-law suite. On the main level, the foyer spills to a tray-ceiling living room with a fireplace and an arched, floor-to-ceiling window wall. Up from the foyer, a hall introduces a vaulted family room with a built-in media center and French doors that open to an expansive railed deck. Featured in the gourmet kitchen are a preparation island with a salad sink, a double-door pantry, a corner window sink and a breakfast bay. The vaulted master bedroom opens to the deck, and the master bath offers a raised whirlpool spa and a double-bowl vanity under a skylight. Two family bedrooms share a compartmented bath.

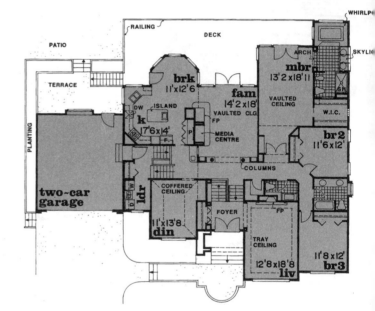

184

DEN
13/0 X 10/10

GARAGE
29/10 X 24/10

FOYER

UP

W D

Width 60' 0"
Depth 26'-0"

SPA

MASTER
16/0 X 13/0
(9' CLG)

OPEN TO
BELOW

MEDIA
CENTER

STOR

UP

UP DN

REF PAN

VAULTED

NOOK

PLANT SHELF OVER

VAULTED
LIVING/DINING
28/0 X 16/0

BR. 2
10/2 X 11/2

BR. 3
10/8 X 11/2

LIN

DN

DN

DN

DESIGN 7518

Main Level: 1,362 square feet
Upper Level: 400 square feet
Lower Level: 538 square feet
Total: 2,300 square feet

This home is designed for lots that slope up from the street. Featuring rafter tails, horizontal siding and stonework, this is a Craftsman home with lots of class. The foyer opens on the lower level, giving access to a large den, a full bath and a laundry room. Up one flight of stairs is the main living level. Here a huge living/dining room awaits and features a fireplace, built-ins and a snack bar from the vaulted galley kitchen. A built-in nook area to one end of the kitchen provides space for casual meals. The lavish owners suite, also on this level, offers many amenities, such as a walk-in closet, private balcony and pampering bath. Two family bedrooms and a shared bath comprise the upper level.

Design by
©ALAN MASCORD DESIGN
ASSOCIATES, INC.

COPYRIGHT LARRY E. BELK

DESIGN 8145

Main Level: 2,959 square feet
Upper Level: 1,055 square feet
Total: 4,014 square feet
Lower Level: 1,270 square feet

Designed for a sloping lot, this fantastic Mediterranean home features all the views to the rear, making it the perfect home for an ocean, lake or golf-course view. Inside, the two-story great room features a full window wall to the rear. The breakfast room, kitchen, dining room and master suite also have rear views. A tri-level series of porches is located on the back for outdoor relaxing. Two bedroom suites are found upstairs, each with a private bath and a porch. The basement of this home features another bedroom suite and a large game room. An expandable area can be used as an office or Bedroom 5. This home may also be built with a slab foundation. Please specify your preference when ordering.

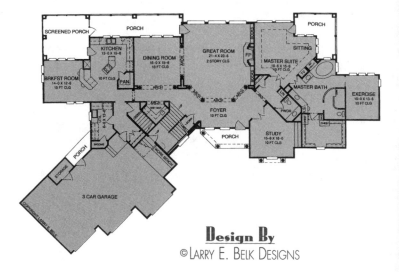

Design By
©LARRY E. BELK DESIGNS

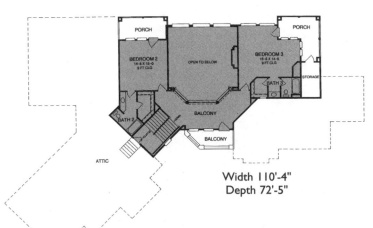

Width 110'-4"
Depth 72'-5"

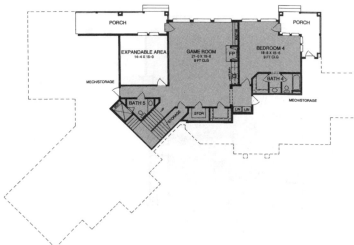

DESIGN 7554

Mail Level: 2,813 square feet
Upper Level: 1,058 square feet
Total: 3,871 square feet
Unfinished Lower Level: 806 square feet

Width 83'-0"
Depth 61'-0"

Design By
© ALAN MASCORD
DESIGN ASSOCIATES, INC.

For an extra-luxurious hillside home, with unfinished space on the lower level, look no farther than this grand design. The main and upper levels include over 3,500 square feet of livability and have spacious living and sleeping areas, a service kitchen for the formal dining room, a den and gourmet kitchen. Two family bedrooms with shared bath sit on the main level, while the master suite has the entire upper floor to itself. The lower level holds the three-car garage and a games room and shop, plus a full bath.

DESIGN 9537

Main Level: 1,687 square feet
Lower Level: 1,251 square feet
Total: 2,938 square feet

This striking home is perfect for daylight basement lots. An elegant dining room fronts the plan. It is near an expansive kitchen that features plenty of cabinet and counter space. A nook surrounded by a deck adds character. The comfortable great room, with a raised ceiling and a fireplace, shares space with these areas. The master bedroom suite includes private deck access and a superb bath with a spa tub and dual lavatories. Downstairs, two bedrooms, a laundry room with lots of counter space and a rec room with a fireplace cap off the plan.

Design By
© ALAN MASCORD
DESIGN ASSOCIATES, INC.

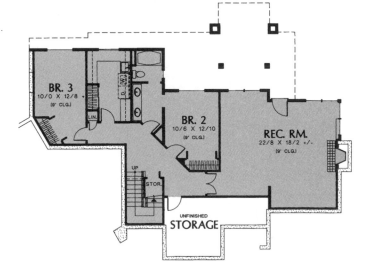

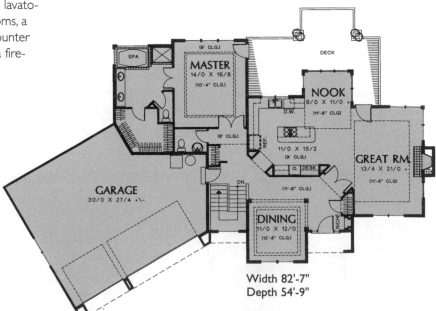

Width 82'-7"
Depth 54'-9"

COVERED DECK

DECK

DINING
10/8 X 14/0

BUILT-INS

LIVING
16/8 X 15/0

NOOK
10/0 X 10/4

FAMILY
14/8 X 16/0

BOOKSHELF

MASTER
17/8 X 15/0

SPA

GALLERY

DN.

GARAGE
32/4 X 23/2 +/-

BUILT-IN

DEN
12/4 X 14/4 +/-

Width 71'-0"
Depth 56'-0"

GAMES RM.
26/8 X 19/0

BR. 2
12/8 X 12/8 +

OPTIONAL WET BAR

UP

STOR.

LINEN

BR. 3
13/0 X 13/0

BR. 4
11/0 X 11/6

Design By
© ALAN MASCORD
DESIGN ASSOCIATES, INC.

Rear View

DESIGN 9417

Main Level: 2,196 square feet
Lower Level: 1,542 square feet
Total: 3,738 square feet

This refined hillside home is designed for lots that fall off toward the rear and works especially well with a view out the back. The kitchen and eating nook wrap around the vaulted family room where arched transom windows flank the fireplace. Formal living is graciously centered in the living room that's directly off the foyer and the adjoining dining room. A grand master suite is located on the main level for convenience and privacy. Downstairs, three family bedrooms share a compartmented hall bath.

DESIGN HPTHH20010

Main Level: 1,544 square feet
Lower Level: 1,018 square feet
Total: 2,562 square feet

A cozy bungalow, this design includes Craftsman details such as a pillared front entry, cedar shake detailing on the gable ends and an arched window. The main level holds living and dining areas as well as the owners suite. The great room is vaulted and opens to a rear deck through double doors. The owners bedroom also opens to this deck. The L-shaped kitchen features an island work center. The den at the front of this level could be used as an additional bedroom. The lower level holds a games room with fireplace and patio access. Plus, there are two bedrooms sharing a full bath on this level.

Width 40'-0"
Depth 60'-0"

Design by
©ALAN MASCORD DESIGN
ASSOCIATES, INC.

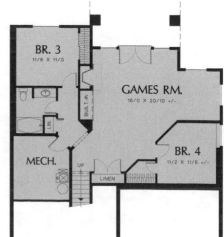

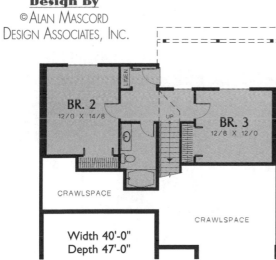

BR. 2
12/0 X 14/8

LINEN

UP

BR. 3
12/8 X 12/0

CRAWLSPACE

CRAWLSPACE

Width 40'-0"
Depth 47'-0"

DESIGN 7519

Main Level: 1,120 square feet
Lower Level: 620 square feet
Total: 1,740 square feet

VAULTED
MASTER
11/8 X 15/0

VAULTED
GREAT RM.
15/8 X 16/8

PLANT SHELF OVER

DN

VAULTED
DINING
11/0 X 10/0 +/-

GARAGE
19/0 X 21/6

REF PAN

VAULTED
KIT
13/0 X 8/4

PLANTER

Cozy in a style reminiscent of Craftsman homes, this three-bedroom plan has livability on two levels. The main level has a vaulted great room with corner fireplace, a vaulted dining room and a vaulted modified-U-shaped kitchen. A half bath sits in the hall to the master suite. A vaulted ceiling also graces the master bedroom. The master bath has double sinks and a walk-in closet. Two family bedrooms are on the lower level and share a full bath. Doors on the lower level lead out to a covered patio. The master bedroom and the great room also have doors to a deck in the back.

DESIGN 3800

Main Level: 1,946 square feet
Lower Level: 956 square feet
Total: 2,902 square feet

The simple, Pueblo-style lines borrowed from the early Native American dwellings combine with contemporary planning for the best possible design. From the front, this home appears to be a one-story. However, a lower level provides a two-story rear elevation, making it ideal for sloping lots. The unique floor plan places a circular staircase to the left of the angled foyer. To the right is an L-shaped kitchen with a walk-in pantry, a sun-filled breakfast room and a formal dining room. Half walls border the entrance to the formal living room that is warmed by a beehive fireplace. The adjacent covered deck provides shade to the patio below. A roomy master suite, secondary bedroom, full bath and laundry room complete the first floor. The lower level contains a great room, a full bath and two family bedrooms.

Design By
© HOME PLANNERS

Width 51'-6"
Depth 70'-2"

QUOTE ONE®
Cost to build? See page 214 to order complete cost estimate to build this house in your area!

Rear View

DESIGN 3645

First Floor: 2,024 square feet
Second Floor: 800 square feet
Total: 2,824 square feet

L

Tame the wild West with this handsome adobe-style home. Suitable for side-sloping lots, it contains a wealth of livability. A beehive fireplace graces the living room to enhance formal entertaining. The formal dining room is nearby. An office or TV room is located near the master bedroom suite. All will enjoy the family room, which opens to outdoor spaces. Three secondary bedrooms include a guest room with its own bath. Split styling puts the master bedroom suite on the right side of the plan. Here, a walk-in closet, a curved shower and dual vanities bring a touch of luxury.

Design By
© HOME PLANNERS

Width 80'-10"
Depth 54'-0"

QUOTE ONE®
Cost to build? See page 214 to order complete cost estimate to build this house in your area!

DESIGN T204

Square Footage: 2,127
Unfinished Lower Level:
1,421 square feet

The foyer of this quaint French cottage is set apart from the formal dining room with stately columns. The great room will accommodate easy living with a grand fireplace and doors to the rear porch. A gourmet-style kitchen has a cooktop island and a bayed breakfast nook. The master suite has twin walk-in closets and a luxury bath. Two secondary bedrooms share a hall bath. An additional bedroom and bath off the kitchen would make a nice guest suite or a home office. This home is designed with a basement foundation.

Design By
STEPHEN FULLER

Width 61'-0"
Depth 73'-8"

Rear View

Porch

Master Bedroom
16^3 x 13^6

Bedroom Office
10^3 x 11^0

Breakfast
13^3 x 9^0

Great Room
17^0 x 17^9

Bedroom No. 2
10^3 x 12^0

Kitchen
13^3 x 10^6

Dining Room
11^3 x 12^9

Bedroom No. 3
11^3 x 12^0

Two Car Garage
20^6 x 19^6

© American Home Gallery, Ltd.

Design T039

Square Footage: 1,684
Unfinished Lower Level: 1,650 square feet

Charmingly compact, this one-story home is as beautiful as it is practical. The impressive arch over the double front door is repeated with an arched window in the formal dining room. This room opens to a spacious great room with fireplace and is near the kitchen and bayed breakfast area. Split sleeping arrangements put the master suite with His and Hers walk-in closets at the right of the plan and two family bedrooms at the left. Additional space in the basement can later be developed as the family grows.

Design By
STEPHEN FULLER

Width 55'-6"
Depth 57'-6"

Cost to build? See page 214 to order complete cost estimate to build this house in your area!

195

DESIGN T081

Square Footage: 2,377
Unfinished Lower Level:
1,451 square feet

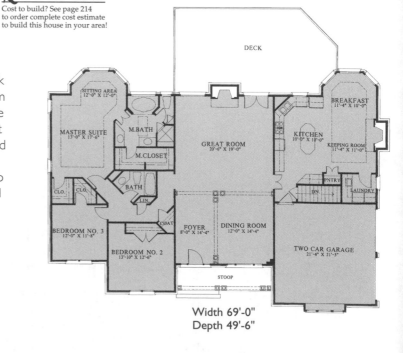

QUOTE ONE®

Cost to build? See page 214
to order complete cost estimate
to build this house in your area!

One-story living takes a traditional turn in this lovely brick home. The entry foyer opens directly to the dining room and great room, with columned accents to separate the areas. A large island kitchen adjoins a combination breakfast room/keeping room with fireplace. The bedrooms are found to the left of the plan. A master suite is cloistered to the rear and has a large master bath and bayed sitting area. Two additional bedrooms share a full bath. This home is designed with a walkout basement foundation.

DECK

SITTING AREA
12'-0" X 12'-0"

MASTER SUITE
13'-0" X 17'-6"

M. BATH

M. CLOSET

BREAKFAST
11'-4" X 10'-0"

GREAT ROOM
20'-6" X 19'-0"

KITCHEN
10'-0" X 18'-0"

KEEPING ROOM
11'-4" X 11'-0"

PNTRY

BATH

CLO. CLO.

LIN.

DN LAUNDRY

BEDROOM NO. 3
12'-0" X 11'-8"

COAT

BEDROOM NO. 2
13'-10" X 12'-6"

FOYER
8'-0" X 14'-4"

DINING ROOM
12'-0" X 14'-4"

TWO CAR GARAGE
21'-4" X 21'-5"

STOOP

Width 69'-0"
Depth 49'-6"

Rear View

Design By
STEPHEN FULLER

196

DECK

NOOK/KIT.
15/6 X 18/0
(11'-8" CLG.)

VAULTED
GREAT RM.
19/0 X 16/6

DINING
11/0 X 12/0
(12'-8" CLG.)

MASTER
14/0 X 15/8
(10' CLG.)

SPA

DN

GARAGE
32/2 X 21/4 +/-

DECK

DEN/BR.4
12/10 X 11/2

GAMES RM.
19/0 X 16/6

BUILT-IN

LINEN

STOR.

UP

BR. 3
11/10 X 12/10

BR. 2
11/0 X 16/6

LINEN

MECHANICAL

CRAWLSPACE

D.W.

Width 76'-0"
Depth 43'-0"

Design By
© ALAN MASCORD
DESIGN ASSOCIATES, INC.

Rear View

DESIGN 9484

Main Level: 1,573 square feet
Lower Level: 1,404 square feet
Total: 2,977 square feet

There's something for every member of the family in this captivating hillside plan. The first floor holds a huge great room for family and formal gatherings, a dining room distinguished by columns, an island kitchen with attached nook and an outdoor deck area. The master suite has a lavish bath. The game room downstairs is joined by three bedrooms, or two bedrooms and a den. Look for another deck at this level.

DESIGN 7222

Main Level: 1,887 square feet
Lower Level: 1,338 square feet
Total: 3,225 square feet

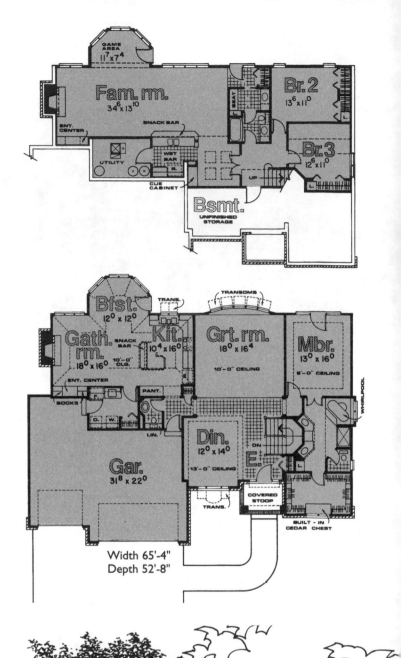

A majestic window and a brick exterior provide an extra measure of style to this handsome traditional home. Straight ahead, upon entering the foyer, is the spacious great room where bowed windows coupled with a high ceiling promote a light and airy feeling. The kitchen and breakfast area are integrated with the gathering room, which features a fireplace and an entertainment center with built-in bookshelves, making this area a favorite for family gatherings. For more formal occasions, entertaining is easy in the adjacent dining room. The large, private master suite is highlighted by double doors opening into the master dressing area, which features angled lavs and a huge walk-in closet complete with a cedar chest. The basement is designed for finishing as space is needed.

Design By
© DESIGN BASICS, INC.

Width 65'-4"
Depth 52'-8"

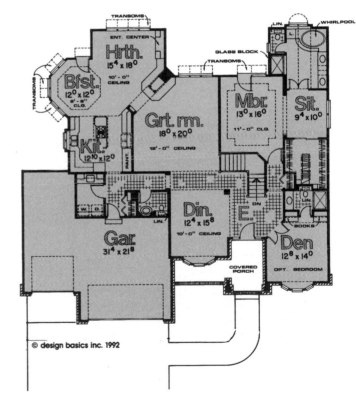

DESIGN 9393

Square Footage: 2,317
Lower Level: 1,475 square feet

A lower-level option turns this tidy one-story home into a much larger plan—and accommodates a hillside nicely. The main level contains the basic living areas: a great room with through-fireplace to the hearth room, a formal dining room with bay window, and a kitchen with informal eating space. The master bedroom, also on this level, has a wonderfully appointed bath and its own sitting room. An additional bedroom may serve as a den. The lower level, when finished, contains space for a family room with wet bar and snack counter, plus two bedrooms and a bath.

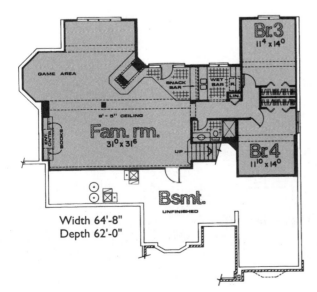

Width 64'-8"
Depth 62'-0"

Design By
© DESIGN BASICS, INC.

© design basics inc. 1992

DESIGN 9568

Main Level: 1,972 square feet
Lower Level: 837 square feet
Total: 2,809 square feet

A gracious facade welcomes all into this delightful family plan. A formal zone, consisting of living and dining rooms, greets you at the foyer. To the right, a double-door den provides a peaceful place to work or relax. The spacious kitchen has a cooktop island, a pantry and a window-laden breakfast nook. The family room offers passage to the rear deck. The master suite does the same. You'll also find a private bath and a walk-in closet here. Bedroom 2 is nestled in front by a full hall bath. Downstairs, two bedrooms flank a games room. A two-car garage opens to a laundry room.

Design By
© ALAN MASCORD
DESIGN ASSOCIATES, INC.

DESIGN 9567

Main Level: 1,644 square feet
Lower Level: 1,012 square feet
Total: 2,656 square feet

The character of this home is purely traditional. At the forefront is an elegant dining room open to the great room. The spacious kitchen is centered around a cooktop island. Double doors lead to a rear deck. The main-level master suite also opens to this area. A den or bedroom faces the front and is not far from a full bath, making it an ideal guest room. On the lower level, a games room and two more bedrooms reside. Built-ins and outdoor access make the games room versatile.

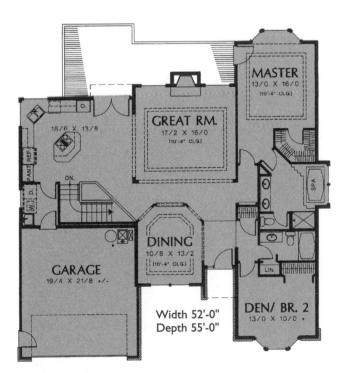

GARAGE
19/4 X 21/8 +/-

DINING
10/8 X 13/2
(10'-4" CLG.)

DEN/ BR. 2
13/0 X 10/0 +

GREAT RM.
17/2 X 16/0
(10'-4" CLG.)

18/6 X 13/8

MASTER
13/0 X 16/0
(10'-4" CLG.)

SPA

Width 52'-0"
Depth 55'-0"

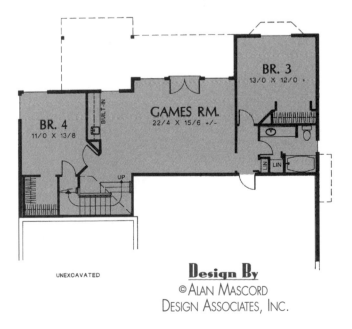

BR. 4
11/0 X 13/8

GAMES RM.
22/4 X 15/6 +/-

BR. 3
13/0 X 12/0 +

BUILT-IN

UP

UNEXCAVATED

Design By
© ALAN MASCORD
DESIGN ASSOCIATES, INC.

Design 7281

Main Level: 1,595 square feet
Lower Level: 790 square feet
Total: 2,385 square feet

A columned entry and large windows mark this home's charming elevation. In the great room, a ten-foot ceiling and an angled, see-through fireplace create a cozy atmosphere. The dining room also features a ten-foot ceiling. The kitchen has room for a planning desk and an island counter. The breakfast area is served by the snack bar. An entertainment center is available in the bay-windowed hearth room. The master bedroom overlooks a private, covered deck. The master bath includes a walk-in closet, a whirlpool tub and a dual-sink vanity. The optional finished basement has plans for additional bedrooms and a family room.

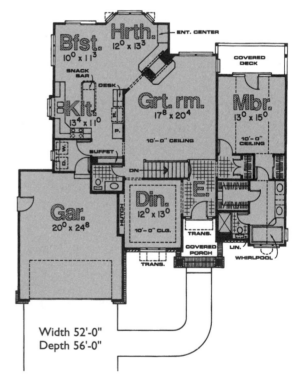

Width 52'-0"
Depth 56'-0"

Design By
©Design Basics, Inc.

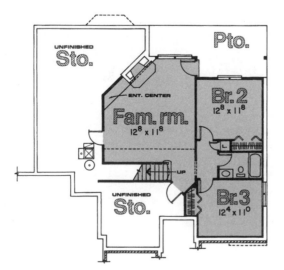

DESIGN 6622

Square Footage: 2,190
Lower Level: 1,966 square feet

A strikingly simple staircase leads to the dramatic entry of this contemporary design. The foyer opens to an expansive grand room with a fireplace and a built-in entertainment center. An expansive lanai opens from the living area and offers good inside/outside relationships. For more traditional occasions and planned events, a front-facing dining room offers a place for quiet, elegant entertaining. The master suite features a lavish bath with two sizable walk-in closets, a windowed whirlpool tub, twin lavatories and a compartmented toilet. Double doors open from the gallery hall to a secluded study that is convenient to the master bedroom. Two additional bedrooms share a private hall and a full bath on the opposite side of the plan.

©The Sater Group, Inc.

lanai
58'-0" x 10'-8"

master suite
13'-0" x 15'-0"
9'-4" stepped clg.

grand room
20'-0" x 18'-0" avg.
tray ceiling

nook
11'-0" x 9'-4"

br. 2
13'-0" x 11'-4"
9'-4" flat clg.

built ins

fireplace

kitchen
11' x 11'

built ins

opt. aquarium

arch

utility

foyer

down

study
11'-0" x 11'-0"
9'-4" flat clg.

dining
10'-10" x 15'-0"
9'-4" flat clg.

br. 3
12'-0" x 11'-0"
9'-4" flat clg.

entry porch

planter

verandah
58'-0" x 12'-0"

recreation
25'-0" x 35'-0"

storage

garage
23'-4" x 24'-0"

up

up

Width 58'-0"
Depth 54'-0"

QUOTE ONE®
Cost to build? See page 214
to order complete cost estimate
to build this house in your area!

Design By
©THE SATER
DESIGN COLLECTION

DESIGN 6615

Main Level: 1,736 square feet
Upper Level: 640 square feet
Total: 2,376 square feet
Lower Level: 840 square feet

Lattice door panels, shutters, a balustrade and a metal roof add character to this delightful coastal home. Double doors flanking a fireplace open to the side sun deck from the spacious great room sporting a vaulted ceiling. Access to the rear veranda is provided from this room also. An adjacent dining room provides views of the rear grounds and space for formal and informal entertaining. The glassed-in nook shares space with the L-shaped kitchen containing a center work island. Bedrooms 2 and 3, a full bath and a utility room complete this floor. Upstairs, a sumptuous master suite awaits. Double doors extend to a private deck from the master bedroom. His and Hers walk-in closets lead the way to a grand master bath featuring an arched whirlpool tub, a double-bowl vanity and a separate shower.

Design By
© THE SATER
DESIGN COLLECTION

Width 54'-0"
Depth 44'-0"

QUOTE ONE®
Cost to build? See page 214
to order complete cost estimate
to build this house in your area!

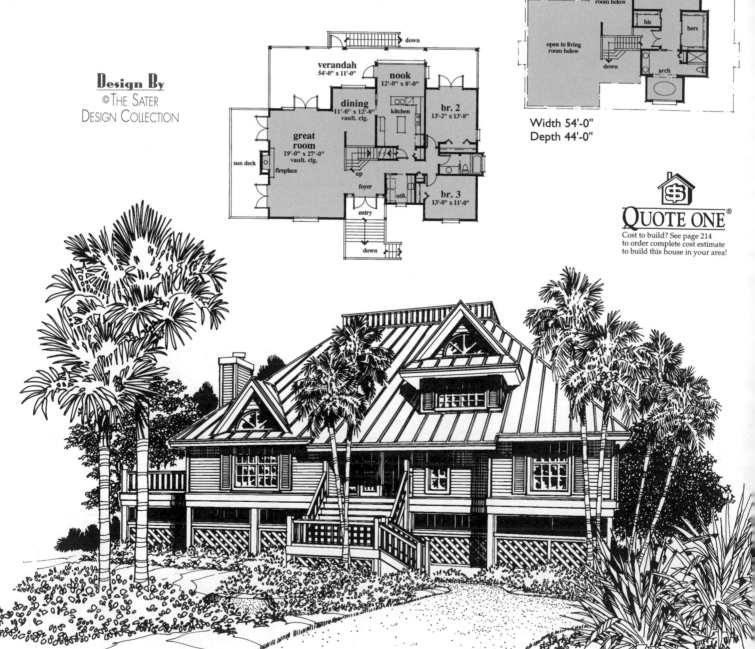

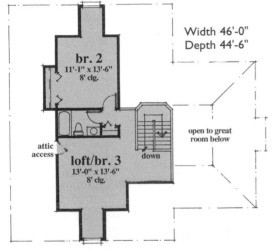

br. 2
11'-1" x 13'-6"
8' clg.

attic access

loft/br. 3
13'-0" x 13'-6"
8' clg.

down

open to great room below

Width 46'-0"
Depth 44'-6"

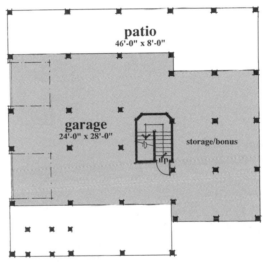

patio
46'-0" x 8'-0"

garage
24'-0" x 28'-0"

storage/bonus

up

Design By
© The Sater
Design Collection

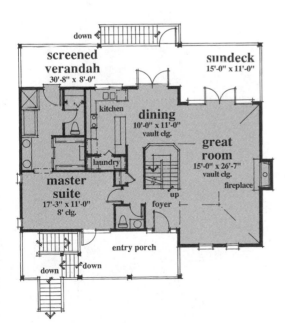

down

screened verandah
30'-8" x 8'-0"

sundeck
15'-0" x 11'-0"

kitchen

dining
10'-0" x 11'-0"
vault clg.

laundry

great room
15'-0" x 26'-7"
vault clg.

fireplace

master suite
17'-3" x 11'-0"
8' clg.

up

foyer

entry porch

down

Design 6617

Main Level: 1,189 square feet
Upper Level: 575 square feet
Total: 1,764 square feet
Lower Level: 2,208 square feet

An abundance of porches and a sun deck encourage year-round indoor-outdoor relationships in this classic two-story home. The spacious living room and the adjacent dining room, both with access to the screened veranda and sun deck, work well for informal gatherings or formal entertaining. The master suite accesses the veranda and leads into a relaxing compartmented bath complete with a separate tub and shower, double-bowl vanity and walk-in closet. A U-shaped staircase looks over the great room, adding a greater sense of space. Bedroom 2 shares the second floor with a full bath and a loft, which may be used as a third bedroom.

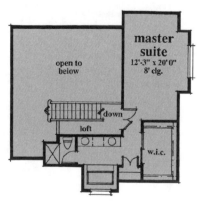

Design 6616

Main Level: 1,136 square feet
Upper Level: 636 square feet
Total: 1,772 square feet
Lower Level: 1,928 square feet

This two-story home's pleasing exterior is complemented by its warm character and decorative "widow's walk." The covered entry—with its dramatic transom window—leads to a spacious great room highlighted by a warming fireplace. To the right, the dining room and kitchen combine to provide a delightful place for mealtimes inside or out, with access to a side deck through double doors. Two bedrooms and a full bath complete the first floor. The luxurious master suite is located on the second floor for privacy and features an oversized walk-in closet and a separate dressing area. The pampering master bath enjoys a relaxing whirlpool tub, a double-bowl vanity and a compartmented toilet.

down

screened verandah
20'-0" x 7'-8"

kitchen

great room
21'-0" x 14'-0"
vault. clg.

fireplace

dining
12'-6" x 9'-0"
8' clg.

sundeck

up

down

foyer

study
10'-0" x 13'-0"
8' clg.

br. 2
11'-8" x 11'-6"
8' clg.

entry porch

down

Width 41'-9"
Depth 45'-0"

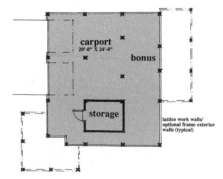

carport
20'-0" X 24'-0"

bonus

storage

lattice work walls/
optional frame exterior
walls (typical)

open to below

master suite
12'-3" x 20'-0"
8' clg.

down

loft

w.i.c.

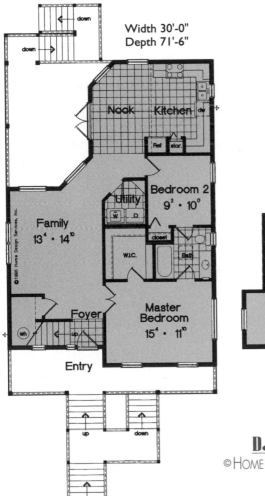

Width 30'-0"
Depth 71'-6"

Nook   Kitchen

Ref   stor.

Utility

Bedroom 2
9² · 10⁰

W   D

closet

Family
13⁴ · 14¹⁰

W.I.C.   Bath

Foyer

Master Bedroom
15⁴ · 11¹⁰

wh

up

Entry

up   down

© 1996 Home Design Services, Inc.

Bedroom 4
13⁰ · 11⁸

a.c.   closet

Bath

down

stor.

Bedroom 3
10⁸ · 11⁸

Design By
© HOME DESIGN SERVICES

DESIGN 8744

Main Level: 1,073 square feet
Upper Level: 470 square feet
Total: 1,543 square feet

Holding the narrowest of footprints, this adorable little plan is big on interior space, while encapsulating it in one of the cutest elevations. It's a perfect plan for low-lying beachfront areas or even high mountain views. The secret to good design in small homes is zero hallways. This design boasts plenty of space with no hallways. The country kitchen expands into the large dining area and family gathering space. The large master suite can have doors onto the deck for sunset watching and the large closet and unique dual-use bath make it a special retreat. The upper level holds two ample bedrooms with a bath. Bedroom 4 has a "study space" that leads to its own widow's walk. A third bedroom is found on the main level and can be used as a study. The ground level can be converted to garage space or storage areas.

Design 6621

Main Level: 1,642 square feet
Upper Level: 927 square feet
Total: 2,569 square feet
Lower Level: 1,642 square feet

Design By
©The Sater
Design Collection

Luxury abounds in this Floridian home. A game room just to the right of the entry gains attention. Up the stairs, livability takes off with an open dining room and grand room that stretches across the back of the plan. Two bedrooms occupy the right side of this level and share a full hall bath with dual lavs and a separate tub and shower. The master retreat on the upper level pleases with its own library, a morning kitchen, a large walk-in closet and a pampering bath with a double-bowl vanity, a compartmented toilet and bidet, a whirlpool tub and a shower that opens outside. A private deck allows outdoor enjoyments.

Quote One®
Cost to build? See page 214 to order complete cost estimate to build this house in your area!

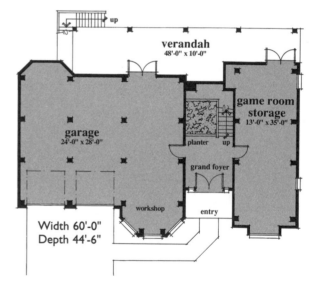

Width 60'-0"
Depth 44'-6"

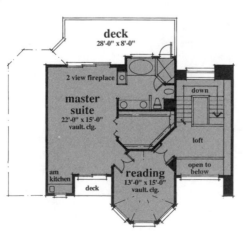

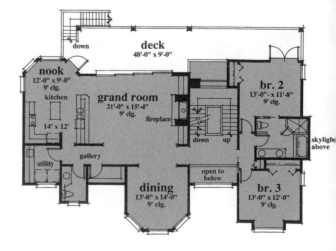

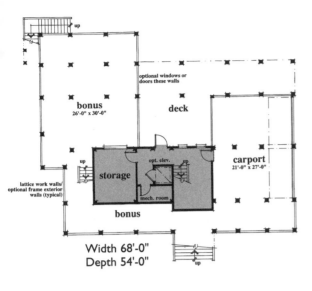

bonus
26'-0" x 30'-0"

optional windows or
doors these walls

deck

up

carport
21'-0" x 27'-0"

storage

opt. elev.

up

mech. room

lattice work walls/
optional frame exterior
walls (typical)

bonus

Width 68'-0"
Depth 54'-0"

DESIGN 6618

Main Level: 1,944 square feet
Upper Level: 1,196 square feet
Basement Entry/Storage:
195 square feet
Total: 3,335 square feet
Unfinished Lower Level:
2,563 square feet

Design By
© THE SATER
DESIGN COLLECTION

In the deluxe grand room of this Floridian home, family and friends will enjoy the ambience created by arches and access to a veranda. Two guest rooms flank a full bath—one of the guest rooms also sports a private deck. The kitchen serves a circular breakfast nook. Upstairs, a balcony overlook furthers the drama of the grand room. The master suite, with a deck and a private bath opening through a pocket door, will be a pleasure to occupy. Another bedroom—or use this room for a study—sits at the other side of this floor. It extends a curved bay window, an expansive deck, built-ins and a full bath. The lower level contains enough room for two cars in its carport and offers plenty of storage and bonus room.

down

verandah
26'-0" x 16'-0"

verandah

nook   kitchen

15' x 14'

grand room
28'-0" x 17'-0"
vaulted clg.

guest
12'-8" x 14'-8"
9'-4" clg.

arch   arch   arch

deck

down

gallery

up   down

elev.

util.

foyer

guest
15'-0" x 12'-8"
9'-4" clg.

entry porch

© The Sater Group, Inc.

deck
18'-0" x 16'-0"

deck
17'-0" x 8'-0"

curved bay
window

br./stdy.
15'-6" x 11'-5"
9'-4" clg.

open to grand
room below

master
suite
15'-0" x 19'-0"
9'-4" clg.

rail

clg. ridge line

built
ins

overlook

down

elev.

mech.

© The Sater Group, Inc.

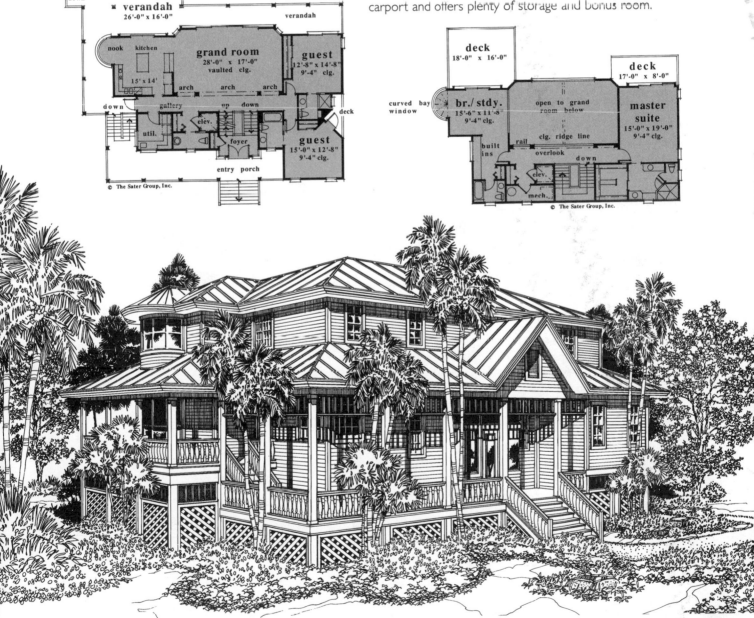

DESIGN 6619

Main Level: 2,725 square feet
Upper Level: 1,418 square feet
Total: 4,143 square feet
Lower Level: 2,813 square feet

Design By
© THE SATER
DESIGN COLLECTION

Florida living takes off in this design. A grand room gains attention as a superb entertaining area. A through-fireplace here connects this room to the dining room. Sets of sliding glass doors offer passage to an expansive rear deck. In the bayed study, quiet time is assured—or slip out onto the deck for a breather. A full bath connects the study and Bedroom 2. Bedroom 3 sits on the opposite side of the house and enjoys its own bath. The kitchen is fully functional with a large work island and a sunny connecting breakfast nook. Upstairs, the master bedroom suite is something to behold. His and Hers baths, a through-fireplace and access to an upper deck add character to this room. A guest bedroom suite with a bay window is located on the other side of the upper floor and will make visits a real pleasure.

Quote One®
Cost to build? See page 214
to order complete cost estimate
to build this house in your area!

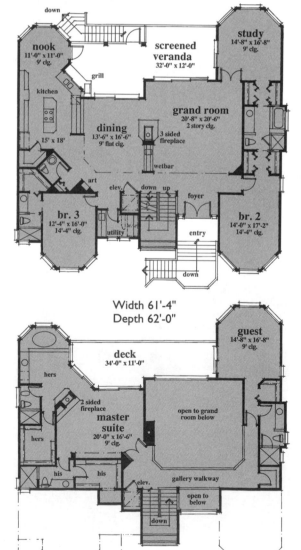

Width 61'-4"
Depth 62'-0"

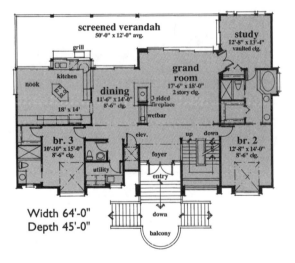

screened verandah
50'-0" x 12'-0" avg.

grill

study
12'-8" x 13'-4"
vaulted clg.

kitchen

nook

dining
11'-6" x 14'-0"
8'-6" clg.

grand
room
17'-6" x 18'-0"
2 story clg.

18' x 14'

3 sided
fireplace

wetbar

br. 3
10'-10" x 15'-0"
8'-6" clg.

elev.

up

down

br. 2
12'-8" x 14'-0"
8'-6" clg.

foyer

utility

entry

Width 64'-0"
Depth 45'-0"

down

balcony

DESIGN 6620

Main Level: 2,066 square feet
Upper Level: 810 square feet
Total: 2,876 square feet
Lower Level: 1,260 square feet

This striking Floridian plan is designed for entertaining. A large, open floor plan offers soaring, sparkling space for planned gatherings. The foyer leads to the grand room, highlighted by a glass fireplace, a wet bar and wide views of the outdoors. Both the grand room and the formal dining room open to a screened veranda. The first floor includes two spacious family bedrooms and a secluded study that opens from the grand room. The second-floor master suite offers sumptuous amenities, including a private deck and spa, a three-sided fireplace, a sizable walk-in closet and a gallery hall with an overlook to the grand room.

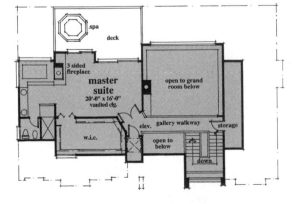

spa

deck

3 sided
fireplace

master
suite
20'-0" x 16'-0"
vaulted clg.

open to grand
room below

elev.

gallery walkway

storage

w.i.c.

open to
below

down

Design By
© THE SATER
DESIGN COLLECTION

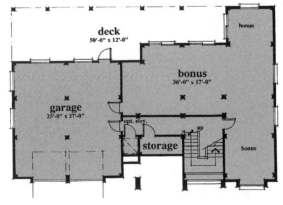

deck
50'-0" x 12'-0"

bonus

garage
25'-0" x 27'-0"

bonus
36'-0" x 17'-0"

opt. elev.

up

storage

bonus

LET US SHOW YOU OUR HOME BLUEPRINT PACKAGE.

Building a home? Planning a home? Our Blueprint Package has nearly everything you need to get the job done right, whether you're working on your own or with help from an architect, designer, builder or subcontractors. Each Blueprint Package is the result of many hours of work by licensed architects or professional designers.

QUALITY

Hundreds of hours of painstaking effort have gone into the development of your blueprint set. Each home has been quality-checked by professionals to insure accuracy and buildability.

VALUE

Because we sell in volume, you can buy professional quality blueprints at a fraction of their development cost. With our plans, your dream home design costs only a few hundred dollars, not the thousands of dollars that architects charge.

SERVICE

Once you've chosen your favorite home plan, you'll receive fast, efficient service whether you choose to mail or fax your order to us or call us toll free at 1-800-521-6797. For customer service, call toll free 1-888-690-1116.

SATISFACTION

Over 50 years of service to satisfied home plan buyers provide us unparalleled experience and knowledge in producing quality blueprints.

ORDER TOLL FREE 1-800-521-6797

After you've looked over our Blueprint Package and Important Extras on the following pages, simply mail the order form on page 221 or call toll free on our Blueprint Hotline: 1-800-521-6797. We're ready and eager to serve you. For customer service, call toll free 1-888-690-1116.

Each set of blueprints is an interrelated collection of detail sheets which includes components such as floor plans, interior and exterior elevations, dimensions, cross-sections, diagrams and notations. These sheets show exactly how your house is to be built.

AMONG THE SHEETS INCLUDED MAY BE:

FRONTAL SHEET

This artist's sketch of the exterior of the house gives you an idea of how the house will look when built and landscaped. Large floor plans show all levels of the house and provide an overview of your new home's livability, as well as a handy reference for deciding on furniture placement.

FOUNDATION PLANS

This sheet shows the foundation layout including support walls, excavated and unexcavated areas, if any, and foundation notes. If slab construction rather than basement, the plan shows footings and details for a monolithic slab. This page, or another in the set, may include a sample plot plan for locating your house on a building site.

DETAILED FLOOR PLANS

These plans show the layout of each floor of the house. Rooms and interior spaces are carefully dimensioned and keys are given for cross-section details provided later in the plans. The positions of electrical outlets and switches are shown.

HOUSE CROSS-SECTIONS

Large-scale views show sections or cut-aways of the foundation, interior walls, exterior walls, floors, stairways and roof details. Additional cross-sections may show important changes in floor, ceiling or roof heights or the relationship of one level to another. Extremely valuable for construction, these sections show exactly how the various parts of the house fit together.

INTERIOR ELEVATIONS

Many of our drawings show the design and placement of kitchen and bathroom cabinets, laundry areas, fireplaces, bookcases and other built-ins. Little "extras," such as mantelpiece and wainscoting drawings, plus molding sections, provide details that give your home that custom touch.

EXTERIOR ELEVATIONS

These drawings show the front, rear and sides of your house and give necessary notes on exterior materials and finishes. Particular attention is given to cornice detail, brick and stone accents or other finish items that make your home unique.

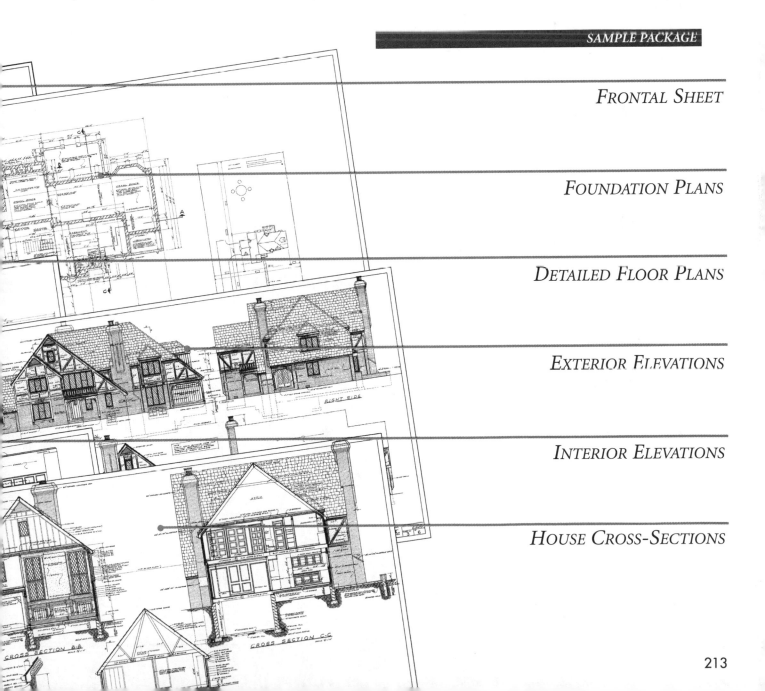

SAMPLE PACKAGE

FRONTAL SHEET

FOUNDATION PLANS

DETAILED FLOOR PLANS

EXTERIOR ELEVATIONS

INTERIOR ELEVATIONS

HOUSE CROSS-SECTIONS

IMPORTANT EXTRAS TO DO THE JOB RIGHT!

INTRODUCING
EIGHT IMPORTANT
PLANNING AND
CONSTRUCTION AIDS
DEVELOPED BY OUR
PROFESSIONALS TO
HELP YOU SUCCEED
IN YOUR HOME-
BUILDING PROJECT

MATERIALS LIST

For many of the designs in our portfolio, we offer a customized materials take-off that is invaluable in planning and estimating the cost of your new home. This Materials List outlines the quantity, type and size of materials needed to build your house (with the exception of mechanical system items). Included are framing lumber, windows and doors, kitchen and bath cabinetry, rough and finish hardware, and much more. This handy list helps you or your builder cost out materials and serves as a reference sheet when you're compiling bids. A Materials List cannot be ordered before blueprints are ordered.

(Note: Because of the diversity of local building codes, our Materials List does not include mechanical materials.)

SPECIFICATION OUTLINE

This valuable 16-page document is critical to building your house correctly. Designed to be filled in by you or your builder, this book lists 166 stages or items crucial to the building process. It provides a comprehensive review of the construction process and helps in choosing materials. When combined with the blueprints, a signed contract, and a schedule, it becomes a legal document and record for the building of your home.

QUOTE ONE®

SUMMARY COST REPORT / MATERIALS COST REPORT

A new service for estimating the cost of building select designs, the Quote One® system is available in two separate stages: The Summary Cost Report and the Materials Cost Report.

The **Summary Cost Report** is the first stage in the package and shows the total cost per square foot for your chosen home in your zip-code area and then breaks that cost down into various categories showing the costs for building materials, labor and installation. The report includes three grades: Budget, Standard and Custom. These reports allow you to evaluate your building budget and compare the costs of building a variety of homes in your area.

Make even more informed decisions about your home-building project with the second phase of our package, our **Materials Cost Report.** This tool is invaluable in planning and estimating the cost of your new home. The material and installation (labor and equipment) cost is shown for each of over 1,000 line items provided in the Materials List (Standard grade), which is included when you purchase this estimating tool. It allows you to determine building costs for your specific zip-code area and for your chosen home design. Space is allowed for additional estimates from contractors and subcontractors, such as for mechanical materials, which are not included in our packages.

This invaluable tool includes a Materials List. For most plans, a Materials Cost Report cannot be ordered before blueprints are ordered. Call for details. In addition, ask about our Home Planners Estimating Package.

The Quote One® program is continually updated with new plans. If you are interested in a plan that is not indicated as Quote One®, please call and ask our sales reps. They will be happy to verify the status for you. To order these invaluable reports, use the order form on page 221 or call 1-800-521-6797.

CONSTRUCTION INFORMATION

If you want to know more about techniques—and deal more confidently with subcontractors—we offer these useful sheets. Each set is an excellent tool that will add to your understanding of these technical subjects. These helpful details provide general construction information and are not specific to any single plan.

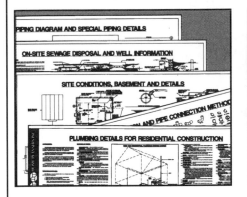

PLUMBING

The Blueprint Package includes locations for all the plumbing fixtures, including sinks, lavatories, tubs, showers, toilets, laundry trays and water heaters. However, if you want to know more about the complete plumbing system, these Plumbing Details will prove very useful. Prepared to meet requirements of the National Plumbing Code, these fact-filled sheets give general information on pipe schedules, fittings, sump-pump details, water-softener hookups, septic system details and much more. Sheets also include a glossary of terms.

ELECTRICAL

The locations for every electrical switch, plug and outlet are shown in your Blueprint Package. However, these Electrical Details go further to take the mystery out of household electrical systems. Prepared to meet requirements of the National Electrical Code, these comprehensive drawings come packed with helpful information, including wire sizing, switch-installation schematics, cable-routing details, appliance wattage, doorbell hookups, typical service panel circuitry and much more. A glossary of terms is also included.

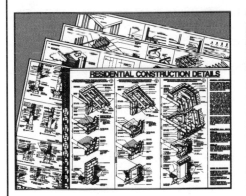

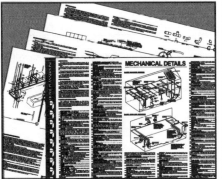

CONSTRUCTION

The Blueprint Package contains everything an experienced builder needs to construct a particular house. However, it doesn't show all the ways that houses can be built, nor does it explain alternate construction methods. To help you understand how your house will be built—and offer additional techniques—this set of Construction Details depicts the materials and methods used to build foundations, fireplaces, walls, floors and roofs. Where appropriate, the drawings show acceptable alternatives.

MECHANICAL

These Mechanical Details contain fundamental principles and useful data that will help you make informed decisions and communicate with subcontractors about heating and cooling systems. Drawings contain instructions and samples that allow you to make simple load calculations, and preliminary sizing and costing analysis. Covered are today's most commonly used systems from heat pumps to solar fuel systems. The package is filled with illustrations and diagrams to help you visualize components and how they relate to one another.

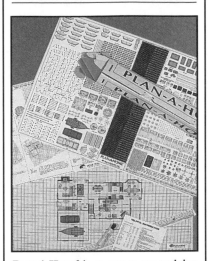

THE FINISHING TOUCHES...

THE DECK BLUEPRINT PACKAGE

Many of the homes in this book can be enhanced with a professionally designed Home Planners Deck Plan. Those home plans highlighted with a **D** have a matching Deck Plan, sold separately, which includes a Deck Plan Frontal Sheet, Deck Framing and Floor Plans, Deck Elevations and a Deck Materials List. A Standard Deck Details Package, also available, provides all the how-to information necessary for building *any* deck. Our Complete Deck Building Package contains one set of Custom Deck Plans of your choice, plus one set of Standard Deck Building Details, all for one low price. Our plans and details are carefully prepared in an easy-to-understand format that will guide you through every stage of your deck-building project. This page contains a sampling of six different Deck layouts (and a front-yard landscape) to match your favorite house. See page 218 for prices and ordering information.

EUROPEAN-FLAIR HOME
Landscape OLA088

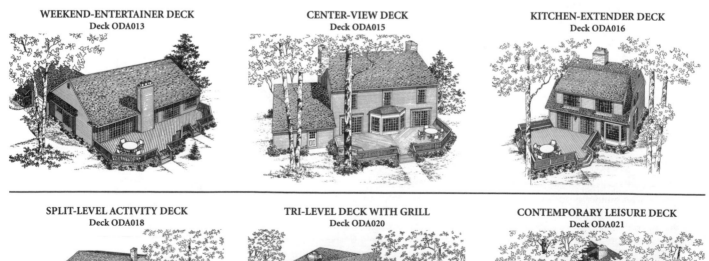

WEEKEND-ENTERTAINER DECK
Deck ODA013

CENTER-VIEW DECK
Deck ODA015

KITCHEN-EXTENDER DECK
Deck ODA016

SPLIT-LEVEL ACTIVITY DECK
Deck ODA018

TRI-LEVEL DECK WITH GRILL
Deck ODA020

CONTEMPORARY LEISURE DECK
Deck ODA021

THE LANDSCAPE BLUEPRINT PACKAGE

For the homes marked with an **L** in this book, Home Planners has created a front-yard Landscape Plan that matches or is complementary in design to the house plan. These comprehensive blueprint packages include a Frontal Sheet, Plan View, Regionalized Plant & Materials List, a sheet on Planting and Maintaining Your Landscape, Zone Maps and Plant Size and Description Guide. These plans will help you achieve professional results, adding value and enjoyment to your property for years to come. Each set of blueprints is a full 18" x 24" in size with clear, complete instructions and easy-to-read type. Six of the forty front-yard Landscape Plans to match your favorite house are shown below.

Regional Order Map

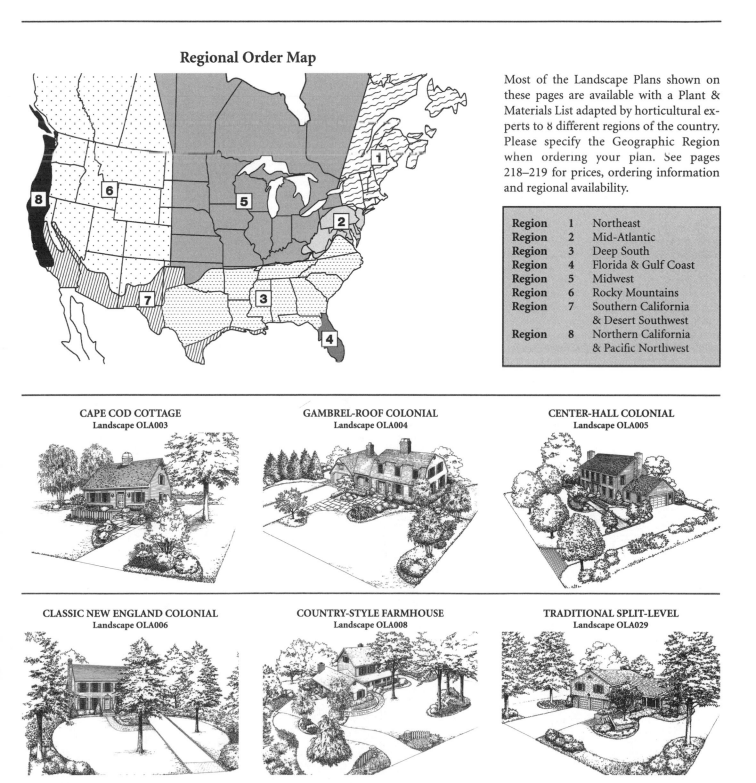

Most of the Landscape Plans shown on these pages are available with a Plant & Materials List adapted by horticultural experts to 8 different regions of the country. Please specify the Geographic Region when ordering your plan. See pages 218–219 for prices, ordering information and regional availability.

Region	1	Northeast
Region	2	Mid-Atlantic
Region	3	Deep South
Region	4	Florida & Gulf Coast
Region	5	Midwest
Region	6	Rocky Mountains
Region	7	Southern California & Desert Southwest
Region	8	Northern California & Pacific Northwest

CAPE COD COTTAGE
Landscape OLA003

GAMBREL-ROOF COLONIAL
Landscape OLA004

CENTER-HALL COLONIAL
Landscape OLA005

CLASSIC NEW ENGLAND COLONIAL
Landscape OLA006

COUNTRY-STYLE FARMHOUSE
Landscape OLA008

TRADITIONAL SPLIT-LEVEL
Landscape OLA029

HOUSE BLUEPRINT PRICE SCHEDULE

Prices guaranteed through December 31, 2001

TIERS	1-SET STUDY PACKAGE	4-SET BUILDING PACKAGE	8-SET BUILDING PACKAGE	1-SET REPRODUCIBLE	HOME CUSTOMIZER® PACKAGE
P1	$20	$50	$90	$140	N/A
P2	$40	$70	$110	$160	N/A
P3	$60	$90	$130	$180	N/A
P4	$80	$110	$150	$200	N/A
P5	$100	$130	$170	$230	N/A
P6	$120	$150	$190	$250	N/A
A1	$420	$460	$520	$625	$680
A2	$460	$500	$560	$685	$740
A3	$500	$540	$600	$745	$800
A4	$540	$580	$640	$805	$860
C1	$585	$625	$685	$870	$925
C2	$625	$665	$725	$930	$985
C3	$675	$715	$775	$980	$1035
C4	$725	$765	$825	$1030	$1085
L1	$785	$825	$885	$1090	$1145
L2	$835	$875	$935	$1140	$1195
L3	$935	$975	$1035	$1240	$1295
L4	$1035	$1075	$1135	$1340	$1395

OPTIONS FOR PLANS IN TIERS A1–L4

Additional Identical Blueprints in same order for "A1–L4" price plans ....$50 per set

Reverse Blueprints (mirror image) with 4- or 8-set order for "A1–L4" price plans ....$50 fee per order

Specification Outlines ....$10 each

Materials Lists for "A1–C3" price plans ....$60 each

Materials Lists for "C4–L4" price plans ....$70 each

OPTIONS FOR PLANS IN TIERS P1–P6

Additional Identical Blueprints in same order for "P1–P6" price plans ....$10 per set

Reverse Blueprints (mirror image) for "P1–P6" price plans ....$10 per set

1 Set of Deck Construction Details ....$14.95 each

Deck Construction Package ....add $10 to Building Package price (includes 1 set of "P1–P6" price plans, plus 1 set Standard Deck Construction Details)

1 Set of Gazebo Construction Details ....$14.95 each

Gazebo Construction Package ....add $10 to Building Package price (includes 1 set of "P1–P6" price plans, plus 1 set Standard Gazebo Construction Details)

IMPORTANT NOTES

The 1-set study package is marked "not for construction."
Prices for 4- or 8-set Building Packages honored only at time of original order. Some basement foundations carry a $225 surcharge. Right-reading reverse blueprints, if available, will incur a $165 surcharge.

INDEX

To use the Index below, refer to the design number listed in numerical order (a helpful page reference is also given). Note the price index letter and refer to the House Blueprint Price Schedule above for the cost of one, four or eight sets of blueprints or the cost of a reproducible drawing. Additional prices are shown for identical and reverse blueprint sets, as well as a very useful Materials List for some of the plans. Also note in the Index below those plans that have matching or complementary Deck Plans or Landscape Plans. Refer to the schedules above for prices of these plans. All plans in this publication are customizable. However, only Home Planners plans can be customized with the Home Planners Home Customizer® Package. These plans are indicated below with the letter "Y." See page 221 for more information. The letter "Y" also identifies plans that are part of our Quote One® estimating service and those that offer Materials Lists. See page 214 for more information.

To Order: Fill in and send the order form on page 221—or call toll free 1-800-521-6797 or 520-297-8200. FAX: 1-800-224-6699 or 520-544-3086

DESIGN	PRICE	PAGE	MATERIALS LIST	CUSTOMIZABLE®	QUOTE ONE®	DECK	DECK PRICE	LANDSCAPE	LANDSCAPE PRICE	REGIONS
1378	A4	113	Y	Y						
1850	C1	111	Y	Y						
1974	C2	63	Y	Y						
2254	C2	138	Y	Y						
2354	C1	163	Y	Y						
2502	C3	109	Y	Y				OLA013	P4	12345678
2511	C1	104	Y	Y	Y	ODA009	P2	OLA030	P3	12345678
2583	C3	108	Y	Y						
2608	A4	128	Y	Y	Y	ODA013	P2	OLA029	P3	12345678
2624	C1	137	Y	Y		ODA013	P2	OLA029	P3	12345678
2679	C3	147	Y	Y						
2716	C1	106	Y	Y				OLA030	P3	12345678
2761	C1	103	Y	Y				OLA030	P3	12345678
2788	C1	139	Y	Y						
2843	C2	97	Y	Y				OLA029	P3	12345678
2846	C3	61	Y	Y						
2847	C2	162	Y	Y	Y			OLA021	P3	123568
2894	C1	95	Y	Y				OLA030	P3	12345678
2901	C1	146	Y	Y				OLA030	P3	12345678
2926	C3	96	Y	Y						
2937	C3	107	Y	Y				OLA030	P3	12345678
3311	C4	58	Y	Y	Y	ODA010	P3	OLA021	P3	123568
3360	L1	73	Y	Y				OLA008	P4	1234568
3361	L2	102	Y	Y	Y			OLA031	P4	12345678
3362	C2	105	Y	Y	Y					
3366	C2	110	Y	Y	Y			OLA021	P3	123568
3493	C3	150	Y	Y	Y			OLA021	P3	123568
3516	C2	183	Y	Y	Y			OLA003	P3	123568
3645	C1	193	Y	Y				OLA038	P3	7
3713	A3	112	Y	Y						
3800	C3	192	Y	Y	Y			OLA038	P3	7
4308	C2	149	Y	Y				OLA032	P4	12345678
6615	C2	204	Y	Y	Y			OLA024	P4	123568
6616	A4	206						OLA024	P4	123568
6617	A4	205						OLA024	P4	123568
6618	C2	209						OLA024	P4	123568
6619	C4	210	Y	Y	Y			OLA024	P4	123568
6620	C4	211	Y					OLA004	P3	123568
6621	C2	208	Y	Y	Y			OLA024	P4	123568
6622	C1	203	Y	Y	Y					
7222	A4	198	Y							
7277	A2	153	Y							
7278	A2	13	Y							
7279	A2	117	Y							
7280	A2	10	Y							
7281	C1	202	Y							
7402	C2	28								
7412	C1	145								
7421	A4	140								
7422	A4	40	Y							

DESIGN	PRICE	PAGE	MATERIALS LIST	CUSTOMIZABLE	QUOTE ONE	DECK	DECK PRICE	LANDSCAPE	LANDSCAPE PRICE	REGIONS
7428	L1	92								
7432	C2	34								
7434	A3	42								
7435	C1	176								
7439	A4	37								
7441	C2	25								
7442	C2	31	Y							
7467	A3	166								
7469	A3	22								
7474	C1	24								
7501	A4	39								
7503	C1	29								
7507	C1	33								
7508	A4	5								
7509	A3	19								
7510	A3	18								
7515	A3	23								
7516	A3	21								
7517	A4	11								
7518	A4	185								
7519	A3	191	Y							
7520	A3	177	Y							
7529	C3	99								
7546	C2	98								
7548	C1	43	Y							
7550	C3	56								
7551	C4	57								
7552	A4	178								
7553	C1	179								
7554	C3	187								
7632	A3	51	Y							
7665	C1	62	Y							
7693	C3	55	Y							
7707	L1	159	Y							
7747	C1	54	Y							
7784	C3	50	Y							
7797	C3	53								
7804	C4	49								
8145	L1	186								
8147	L1	72								
8153	C4	60								
8160	L1	160								
8273	L1	172								
8648	C2	161								
8722	A3	136								
8744	A3	207								
8793	C1	59								
9291	A2	125	Y							
9345	A3	124	Y							
9393	C1	199	Y							
9410	C2	14	Y					OLA001	P3	123568
9417	C3	189	Y					OLA001	P3	123568
9484	C1	197	Y					OLA004	P3	123568
9509	A3	20	Y					OLA004	P3	123568
9537	C1	188	Y					OLA004	P3	123568
9538	C1	32	Y					OLA001	P3	123568
9539	C3	100	Y					OLA004	P3	123568
9543	C2	65	Y					OLA001	P3	123568
9554	C3	26	Y		Y					
9561	C2	27	Y							
9567	C1	201	Y							
9568	C1	200	Y							
9573	A4	17	Y							
9576	C2	144	Y							
A215	L3	90								
HPTHH20001	C1	15		Y						
HPTHH20002	C4	16		Y						
HPTHH20003	A3	41		Y						
HPTHH20004	A3	45		Y						
HPTHH20005	A3	64		Y						
HPTHH20006	A3	148		Y						
HPTHH20008	A3	181	Y	Y						
HPTHH20010	C1	190		Y						
P140	A3	8								
P155	C1	35								
P213	A3	7								
P217	A3	141								
P237	C1	46								
P240	A2	4								
P302	A2	12								
P345	A2	6								
P365	C1	30								
P366	A4	9								
P368	A3	157								
P415	A2	158								
P451	A3	156								
Q213	A2	165	Y							
Q216	A2	116	Y							
Q218	A2	129	Y							
Q223	A3	67	Y							
Q225	A2	180	Y							
Q230	A2	130	Y							
Q238	A2	44	Y							
Q245	A2	122	Y							
Q262	A1	123	Y							
Q263	A2	36	Y							
Q264	A2	121	Y							
Q265	A2	119	Y							
Q266	A2	133	Y							
Q268	A2	115	Y							
Q289	A2	118	Y							
Q312	C1	151	Y							
Q315	A2	155	Y							
Q324	A4	143	Y							
Q339	A2	120	Y							
Q340	A2	169	Y							
Q341	A2	164	Y							
Q342	A2	154	Y		Y					
Q349	A2	132	Y							
Q355	A2	170	Y							
Q356	A2	171	Y							
Q360	A2	126	Y							
Q423	A2	131	Y							
Q426	A2	152	Y		Y					
Q432	C2	184	Y							
Q467	A2	127	Y							
Q469	A2	114	Y							
Q478	A4	167	Y							
Q518	A2	66	Y							
Q571	A4	168	Y							
Q606	C4	101								
T013	C2	77	Y		Y					
T021	C3	48	Y		Y					
T022	C3	88	Y		Y					
T023	C3	84	Y		Y					
T027	C4	182	Y							
T038	C1	47								
T039	C1	195	Y		Y					
T049	C3	85	Y		Y					
T051	C3	74								
T052	C2	69	Y		Y					
T068	C3	75	Y		Y					
T081	C2	196	Y		Y					
T088	C2	89	Y		Y					
T093	C1	142								
T105	L1	68	Y							
T109	C1	134	Y		Y					
T112	C1	38								
T137	C1	135								
T155	C4	76								
T167	C4	81								
T169	C4	82								
T170	C4	86								
T172	L1	87								
T179	L1	70								
T180	C4	174								
T181	C4	175								
T182	C4	173								
T190	C3	91								
T195	C4	83								
T197	C4	80								
T198	C4	79								
T199	C3	94								
T201	C3	71								
T204	C2	194								
T243	C3	52								
T244	L2	78								

BEFORE FILLING OUT THE COUPON AT RIGHT OR CALLING US ON OUR TOLL-FREE BLUEPRINT HOTLINE, YOU MAY WANT TO LEARN MORE ABOUT OUR SERVICES AND PRODUCTS. HERE'S SOME INFORMATION YOU WILL FIND HELPFUL.

OUR EXCHANGE POLICY
Since blueprints are printed in response to your order, we cannot honor requests for refunds. However, we will exchange your entire first order for an equal or greater number of blueprints within our plan collection within 90 days of the original order. The entire content of your original order must be returned to our offices before an exchange will be processed. If the returned blueprints look used, redlined or copied, we will not honor your exchange. Fees for exchanging your blueprints are as follows: 20% of the amount of the original order...*plus* the difference in cost if exchanging for a design in a higher price bracket or *less* the difference in cost if exchanging for a design in lower price bracket. **(Reproducible blueprints are not exchangeable.)** Please add $25 for postage and handling via Regular Service; $35 via Priority Service; $45 via Express Service. Shipping and handling charges are not refundable.

ABOUT REVERSE BLUEPRINTS
If you want to build in reverse of the plan as shown, we will include any number of reverse blueprints (mirror image) from a 4- or 8-set package for an additional fee of $50. Although lettering and dimensions will appear backward, reverses will be a useful aid if you decide to flop the plan.

REVISING, MODIFYING AND CUSTOMIZING PLANS
The wide variety of designs available in this publication allows you to select ideas and concepts for a home to fit your building site and match your family's needs, wants and budget. Like many homeowners who buy these plans, you and your builder, architect or engineer may want to make changes to them. Some changes may be made by your builder, but we recommend that most changes be made by a licensed architect or engineer. If you need to make alterations to a design that is customizable, you need only order our Home Customizer® Package to get you started. As set forth below, we cannot assume any responsibility for blueprints which have been changed, whether by you, your builder or by professionals selected by you or referred to you by us, because such individuals are outside our supervision and control.

ARCHITECTURAL AND ENGINEERING SEALS
Some cities and states are now requiring that a licensed architect or engineer review and "seal" a blueprint, or officially approve it, prior to construction due to concerns over energy costs, safety and other factors. Prior to application for a building permit or the start of actual construction, we strongly advise that you consult your local building official who can tell you if such a review is required.

ABOUT THE DESIGNS
The architects and designers whose work appears in this publication are among America's leading residential designers. Each plan was designed to meet the requirements of a nationally recognized model building code in effect at the time and place the plan was drawn. Because national building codes change from time to time, plans may not comply with any such code at the time they are sold to a customer. In addition, building officials may not accept these plans as final construction documents of record as the plans may need to be modified and additional drawings and details added to suit local conditions and requirements. We strongly advise that purchasers consult a licensed architect or engineer, and their local building official, before starting any construction related to these plans.

LOCAL BUILDING CODES AND ZONING REQUIREMENTS
At the time of creation, our plans are drawn to specifications published by the Building Officials and Code Administrators (BOCA) International, Inc.; the Southern Building Code Congress (SBCCI) International, Inc.; the International Conference of Building Officials (ICBO); or the Council of American Building Officials (CABO). Our plans are designed to meet or exceed national building standards. Because of the great differences in geography and climate throughout the United States and Canada, each state, county and municipality has its own building codes, zone requirements, ordinances and building regulations. Your plan may need to be modified to comply with local requirements regarding snow loads, energy codes, soil and seismic conditions and a wide range of other matters. In addition, you may need to obtain permits or inspections from local governments before and in the course of construction. Prior to using blueprints ordered from us, we strongly advise that you consult a licensed architect or engineer—and speak with your local building official—before applying for any permit or beginning construction. We authorize the use of our blueprints on the express condition that you strictly comply with all local building codes, zoning requirements and other applicable laws, regulations, ordinances and requirements. **Notice: Plans for homes to be built in Nevada must be re-drawn by a Nevada-registered professional. Consult your building official for more information on this subject.**

FOUNDATION AND EXTERIOR WALL CHANGES
Depending on your specific climate or regional building practices, you may wish to change a full basement to a slab or crawlspace foundation. Most professional contractors and builders can easily adapt your plans to alternate foundation types. Likewise, most can easily change 2x4 wall construction to 2x6, or vice versa.

DISCLAIMER
We and the designers we work with have put substantial care and effort into the creation of our blueprints. However, because we cannot provide on-site consultation, supervision and control over actual construction, and because of the great variance in local building requirements, building practices and soil, seismic, weather and other conditions, WE CANNOT MAKE ANY WARRANTY, EXPRESS OR IMPLIED, WITH RESPECT TO THE CONTENT OR USE OF OUR BLUEPRINTS, INCLUDING BUT NOT LIMITED TO ANY WARRANTY OF MERCHANTABILITY OR OF FITNESS FOR A PARTICULAR PURPOSE.

TERMS AND CONDITIONS
These designs are protected under the terms of United States Copyright Law and may not be copied or reproduced in any way, by any means, unless you have purchased Sepias or Reproducibles which clearly indicate your right to copy or reproduce. We authorize the use of your chosen design as an aid in the construction of one single family home only. You may not use this design to build a second or multiple dwellings without purchasing another blueprint or blueprints or paying additional design fees.

HOW MANY BLUEPRINTS DO YOU NEED?
A single set of blueprints is sufficient to study a home in greater detail. However, if you are planning to obtain cost estimates from a contractor or subcontractors—or if you are planning to build immediately—you will need more sets. Because additional sets are cheaper when ordered in quantity with the original order, make sure you order enough blueprints to satisfy all requirements. The following checklist will help you determine how many you need:

__ Owner

__ Builder (generally requires at least three sets; one as a legal document, one to use during inspections, and at least one to give to subcontractors)

__ Local Building Department (often requires two sets)

__ Mortgage Lender (usually one set for a conventional loan; three sets for FHA or VA loans)

__ TOTAL NUMBER OF SETS

The Home Customizer®

"This house is perfect...if only the family room were two feet wider." Sound familiar? In response to the numerous requests for this type of modification, Home Planners has developed **The Home Customizer® Package**. This exclusive package offers our top-of-the-line materials to make it easy for anyone, anywhere to customize any Home Planners design to fit their needs. Check the index on page 218-219 for those plans which are customizable.

Some of the changes you can make to any of our plans include:

- exterior elevation changes
- kitchen and bath modifications
- roof, wall and foundation changes
- room additions and more!

The Home Customizer® Package includes everything you'll need to make the necessary changes to your favorite Home Planners design. The package includes:

- instruction book with examples
- architectural scale and clear work film
- erasable red marker and removable correction tape
- ¼"-scale furniture cutouts
- 1 set reproducible drawings
- 1 set study blueprints for communicating changes to your design professional
- a copyright release letter so you can make copies as you need them
- referral letter with the name, address and telephone number of the professional in your region who is trained in modifying Home Planners designs efficiently and inexpensively.

The Home Customizer® Package will not only save you 25% to 75% of the cost of drawing the plans from scratch with an architect or engineer, it will also give you the flexibility to have your changes and modifications made by our referral network or by the professional of your choice. Now it's even easier and more affordable to have the custom home you've always wanted.

ORDER TOLL FREE!
FOR INFORMATION ABOUT ANY OF OUR SERVICES OR TO ORDER CALL

1-800-521-6797 OR 520-297-8200
Browse our website:
www.eplans.com

BLUEPRINTS ARE NOT REFUNDABLE EXCHANGES ONLY

FOR CUSTOMER SERVICE,
CALL TOLL FREE **1-888-690-1116.**

HOME PLANNERS, LLC wholly owned by Hanley-Wood, LLC
3275 WEST INA ROAD, SUITE 110 • TUCSON, ARIZONA • 85741

THE BASIC BLUEPRINT PACKAGE
Rush me the following (please refer to the Plans Index and Price Schedule in this section):
____ Set(s) of blueprints for plan number(s) _____. $_____
____ Set(s) of reproducibles for plan number(s) _____. $_____
____ Home Customizer® Package for plan(s)_____. $_____
____ Additional identical blueprints (standard or reverse) in same order @ $50 per set. $_____
____ Reverse blueprints @ $50 fee per order. Right-reading reverse @ $165 surcharge $_____

IMPORTANT EXTRAS
Rush me the following:
____ Materials List: $60 (Must be purchased with Blueprint set.) Add $10 for Schedule C4–L4 plans. $_____
____ **Quote One®** Summary Cost Report @ $29.95 for one, $14.95 for each additional,
for plans _____ $_____
Building location: City _____ Zip Code _____
____ **Quote One®** Materials Cost Report @ $120 Schedules P1–C3; $130 Schedules C4–L4,
for plan _____ (Must be purchased with Blueprints set.) $_____
Building location: City _____ Zip Code _____
____ Specification Outlines @ $10 each. $_____
____ Detail Sets @ $14.95 each; any two $22.95; any three $29.95; all four for $39.95 (save $19.85). $_____
____ ❑ Plumbing ❑ Electrical ❑ Construction ❑ Mechanical
____ Plan-A-Home® @ $29.95 each. $_____

DECK BLUEPRINTS
(Please refer to the Plans Index and Price Schedule in this section)
____ Set(s) of Deck Plan _____. $_____
____ Additional identical blueprints in same order @ $10 per set. $_____
____ Reverse blueprints @ $10 per set. $_____
____ Set of Standard Deck Details @ $14.95 per set. $_____
____ Set of Complete Deck Construction Package (Best Buy!) Add $10 to Building Package
Includes Custom Deck Plan _____ Plus Standard Deck Details

LANDSCAPE BLUEPRINTS
(Please refer to the Plans Index and Price Schedule in this section)
____ Set(s) of Landscape Plan _____. $_____
____ Additional identical blueprints in same order @ $10 per set. $_____
____ Reverse blueprints @ $10 per set. $_____
Please indicate the appropriate region of the country for Plant & Material List.
(See map on page 217): Region _____

POSTAGE AND HANDLING	1–3 sets	4+ sets
Signature is required for all deliveries. **DELIVERY** No CODs (Requires street address—No P.O. Boxes)		
•Regular Service (Allow 7–10 business days delivery)	❑ $20.00	❑ $25.00
•Priority (Allow 4–5 business days delivery)	❑ $25.00	❑ $35.00
•Express (Allow 3 business days delivery)	❑ $35.00	❑ $45.00
OVERSEAS DELIVERY	fax, phone or mail for quote	

Note: All delivery times are from date Blueprint Package is shipped.

POSTAGE (From box above) $_____
SUBTOTAL $_____
SALES TAX (AZ & MI residents, please add appropriate state and local sales tax.) $_____
TOTAL (Subtotal and tax) $_____

YOUR ADDRESS (please print)

Name _____

Street _____

City _____ State _____ Zip _____

Daytime telephone number (_____) _____

FOR CREDIT CARD ORDERS ONLY

Credit card number _____ Exp. Date: (M/Y) _____

Check one ❑ Visa ❑ MasterCard ❑ Discover Card ❑ American Express

Signature _____

Please check appropriate box: ❑ Licensed Builder-Contractor ❑ Homeowner

ORDER TOLL FREE!
1-800-521-6797 or 520-297-8200

Order Form Key

HPTHH-2

HOME PLANNERS WANTS YOUR BUILDING EXPERIENCE TO BE AS PLEASANT AND TROUBLE-FREE AS POSSIBLE.

That's why we've expanded our library of Do-It-Yourself titles to help you along. In addition to our beautiful plans books, we've added books to guide you through specific projects as well as the construction process. In fact, these are titles that will be as useful after your dream home is built as they are right now.

BIGGEST & BEST
1. 1001 of our best-selling plans in one volume. 1,074 to 7,275 square feet. 704 pgs $12.95 1K1

ONE-STORY
2. 450 designs for all lifestyles. 800 to 4,900 square feet. 384 pgs $9.95 OS

MORE ONE-STORY
3. 475 superb one-level plans from 800 to 5,000 square feet. 448 pgs $9.95 MOS

TWO-STORY
4. 443 designs for one-and-a-half and two stories. 1,500 to 6,000 square feet. 448 pgs $9.95 TS

VACATION
5. 465 designs for recreation, retirement and leisure. 448 pgs $9.95 VSH

HILLSIDE
6. 208 designs for split-levels, bi-levels, multi-levels and walkouts. 224 pgs $9.95 HH

FARMHOUSE
7. 200 country designs from classic to contemporary by 7 winning designers. 224 pgs $8.95 FH

COUNTRY HOUSES
8. 208 unique home plans that combine traditional style and modern livability. 224 pgs $9.95 CN

BUDGET-SMART
9. 200 efficient plans from 7 top designers, that you can really afford to build! 224 pgs $8.95 BS

BARRIER FREE
10. Over 1,700 products and 51 plans for accessible living. 128 pgs $15.95 UH

ENCYCLOPEDIA
11. 500 exceptional plans for all styles and budgets—the best book of its kind! 528 pgs $9.95 ENC

ENCYCLOPEDIA II
12. 500 completely new plans. Spacious and stylish designs for every budget and taste. 352 pgs $9.95 E2

AFFORDABLE
13. Completely revised and updated, featuring 300 designs for modest budgets. 256 pgs $9.95 AF

VICTORIAN
14. NEW! 210 striking Victorian and Farmhouse designs from today's top designers. 224 pgs $15.95 VDH2

ESTATE
15. Dream big! Twenty-one designers showcase their biggest and best plans. 208 pgs $15.95 EDH

LUXURY
16. 154 fine luxury plans—loaded with luscious amenities! 192 pgs $14.95 LD2

EUROPEAN STYLES
17. 200 homes with a unique flair of the Old World. 224 pgs $15.95 EURO

COUNTRY CLASSICS
18. Donald Gardner's 101 best Country and Traditional home plans. 192 pgs $17.95 DAG

WILLIAM POOLE
19. 70 romantic house plans that capture the classic tradition of home design. 160 pgs $17.95 WEP

TRADITIONAL
20. 85 timeless designs from the Design Traditions Library. 160 pgs $17.95 TRA

COTTAGES
21. 25 fresh new designs that are as warm as a tropical breeze. A blend of the best aspects of many coastal styles. 64 pgs. $19.95 CTG

CLASSIC
22. Timeless, elegant designs that always feel like home. Gorgeous plans that are as flexible and up-to-date as their occupants. 240 pgs. $9.95 CS

CONTEMPORARY
23. The most complete and imaginative collection of contemporary designs available anywhere. 240 pgs. $9.95 CM

EASY-LIVING
24. 200 efficient and sophisticated plans that are small in size, but big on livability. 224 pgs $8.95 EL

SOUTHERN
25. 207 homes rich in Southern styling and comfort. 240 pgs $8.95 SH

SOUTHWESTERN
26. 138 designs that capture the spirit of the Southwest. 144 pgs $10.95 SW

WESTERN
27. 215 designs that capture the spirit and diversity of the Western lifestyle. 208 pgs $9.95 WH

NEIGHBORHOOD
28. 170 designs with the feel of main street America. 192 pgs $12.95 TND

CRAFTSMAN
29. 170 Home plans in the Craftsman and Bungalow style. 192 pgs $12.95 CC

COLONIAL HOUSES
30. 181 Classic early American designs. 208 pgs $9.95 COL

DUPLEX & TOWNHOMES
31. Over 50 designs for multi-family living. 64 pgs $9.95 DTP

WATERFRONT
32. 200 designs perfect for your waterside wonderland. 208 pgs $10.95 WF

Design 7517, page 11

OVER 3 MILLION BLUEPRINTS SOLD

"We instructed our builder to follow the plans including all of the many details which make this house so elegant…Our home is a fine example of the results one can achieve by purchasing and following the plans which you offer…Everyone who has seen it has assured us that it belongs in 'a picture book.' I truly mean it when I say that my home 'is a DREAM HOUSE.' "

S.P.
Anderson, SC

"We have had a steady stream of visitors, many of whom tell us this is the most beautiful home they've seen. Everyone is amazed at the layout and remarks on how unique it is. Our real estate attorney, who is a Chicago dweller and who deals with highly valued properties, told me this is the only suburban home he has seen that he would want to live in."

W. & P.S.
Flossmoor, IL

"Your blueprints saved us a great deal of money. I acted as the general contractor and we did a lot of the work ourselves. We probably built it for half the cost! We are thinking about more plans for another home. I purchased a competitor's book but my husband wants only your plans!"

Grovetown, GA

"We are very happy with the product of our efforts. The neighbors and passersby appreciate what we have created. We have had many people stop by to discuss our house and kindly praise it as being the nicest house in our area of new construction. We have even had one person stop and make us an unsolicited offer to buy the house for much more than we have invested in it."

K. & L.S.
Bolingbrook, IL

"The traffic going past our house is unbelievable. On several occasions, we have heard that it is the 'prettiest house in Batavia.' Also, when meeting someone new and mentioning what street we live on, quite often we're told, 'Oh, you're the one in the yellow house with the wrap-around porch! I love it!' "

A.W.
Batavia, NY

"I have been involved in the building trades my entire life…Since building our home we have built two other homes for other families. Their plans from local professional architects were not nearly as good as yours. For that reason we are ordering additional plan books from you."

T.F.
Kingston, WA

"The blueprints we received from you were of excellent quality and provided us with exactly what we needed to get our successful home-building project underway. We appreciate your invaluable role in our home-building effort."

T.A.
Concord, TN